FIRST FICT

# ff

# FIRST FICTIONS

## Introduction 9

*faber and faber*
LONDON · BOSTON

First published in 1986 by
Faber and Faber Limited
3 Queen Square  London WC1N 3AU
Filmset by Wilmaset Birkenhead Wirral
Printed in Great Britain by
Butler & Tanner  Frome  Somerset

*British Library Cataloguing in Publication Data*

First fictions: Introduction 9
1. Short stories, English  2. English fiction
– 20th century
823'.01'08[FS]  PR1309.S5

ISBN 0–571–13607–9

# CONTENTS

## PUBLISHER'S NOTE

In this collection, the ninth to appear in the INTRODUCTION series, it is our aim once again to introduce new writers to a wider reading public. As before, the number of contributors is restricted to give each the advantage of presenting a substantial amount of work.

The INTRODUCTION series has now provided a number of well-known writers with a first chance to establish their reputations; they include Ted Hughes, Julian Mitchell, Jim Hunter, Francis Hope, Tom Stoppard, Garth St Omer, Christopher Hampton, Kazuo Ishiguro and Anne Devlin. We believe that this new collection maintains the high standard set in the past.

# BIOGRAPHICAL NOTES

*Douglas Glover* was born in Ontario in 1948. He studied philosophy at York University, Toronto, and did an M.Litt. at Edinburgh University. He has had short stories published in Canada by Talon Books and 'Dog Attempts to Drown Man In Saskatoon' won the *Canadian Fiction Magazine* Contributor's Prize. He is currently working on a novel.

*Kristien Hemmerechts* was born in Brussels in 1955, and has lived in Amsterdam and England and travelled in South America. Since 1980 she has worked at the University of Brussels, has just completed a PhD on Jean Rhys, and has been writing stories since 1982.

*Deirdre Madden* was born in Ireland in 1960 and attended Trinity College, Dublin, and the University of East Anglia. She has had short stories published in *The Irish Press*, *Irish Country Woman*, *Icarus* and *Ulster Tatler*, and in 1980 was awarded a Hennessy Literary Award. Part of *Hidden Symptoms* was written while she was at the Tyrone Guthrie Centre in County Monaghan.

*Deborah Moffatt* was born in Vermont in 1953. Since 1971 she has lived in Seattle, Buenos Aires, Montevideo, Boston, Mexico City and currently lives in Auchtermuchty, Scotland. She has had poems published in American and Scottish periodicals and a story published in *New Writing Scotland 3*.

*Dorothy Nimmo* was born in Manchester and now lives in North Yorkshire. She has published short stories in *Spare Rib* and *Writing Women* and poems in *Writing Women*, *Iron*, *Literary Review*, *Spectator* and *Encounter*.

*Jaci Stephen* was born in Cardiff in 1958. She read English at Cardiff University and, after teaching for two years, took an MA in Creative Writing at Lancaster University. She now lives in London where she works as a freelance journalist and in 1984 was winner of the Catherine Pakenham Award. 'The Other Side of Summer' was broadcast on Radio Four's *Morning Story*.

DEBORAH MOFFATT

## When Roger Got Married

Roger is my brother, though we've never lived in the same house or anything. He's my half-brother is all, and that's why we don't look alike. 'But you're a pair, you two,' my mother says. 'You both got the old man's brains, too smart for your own good.'

Roger is twenty-five and I'm thirteen. Roger's mother died when he was just little and then his father married my mom. Roger likes my mom a lot; he says the years she lived out there on their farm were the best. But I never lived out there, so I don't know. When Mom had me she was already pretty sick of Frank, that's our father, and she left that farm and came here. I was born here, in the same house where my mother grew up.

This is a farm, too, but we don't farm it. 'Never did like farming,' my mom tells everyone, including Grandpa, who lives with us, 'and this farm isn't worth it anyways.' Grandpa looks sad when she says that, but she's right. Nowadays farms as small as ours don't make any money, even I know that. Ever since the Armstrongs came to town and started the big dairy farm out on Route 10, none of the small farmers makes any money, at least not much more than they need to get by.

Roger still keeps our father's farm. He's all alone up there now and he manages all right, I guess. 'Don't know how, though,' Mom says. 'After all, his father couldn't manage without putting both me and Roger to work overtime, and me pregnant with you! Well, Frank was just a slave driver and thank God I got away. Made Roger into a good solid worker, though, Frank did. Not a lazy little brat like you!'

She's always telling me I'm lazy but I know she doesn't mean it. She thinks I should study more, work harder, but I don't have to. I get straight A's anyway. Most of the time I'm bored to death in school. I play hookey a lot and run up the back roads to Roger's farm, where I can work and talk with him. He makes a lot more sense than the teachers anyway.

'They're gonna put you in jail if you keep on playing hookey,' he says to me, looking real sad and serious, but I can tell he's just as glad that I'm here with him. He must get pretty bored up there on the farm alone.

'Your Mom'll have to quit, she can't have that job if her kid's in jail.'

Now that always makes me think; Mom would sure hate to lose her job. She's the Town Clerk. She makes the town run – that's what Grandpa says, at least, and he says it real proud like. Mom says it's a whole lot better than cleaning out dirty cow barns and I agree. But Roger says politics is no place for a woman.

'Naw, they won't throw me in jail,' I say. 'Anyway, I could get through the bars.' I only weigh ninety pounds and I'm over five feet tall. I can look Roger right in the eye when he stands up straight. His mother was really short. 'She never was too tall in the first place, but Frank just wore her down into the ground with hard work,' my mother says.

Roger and I are good friends even though we're brother and sister. He went to college when he was eighteen and I was six, and I just cried and cried. But he came back real soon. Now he tells me, 'You don't just need straight As if you wanta go to college, Brenda May. You got to learn a whole lot of other stuff, how to talk right, and you got to buy expensive clothes and go to Europe, all that stuff.'

They laughed at Roger at the college, called him a hick. So he came back here and finished up at the vo-tech in the Junction. Anyway, he had to come back because our father dropped dead and somebody had to take care of the farm.

The only other time I didn't see much of Roger was when he was married. That time we almost stopped being friends, I was so mad at him.

He was twenty-two when he got married. I was ten. There was a lot I couldn't understand then and I still don't, mostly. But Roger had his reasons, though we all thought he'd gone crazy.

He married Linda McWilliams. If you know any of the McWilliams you know why we thought he'd gone crazy. That family is just trash, that's all. They're not the *worst* trash we've got here – there's the Delaroux that keeps pigs and has lice all the time, and the Smiths, out on the Junction road, they do nothing at all but sit and stink.

## When Roger Got Married

Mr McWilliams works at the dump, which is a good place for him. Someday someone's gonna come along and think that the garbage is alive, 'cause that's what he looks like, walking garbage. He stinks like it too. He drinks a lot, and his belly hangs out over his belt. 'Drinker's gut,' Grandpa says.

Mrs McWilliams works in the cafeteria at school. I won't touch the food there on account of her, makes me sick to think of her just being *in* that kitchen. She's got greasy, stringy hair that I don't think she ever washes. She's a fat slob is what she is. She stands around and chews gum in the kitchen all day. Angie La Fourtier – she's a real nice old lady who's always telling me, 'Eat, eat, skinny girl, you'll never get a boyfriend if you don't eat' – she told me that Mrs McWilliams would be fired except that the principal says, 'If I fire her, that family will go on welfare, and it wouldn't be fair for the taxpayers to have to support them.' Angie can't stand Mrs McWilliams.

Linda is the oldest in that family, and there's ten of them at least. She was sixteen when Roger married her. She had just quit school and gone to work in the Dairy Queen in the Junction. Well, she's no Dairy Queen, that's for sure. She's pretty, I guess; she's got big brown eyes and fat lips and great huge tits. But she's a little fat and her clothes are kind of cheap and dirty-looking. And she wears a *ton* of makeup. Anyway, you can see she's gonna end up just like her mother. I mean she's already a little fat, and she'll get fatter and fatter, and then she won't be pretty at all anymore.

Roger married her that February after she dropped out of school. Roger was in danger of getting fat himself, he went to that old Dairy Queen so much. Then he married her and she didn't work there anymore.

Everybody was saying 'what a shame' about the marriage. Lots of people had their eye on Roger, for their daughters, you know; he could have married a lot of other girls in town. Course I didn't think anybody was good enough for him, but nobody was worse than Linda McWilliams!

Roger didn't come around to our farm much after he married her, and nobody else saw much of him, either. Mom went out to the farm once, to give Roger some kitchen stuff that belonged to our father before she married him. 'Now that you're a married man you'll have use for all this,' she told him. When she came back she said, 'Well, I'll say one thing, he didn't marry her for

15

the same reason your father married me – at least, if he did want a workhorse for a wife then he made the wrong choice! That girl does nothing; the kitchen is a right mess! Frank would just die if he could see it.' Dead as he was, I don't think my father would have been as upset as my mother. She doesn't like farming much but she's a real hard worker at home. Our kitchen looks like a hospital or something.

After that I wanted to see for myself but I didn't really want to go over to Roger's farm. I was plenty mad at him for marrying and he didn't even ask my opinion if he should. I would have told him he was out of his gourd if he *had* asked.

In April one day I went up there. April must be the worst month in Vermont. The snow is mostly gone, so you can't play in it, and the ground is too wet and muddy to do much with. Everything is dirty and wet, and it rains a lot. So I can see why anybody might be bored in April.

And Linda was bored, bored, bored. I got there and she was sitting at the kitchen table. Just sitting. Now Grandpa does a lot of sitting, just sitting at the window, but he's old and has a whole long life to think about. Linda was just sitting and I don't think she was even thinking. She looked at me like I was her best friend in the world. 'Course, she didn't have any friends that I ever heard of.

'God,' she said, 'what on earth did your mom ever do out here to keep from going crazy? I bet old Frank was just like Roger – did you know he goes to sleep every night at *ten*?' (So did I, back then, so I didn't see what was wrong with that.) 'We haven't gone out but twice since I got married. Twice!'

'Where'd you go?' Where would Roger take her, anyway? Nobody had ever seen them out together.

'The movies once, some terrible thing about England, or somewhere, wars, I don't know. I fell asleep. We went to a bar for dancing once though, that was fun. I passed for twenty-one.' I wasn't surprised; she looked about thirty to me. 'I got a little drunk, too. Roger don't drink; he's so *dull*.' She pouted with her big fat lips. 'Shit, I wish I had a beer now,' she said. She was showing off, swearing like that and talking about drinking. I was pretty well shocked. My mother never drinks, she says women don't need to drink. Only sometimes when it's really hot, then she has a beer. 'My goodness it's hot out, I'll just have a nice cold beer,' she'll say. 'Don't you want half, Grandpa? I can't possibly finish the bottle.' Grandpa never wants half and Mom always finishes the bottle.

'That'd be something to *do* at least,' Linda said, rolling her eyes way up. 'I'm so bored.'

'You could cook,' I suggested.

'Don't know how. Anyways, Roger is making me diet.'

Not know how to cook? I always thought that came together with growing up. Mom makes me cook, though I don't like to much. But she sure has a fun time looking in recipe books and everything, so I guess you like it when you're older. 'Didn't you cook at home?'

'Naw, all we done was eat out of cans. That don't take any time to fix, though.'

'Well, don't you work?' My mom always tells me how much work there is on a farm.

' 'Work! Now *that's* what I'd like to do. I want to go back to the Dairy Queen. That was fun, seein' people every day, the Rexall was just across the street, I bought a lot of neat makeup, ya wanna see? Come on.' She took my hand and dragged me into the bedroom. On the bureau was a box, full of lipsticks and eyeshadows and powderpuffs and used-up bottles of perfume and I don't know what all jumbled together, powder and ink and dust everywhere.

'Let me make you up!' she said.

Yicchh, I thought. 'I'm allergic,' I said, just like I'd heard my mom say. I wanted to see myself made up, but not with that filthy stuff.

'Oh,' she said, disappointed. 'Well then, I'll do my face and you can watch.' That pleased her, and she set about primping and patting and painting. She looked weirder every minute. 'Just like the models,' she said.

'Well, why don't you go back to the Dairy Queen then?' I asked.

''ogew 'on't let 'ee,' she said through the lipstick she was gooing on. 'Mmmmmmhh; there.' She smacked her lips. 'Says I'm his wife, I don't have to work anymore.'

'Oh.' That didn't make any sense to me, but if Roger said it, well, he must have his reasons. 'Don't you have an awful lot to do up here?'

17

'Naw. Roger says it's a shame to spoil my pretty hands with farmwork. He don't make me do nothing, really. Just one thing.' She looked at me, right in the eye. 'He says I haveta get my high school degree.'

'Oh?' That sounded better; at least Roger was trying to smarten up this dummy.

'But I told him I was *through* with school, know what I mean? So he's teaching me himself here. Trying, anyhow. He expects me to read all this dull history stuff. I told him if he wants me to learn better reading he's gonna have to get me better books. Do you like "True Confessions"?'

I nodded but I must have looked disgusted, like I felt. My mom won't let that kind of stuff in the house.

She stuck up her nose and said, 'Hey, don't you tell nobody he's teaching me or nothing. Ain't nobody gonna think he's better'n me.' She looked down at me real proud like, even with all those silly paints on her face.

I went home and told Mom everything. 'She's lazy and dumb and cheap and dirty.' But Mom just said it was not for us to judge. So I shut up about old Linda and just missed Roger like crazy.

Then in June Linda got sick. Word went around town that Roger was looking real serious 'cause his wife was 'took ill bad'. So my mother cooked up a big casserole to take up there; they could eat off it for days, she said. 'The poor young couple, with her sick I guess they must have to make do with canned pork and beans. Take this on over there,' she told me.

'She can't cook anyways,' I said. 'I told you that.'

'Nonsense. Every woman can cook, now go on.'

I went on up there, carrying the heavy casserole. Even cold it smelled good and if it hadn't been for Roger I would have sat down and eaten it on the way. Waste of good food to take it to *her*, I thought; she'd probably prefer canned beans.

I got up to the farm and found the door locked. That was strange, let me tell you. Around here nobody locks the door, even at night or when they're out. You just never know, a farmer or a kid like me might have to come in and use the phone in a hurry, or the bathroom, and everybody knows everybody anyway. But the door was locked. I put the casserole dish down on the front step and sat there on the steps awhile, to see if Roger or Linda came along.

Nobody came and the June sun was hot. Roger doesn't have a brook up there, like we do, so I couldn't go wading. I looked around for a hose or something. I walked to the back of the house and decided to climb the apple tree there; that was something to do at least. Up in the apple tree I could see into the windows of the house; they were too high for me to see in from the ground. I was looking into the bedroom. There was Linda, sleeping. In the day! But she was supposed to be sick, so it was all right. Except that then I saw that she wasn't lying in that bed alone. There was another head there, on the pillow beside her. Roger has dark hair and this person didn't. This person was a man with blond hair. I didn't get a good look at his face. I was seeing the side of his head, then the head went over Linda's face and she was covered up by him.

Even though I was only ten I was no dummy. I knew what was going on. I could have stayed up there in the apple tree for a good look but I was scared they'd see me. Anyway I felt sick or something, like I wanted to cry. I wanted to run to Roger and tell him. I wanted to tell my mom. But I didn't dare tell anyone. I didn't want Roger to feel bad and I knew he'd feel bad if he knew what Linda was up to.

I didn't go home 'til dinnertime. I didn't want to see anybody. I wanted to forget what I'd seen. I ran as fast as I could to the brook, up where it runs through our field, where there's an old sugar house I use for a hideout. Up there I have my favourite books and a place to write, in summer anyway. It's a secret place; only Roger knows I go there and he won't tell anybody.

My mother was waiting for me when I got home. 'Where on earth have you been? Roger's been calling wondering if you're all right; he says you just left the casserole on the doorstep,' she said, all in one breath and real fast. She worries when I'm out late because I sometimes go far away. One time I couldn't get home before it was night and they had to come and get me.

'Door was locked, nobody home,' I said, washing my hands in the bathroom.

'Roger says Linda was home all day,' Mom said, pursuing me into the bathroom. 'Didn't you knock?'

''Course I knocked. Nobody home.'

She just looked at me funny. Everybody knows Roger doesn't lie, but they know I sometimes do. Mostly I just like to make up stories and pretend they're true. But this wasn't the kind of thing I'd lie about. I thought Mom could see that. Sometimes I think mothers can see right into your brain; you just can't keep a secret from your mother for long.

A week or two later Linda was all better, according to Roger. Mom called him up to ask him to cut up a fallen tree out back, and she bribed him by offering him dinner. He and Linda said they would come.

I tried not to be there. 'Jennifer Farley invited me to the movies that night,' I said. No luck: 'Well, you can't go. Roger is your half-brother and you haven't seen him in ages. Anyway, what's with you? You used to be wild about Roger.'

'Nothing wrong with *me*,' I said. 'Something's wrong with *him*, though, and you know why.'

'Well, even if you don't like Linda, you're going to be civil to her and treat her like a welcome guest in our home.'

There was no way I was going to treat her like even a human being after what I'd seen, so I didn't say any more to my mom.

They came over at three, and Roger went right down to work on the tree. It was a big tree, and after he cut it up with his chain saw there was a lot of logs to be split. I did the smaller ones and Grandpa did some bigger ones. Grandpa shouldn't work like that, but he gets mad and won't talk all day if we tell him he's too old to work.

Roger and Grandpa get along pretty good, though Grandpa calls Frank, our daddy, a woman killer. Roger just laughs.

'Heard your woman was sick,' Grandpa said. 'Gonna work her to death like your old man killed your mother?'

Sick my foot, I thought, bringing the axe down on the wood – soft maple, it split in one blow. Only place she's sick is in the pants, I said to myself. Crrraccckkk. Hot pants. Another log split.

'Nope,' Roger said, between the *grrrs* of his chain saw, looking for the best angle to get at a branch. 'Won't make my wife work. No wife of mine is going to work.' Then he looked Grandpa in the eye: ''Course, no wife of mine is going to get herself mixed up in town politics, either.'

Grandpa chuckled and said, 'Tit for tat.' I don't know what he meant by that but I know Roger doesn't like my mom working in the town office. A lot of people don't: 'That damn pushy woman,' they say about her. 'But she's the only woman that ever stood up to Frank Corson,' they add.

Linda stayed up in the house with my mom. When we went in around six she was sitting there at the kitchen table, and Mom was whistling away while she cooked. I knew Linda wouldn't help Mom out, like guests usually do; Linda couldn't cook. I don't think they had even been talking. Linda just looked bored, like always.

Grandpa looked at her like she was a cow on display at the fair. He looked her up and down. She was so different from the women that usually come to our house. She had on all that makeup and her hair was full of new curls. Her dress was cut kind of low, so you could just see where the crack of her big breasts began. I guess she was sexy. Grandpa didn't say much to her but he stared at her a lot.

She didn't talk at all during dinner, but Mom and Roger and Grandpa talked a lot, about the weather and farming. I was out of school for the summer and not doing much in those days, helping Mom out in the town offices was all I did, so there wasn't much for me to talk about. Anyway, I was mad at Linda and mad at Roger, so I didn't want to talk to them.

I had to serve, that's the way we do it in our house. I always serve and usually do the dishes. When I served Linda, I wanted to pour everything on her lap. But I didn't. I just hurried her up as fast as I could. Roger noticed that I wasn't real polite to her. He looked at me hard after I accidentally skipped her when I went round with the potatoes.

'You forgot Linda,' he said.

'No I didn't,' I said, embarrassed. 'She's too fat for potatoes.'

'Brenda May!' my mother said. Grandpa's eyes went wide and his face got red and he kind of sputtered. I think he was trying not to laugh.

'Apologize this instant, Brenda, or I'll beat your skinny behind,' Roger said calmly.

'I will not,' I said, sticking my chin out and holding the dish of potatoes between me and him like a shield. 'I will not apologize to that fat stupid cow! You didn't used to be stupid, but boy are you getting stupid now! First you married her and then you let her, let her, *screw* somebody right in your own bed and you don't even know about it!' I hadn't meant to say it, I didn't want

21

to say it, but I said it, the first time in my life I'd ever said 'screw' in front of an adult. I dropped the potatoes and ran away. My mom was screaming at me to get back that instant but Roger said, 'Let her go.' That's all I heard. I never even looked at Linda to see what she would look like when she got found out. I knew I was going to catch hell, but I sure hoped she felt worse than I did.

I was up at the sugar house in no time. The sun was going down; I hoped it wouldn't be night too fast, because I was afraid to be there in the dark.

I knew what would be going on down in the house. Mom would be saying I was tired, I was high-strung, I liked making up stories. Linda would maybe cry or maybe laugh. Anyway, she'd say it wasn't true. And Roger would think I was a liar, a liar and a brat.

I started crying when I thought of what Roger would think. I was crying too because it was getting dark and I wanted to go home, but I didn't want to go down and get spanked and be told I was a liar and a bad girl. It wasn't my fault, after all; I had seen what I had seen.

So I was almost glad when Roger appeared in the door of the sugar house, just a shadow in the dark light. 'Brenda?' I guess he couldn't see me. 'I'm in here,' I said, a little scared. I couldn't tell if he was mad enough to spank me.

'You're a nice little brat, Brenda May Corson,' Roger said softly, coming in. I wasn't frightened then, because I heard that his voice was soft and nice. 'I'd be ready to kill you for insulting my wife,' he said, 'if I didn't know that what you said is true.' By now he was near me. He pulled my head up against him and rubbed my hair. Then he slapped me lightly on the cheek, but it was a pretend slap, not a real one. 'And I won't stand for it for you to call me stupid.'

'Well, if you *know*,' I said, 'if you know, why don't you make her go away?'

He breathed a big breath and sat down on the floor beside me. We looked out the door at the first few stars up in the sky; they winked at us. I sat real close to him. I wasn't sorry anymore that I had hurt his feelings; after all, he'd hurt mine by marrying Linda. And now I had him all to myself for awhile, and he was going to tell me all about it, just like friends again.

'A man has to marry sometime, you know,' he began. 'You'll know more about that when you're grown up. But I can't be dating and talking to a lot of women, I'm too shy. It's too hard for me. Linda was just, sort of, there. I've known her since she was a child, and she was always real sweet and pretty. She is pretty, you know, underneath that makeup.'

'Yeah.' I'd agree to that much at least.

'And that life she's had. You don't know, Brenda, what it must be like to grow up in a family like that. She never would have had a chance in that home to make anything of herself. She'd just end up marrying some drunk and getting fat like her mother. She doesn't want that, she's got more than that going for her. She took that job in the Dairy Queen just to get away from her family. But she shouldn't have to work, she should finish school—'

'But Roger, what about that man that – that I saw? She don't really want to make herself better, she just wants a good time.'

'I know, little sister, I know.' He just stared hard out the doorway. I reached up and touched under his eyes; they were dry. I was glad. I've never seen a man cry and I would have been real embarrassed if Roger was crying.

He looked down at me. 'I ain't gonna cry,' he said. 'I don't love her. I'm not sorry she's been unfaithful. I'm just sorry that I turned out to be such a fool. I should have known better than to think I could change a person's life.'

'But you tried!' I said.

'No,' he said. 'That's not the point. Point is – I don't know, exactly, but somehow you gotta both of you want the same thing. She didn't want to be what I want her to be. She don't know what she wants, and she's trying to find out, that's what that, that affair was all about, I guess.'

It was dark now, completely dark. I huddled up even closer to Roger and said that I was scared. I didn't want to talk anymore about Linda. I wanted to go home and go to bed and wake up and work in the fields with Roger the next day.

We walked down from the sugar house together. Before we got home, Roger said, 'You're going to call her up tomorrow and apologize for calling her a fat cow.'

'Okay,' I said. 'But I won't apologize for the other, what I said.'

'No, you don't have to.'

'And after that I don't ever want to talk to her again.'

'You probably won't have to.'

I squeezed his hand, happy that Roger would be my friend again. We're still friends, but sometimes he teases me to death for calling him stupid that time, especially when he beats me at cards; Roger's sharp at cards.

My father was British, a Scot. He was the opposite of a war bride: a war groom. He married an American, my mother, just after the war, a woman who had gone to Scotland to care for orphans – not personally, but as a volunteer for an adoption agency. She knew nothing about the realities of war and couldn't bear to be told about it, as some of the returning soldiers tried to do. She suited my father because he couldn't bear to talk about the war and would not, even if asked.

My father was no orphan but my mother took him under her wing, seeing that he was in quite a state, probably shell-shocked. He was young and good-looking and so was she, and that affected the care she took of him and his attitude towards it. They married, left his small Fife village, where there was little work for mentally incapacitated veterans, and came to America, where there were jobs and other luxuries: butter, gasoline, nylons, long before they were restored to British consumers.

My mother's family got quite a shock when they saw what their daughter had done. She had gone to Britain with a degree from Vassar and came back with a nearly mute coal miner from Fife. They were well off, an old Boston family now settled in a wealthy north-shore suburb. They had not meant for their daughter to marry in Britain, unless it were to royalty. My father was not royalty.

My mother told her parents to leave them alone. 'Willie is a fine man and will make me proud.' She proceeded to insure her proud future by enrolling Willie in a night school, while she herself took a job teaching immigrants English. My father worked days in various jobs, unable to stay long in any one occupation, since he felt inadequate and superfluous in the modern American city which was so different in temperature and tempo from his native land. Still, he did well at the school, where his subject, technology, presented known challenges.

He graduated and asked my mother to please him in one thing now that he had pleased her by acquiring a degree. 'We must move to the country, Sharon,' he said. 'I can't live in this city. I can't see here; I can't see out.'

She agreed and they moved to Vermont where her family had a summer home and Springfield had a job for him. He worked in a factory as an inventor of tooling gadgets. He even gained a patent in his name by the time I was born.

He adapted well to Vermont, pleased by the green farming fields not so different from the fields of Fife. But he quarrelled with the trees, chopping down all those close to the house and many others on our land. He preferred a sea-view, he said, but did not demand another move once he and my mother had settled into Vermont. He took to the hills, climbing Ascutney often and also smaller mountains with fire-towers on top where he would sit for hours just looking out over the land.

He adapted socially, too, enjoying the taciturn company of the local men at church suppers, town meeting, local fairs. He was different from the locals, of course, being foreign, but not so terribly different: not like the Italian barber or the Lithuanian farmers, who spoke foreign languages and ate foreign foods.

I was glad that my father fit in so well. Most of my friends didn't like to go to homes where the adults spoke strange languages; neither did I. We were all afraid of people who spoke languages we could not understand and ate foods made with garlic and spices and offal, which in general our mothers did not use for cooking. In these ways my father was quite normal, not different. He spoke English and ate nothing unpleasant.

In fact, his being British quite interested some of my friends and also many adults, who asked him questions about Scotland and England. My father didn't talk much about Britain and only sometimes reminisced about Scotland. He could get quite worked up though when he heard reports on the news of rising British unemployment, declining factories, race problems, hardship, over there in Britain.

'You know who really won the war?' he would say. 'The Germans. Do the Germans have unemployment? Do they have to tell people there's no more work? Do they have to close down factories?'

Sometimes this would escalate to a diatribe against the

Germans, or the Huns, as he called them. We were not shocked. Vermonters all had personal prejudices: some against Catholics, others against French Canadians, many against blacks, prejudices informed only by ignorance and lack of contact. My father's animosity toward the Germans was no more unusual or out of place than Ralph Peterson's rage at the Koreans, whose northern army had killed his son in the more recent war.

I was proud of my father when I was in high school, because he did not support the Vietnam war. Many people in our town did support it and put flag decals on their car to prove their patriotic spirit. Many others, mostly teenagers, protested against the war, sticking peace signs on guitars and notebooks. When I told my friends that my father was against the war, they were quite impressed.

But my father didn't want me to advertise his objection to the war. 'The war has nothing to do with me, lassie. I'm British. But I'll tell you this: it's a war that won't be won. Nobody wins a war.'

He appreciated the sagacity of our senator, George Aiken, who was the first to suggest that we 'say we won and get out'. Later we tried to do that, of course, only by then we had clearly not won.

'Winning a war is all in the mind,' my father reminded me.

I went away to college not far from home, up the river to Dartmouth, where I was among the first women to infiltrate the previously all-male campus. Father found this funny, but good. He saw it as a slap in the face to the upper class, upsetting their customs and traditions. He regarded most things as a struggle between classes, which I could not really understand. In Springfield, we all thought we were middle class and didn't care if we weren't.

I brought my first boyfriend home from Dartmouth one weekend in May; Jake Stern. He was a sophomore who was sophisticated and brilliant. The girls at Dartmouth considered him extremely handsome and that, more than his sophistication or brilliance, was the source of my attraction to him.

My father had little to say to Jake, but then he had little to say to anybody. But Jake took offence: 'He doesn't like me because I'm Jewish,' he complained as we climbed up Mt Ascutney.

'He doesn't even know you're Jewish,' I said, sprinting ahead to reach the top before Jake. He was a city boy and unused to climbing mountains, no matter how small.

'Is that boy German?' my father asked when Jake had gone down to the store to buy cigarettes.

'He's American, Dad.'

'But his parents were German.'

'Maybe. I don't know. They're Jewish.'

My father said nothing to that.

It was 1974. There had been a war in Israel and then the Arabs embargoed oil. My father thought that a good move.

'Coal will come back now. That's good for the mines in Scotland,' he said as we watched the evening news.

'That's a rather narrow way to look at it,' Jake said. 'I think it's a rotten situation. The damn Arabs are blackmailing the whole world just because we had the nerve to beat them in a war.' Jake was used to speaking his mind to whomever; he had no ideas about respecting his elders' or anybody else's opinions.

'You won the war, did you?' my father asked quietly.

'Damn right. Israel showed we can't be pushed around.'

'Don't talk like that,' I said to Jake. '*You* weren't there fighting. Besides, I thought you were a pacifist.'

'Pacifist? Naw.'

'But Vietnam –'

'Vietnam is an immoral war,' he said to me. He breathed hard through his nose, heaving his chest. He was annoyed at my ignorance; he was often annoyed by the ignorance of those around him. Jake was generally known to be a genius. He had been valedictorian of his high school class, had written letters to the *New York Times* which were actually published, had read Marx, Mao, Che Guevara, all of Ginsberg and Kerouac. I had read little of any of these. He preferred it that way; he enjoyed teaching me, forming my mind.

My father went out for a walk, looking up at the hills. Through the living-room window we watched him walk to the far edge of the lawn, where he picked up an axe and started chopping wood. Firewood heated our house.

'He's in a huff, isn't he?' Jake said.

'No, he likes to be outside is all. He rarely stays indoors for long.'

'Claustrophobe? But he *is* in a huff. Probably doesn't like to hear that Vietnam is an immoral war.'

'No, my father never supported the war,' I said.

'Oh?' Jake walked around the room, examining the book-shelves. He didn't like to hear unexpected things. Nothing was supposed to contradict his notions because normally his notions were correct.

'He doesn't support any war,' I added.

'Quaker?'

'No.'

'What, then? Did he support World War II?'

'He fought.'

'Let's go see Martin,' Jake said, uninterested in my father's peculiarities. Martin was also at Dartmouth, was Jake's good friend, and lived just down the road from me. Martin, like Jake, talked a lot. Jake found my family's silence upsetting; he said so. 'You guys don't exactly have stimulating conversations around here,' he said. 'Let's go to Martin's and talk about our essays on Lowell.'

'I haven't finished mine.'

'So?'

Jake claimed thoughts came better to him if he talked them out; I preferred simply to think them out. We went to Martin's house and they talked about Robert Lowell's poetry for hours, neither listening to the other.

It was Memorial Day weekend. As usual, my father had been asked to join the parade; as usual, he had refused. On the Monday morning we sat in the kitchen working on our essays while my father wandered about the house at loose ends. He hated holidays, for one thing, and also it was raining so he couldn't work outside as he usually did.

The parade passed by our house, the ageing veterans quite wet.

'Silly sods,' my father muttered.

'No Vietnam vets out there,' I observed.

'I don't blame them,' my father said. 'It's raining too hard.'

'It's because they don't feel welcome, Dad,' I explained. 'The older guys think Vietnam vets are all drug addicts or cowards.'

'Mmmmmh,' Jake rumbled, warming up his throat to make a clever pronouncement. 'It's funny, really, how attitudes change. I mean, now we think of soldiers as fascistic, but in their day –' nodding his head towards the window – 'soldiers fought the fascists. Nowadays a CO is a hero, but then an objector was a coward. Of course, objectors in that war were sickos anyway. I mean, to sit back while millions of Jews were being murdered.'

My mother came in. She always slept late and that morning was no exception. 'Good morning, all,' she said, cheerfully, the only cheer in the dreary kitchen. 'Did everybody get breakfast?'

'Yeah,' I said. 'Just coffee for us. I boiled an egg for Dad.'

'You shouldn't have eggs for breakfast,' Jake said to my father. 'Bad for your heart. Too much cholesterol.'

My father said nothing. He was still looking out the window, probably not listening.

'I'll have an egg, too,' my mother said, not heeding Jake's advice. She had never taken anybody's advice in her life; now was no time to start. 'The parade go by?'

'Just now,' I said. 'They're sopping.'

'Oh, is it raining? I wondered why you were still indoors, Willie.'

'I may go out anyway. It's awfully close in here.'

'What does that mean?' Jake asked.

'Hot, sticky,' I explained.

'I think it's cold. I'm always cold since the oil embargo.'

'You're probably used to central heating, anyway,' my mother said. 'We've never had that here, not oil heating, just wood. Willie said oil heating was a pointless luxury and of course it turned out he was right.'

'Where Dad comes from, they just had coal fires,' I told Jake. 'Still do, I guess. There's no money in Britain for things like central heating.'

Jake shivered. 'I couldn't live like that.'

'No, you couldn't,' my father said.

'Of course, the British are all rather old-fashioned, aren't they? They stick to things like coal fires for sentiment as much as anything else, I think. No wonder the British empire collapsed. They had no sense of challenge, change, adventure – no guts.'

My mother slammed the kettle down hard on the stove. 'That's not exactly a tactful thing to say in this house, young man,' she reprimanded Jake.

He blushed, or flushed with anger. He was not often reprimanded by anybody. 'It's true!' he said. He gathered his papers together to leave the room, unwilling to allow us his company any longer.

'Jake,' I said, 'don't argue. You're coming from a different place than they are, don't forget.'

'It may or may not be true,' my father said, and everybody looked at him, or looked at least at his back, which was all we could see of him. 'It doesn't matter. You've won your war, anyway.'

'What war?' Jake squeaked, exasperated by the futile argument or whatever it was he had gotten involved in.

'Your war, the one that gave you central heating in your expensive New York apartment.'

'But I haven't *got* central heating anymore! There's no goddamn oil.'

'You see? There's no winning in the end, is there?'

'Oh, for Christ's sake,' Jake said, standing up. 'Oh!' he said, suddenly grasping, or thinking he had grasped, my father's logic. 'You think because I'm *Jewish* I got the best deal out of the war, don't you? Maybe you wanted to see all the Jews fry in gas ovens, maybe you think the Germans should have –'

'Whssht!' my father spluttered. That meant 'shut up', a phrase he never used. He left the window and walked over to Jake. Neither of them were tall but my father seemed to tower over Jake.

'The Germans, the Jews!' my father said. 'Is that all there was to the war? What about all the soldiers who died? American soldiers, British soldiers. The ones who came back from the war without legs or arms or mute or deaf or just plain insane? What about the Gypsies in the concentration camps? The Catholics, the conscientious Protestants? What about me?'

'Oh, what about you?' Jake taunted. 'What did *you* lose in the war? Looks like you got a pretty good deal, a nice life in America, huh?'

'I lost – pride,' my father said. His voice was hoarse. 'Four years in a prisoner-of-war camp and I've got nothing to show for it at all. No medals. No service to my country. No dignity. Just – fear.'

Jake had no answer for once. My father had nothing more to say, having said plenty already. My mother stood by the stove, her egg boiling away and already far too hard. Her eyes ran with tears of shock and tenderness. 'Willie,' she whispered, 'why have you never said –?'

'Nobody wanted to know,' he said curtly, and went to the door. He looked out at the drizzly day. 'I've got to get out. I never feel free inside anymore.'

He went outside, crossed the lawn, and looked down the street towards the retreating parade. We watched him walk slowly back towards us until he slipped out of sight around the corner of the house. He walked like a man in a narrow tunnel, cautious of the great space hemming him in. We heard the axe on the wood, a regular rhythmic sound that soothed us.

Jake said, 'I guess I'll finish my paper down at Martin's. Do you want to come?'

'No,' I said.

'Maybe I'll spend the night there,' he added.

'Good,' I said.

'Excuse me,' my mother said, leaving the kitchen. We heard the back door open and shut. She had left the egg still boiling. I turned the stove off and ran cold water over the egg.

'To tell the truth,' Jake said, 'I don't feel too comfortable here. I mean, it's not nice knowing your father thinks he's more important than several million Jews.'

'He doesn't think that,' I said, picking up my own papers and books. I had no appetite for Lowell. I thought I might bake something.

'*You* wouldn't know,' he said bitterly. 'You're not Jewish. You people will never understand.'

'I guess not,' I said. 'And you'll never understand war until you've been in one. Maybe then you'll see that you have something to learn.'

'Oh brother,' he said, slapping his books together. 'Now I've heard everything. I hope Martin is in a sensible mood. I've had enough nonsense up here.'

He stamped up the stairs to gather his belongings. I prepared a cup of coffee for my mother: she had not had any breakfast. I made a cup for my father, too, and took the coffee out to them.

My parents were standing arm in arm, looking up at Mt Ascutney, which had recently changed from its winter blue to light yellow-green. It was a glorious sight, even under the heavy grey clouds which were lifting at last. I thought I could understand my father's long-lasting bitterness but wondered that it hadn't entirely vanished in the peaceful years spent in Vermont.

'Coffee, Mom, Dad,' I said.

'Thank you, sweetie,' my mother said, taking both cups from my hands, as my father didn't turn. 'The sun will come out soon, don't you think?'

'It may,' I said, with the caution of a native Vermonter; caution was a trait my mother did not possess. 'I might climb Ascutney again.'

'What about your friend?' my father asked, turning at last to face me with a vague, sombre expression, his usual one. His face only really showed alertness and perhaps the trace of a smile when he reached a mountain-top and could see that no danger lurked anywhere, that he was in fact free.

'He's gone to Martin's. He doesn't understand your point; he's got it all wrong. He thinks he knows everything.'

'I don't *have* a point,' my father said. 'But then, neither does he. He'll find that out soon enough.' He sipped his coffee and smiled at me to say thank-you.

'When the next war comes!' I said vindictively, thinking of Jake silenced by fear and danger.

But 'God forbid' was all my father said.

# The Lodger

Mrs Ward, lying in bed, worried about Jim. The narrow single
bed in the small crowded room held her large rangy body with
little extra room for worries. Worries she kept inside her hidden,
like her faith, from prying eyes. Eyes pried here. Friend or foe,
they were all intent on knowing your past, your future, your
plans (if you allowed yourself the luxury of having any), your
present state of mind, body and soul.

Mrs Ward, lying in bed alone, felt safe from the prying eyes
and the insolent tongues. Even out of bed, in the kitchen or
wandering through her rooms, she considered herself safely out
of the domain of public gossip. Not because there was nothing to
say about Mrs Ward but because it had all been said too many
times. Now there were others to talk about when and if people
felt it safe to talk about others (which was not always, so
innuendo and suggestion were more common than outright
gossip).

True, when Mrs Ward first came to town there was plenty to
see and plenty to say about her, and local gossips came in pairs
and larger groups for tea and sherry. The attractive, not-so-
young widow was fair game for gossip then: after all, she knew
where she was, knew the kind of place it was, knew the rules,
and *still* she broke them one by one. She was asking to be talked
about!

Mrs Ward was a widow and had been since she first came to
town. Her husband had died not long before, leaving her alone
in unfriendly Belfast with a few acquaintances and enough but
not too much money. She sold their house there and moved up
to the coast, buying a decaying old Victorian house that was
detached but closely sandwiched between two other Victorian
houses just like it, looking out over but not on the seafront.
Other people had the same idea: old army colonels and retired
bankers bought the neighbouring houses and after they were

34

made suitable for modern living by local builders these old retired couples moved in and most of them, like Mrs Ward, took in lodgers to supplement their pensions or small savings.

But Mrs Ward hired no local builders. What a shock it was to see her working herself, running in and out of the front door, wearing dirty denim trousers – jeans, she called them – herself hauling out loads of old plaster and rotten wood, then shoving new boards, wallpaper and cans of paint back in, assisted only by some young men she had hired in Belfast.

Obviously, Mrs Ward was foreign; not English, though, and not from the continent. She would be American, people deduced, since she clearly came from somewhere where they didn't care what you did or how you did it. In fact, Mrs Ward was Canadian, but in town they continued to call her American for many years. Some even went wide of the mark and said she was Australian.

The neighbours assumed that once the house was rebuilt Mrs Ward would leave her jeans in the drawer and would wear proper clothing. The other widows in town wore drab woollen suits year in, year out, olive or navy or dun-coloured skirts and matching lambswool sweaters, sweaters usually too tight, cramming their ample though shapeless bosoms into a mammoth lumpiness that was foreboding. Mrs Ward wore no woolly suits, wore no skirts at all, wore jeans and flannelette shirts over her thin torso, shirts that were large and loose. She wore plimsolls, dirty and with holes at the toes, or sandals in summer.

Dressed like that, Mrs Ward was not welcomed into the town's social circles. She was invited to no bridge games and nobody asked her to join the operetta company. Even the Oxfam women left her alone. She, in turn, made no move to participate in these activities; apparently she found other ways to occupy herself.

Going to church was not one of these ways. She did not go to the Church of Ireland or to the Catholic Church. She did not turn up at the Presbyterian Church, or the Baptist Church, or the Congregational Church, or the Methodist Church, or even at the Temple of God. Some wondered if she were Jewish but others said no, how could she be? She was Canadian, after all, not Polish.

Mrs Ward, lying in bed, prayed to no God, sought no passages of scripture for solace. She had been raised in what was called the Episcopal Church in her town, but no longer felt the need to attend services. She had her own faith. She pierced the gloom of her memory from time to time for quotations from Heidegger, Sartre or Arendt; she had studied philosophy and there found guidance.

'Why on earth does she stay?' they asked at first, and still they wondered but no longer asked, taking her word for it that she could not return, had no family or friends left in Canada and no possible income there. But it didn't seem logical that a foreign widow would invest her small fortune in Ulster when that money could have taken her far away.

Mrs Ward knew that it wasn't logical or clever, but somehow it seemed right to remain in the land that her dead husband had loved. Everybody left Ireland; that was easy. It cost money but it was a cheap thing to do. Mrs Ward stayed, and stayed right through the seventies when all hell broke loose and the High Street was bombed, day after day, shop by shop, right down the length of it.

Mrs Ward ran a Bed-and-Breakfast and admitted everybody who asked for lodging, provided there was room. When the dark-skinned students came to the door at the other Bed-and-Breakfast establishments, they were turned away: 'We're full,' they were told, even when there were vacancies. They were sent to Mrs Ward. She did not often have vacancies; usually she was full with African and Indian and Pakistani students and American tourists. Nobody else in town wanted coloureds and nobody wanted Americans. The Americans caused trouble, taking too long baths with too much hot water and getting up far too early in the morning to go off and wastefully spend energy. It was better to have the house full of students, white British students, nice Protestant boys and girls, who knew the value of a good education and the cost of hot water.

Jim was a foreigner, but he was not a student, nor was he exactly a tourist. He had said he would be staying a year, and although he had nothing to do in that year he had once said to Mrs Ward that a year might not be long enough. Whatever he was doing, it kept him away from the house from just after breakfast until after the pubs closed at night.

# The Lodger

Mrs Ward worried about Jim, not because he was foreign and not because he didn't seem to have any particular reason for staying in the town. Nor was it that, like most Americans, he talked too much and too loudly about things which should not be talked about. Jim didn't do that, not really. It was not what he said, Mrs Ward thought, but what he expected others to say that was so disturbing.

She had watched Jim operate, which was what he did. Every moment seemed to have a purpose with him. She had watched him ask questions of her two Irish lodgers, two Protestant lads from Enniskillen who might just as well have been Catholics from Letterkenny for all Mrs Ward cared. Jim cared, though, about their origin, about their religion, about their feelings. He asked them questions about these things and they were questions the Irish students could not answer; they had never been asked such questions before. Questions were not asked in Ireland, Mrs Ward wanted to tell Jim, nor were they answered, not even in one's head.

'Don't look for trouble,' she wanted to tell him. 'There's no trouble here if you don't look for it.'

Jim had courted trouble in other ways. He had gone to every church in town, choosing a different church each Sunday. It took him more than a month to go to all the churches. Once he had attended them all he didn't return to any; Mrs Ward thought that at least was wise.

He came home often smelling of drink, which did not cause trouble because Mrs Ward considered it quite normal for a young man to enjoy the pub. She herself enjoyed a drink and sometimes met Jim at the door smelling slightly of drink herself. She did not go often to the pub, since she had to go alone and that, she knew, was considered a little odd. So she often had some lager or wine at home, and when she met Jim at the door at night to give him a hot-water bottle, she sometimes wished she could invite him to have a drink with her in the kitchen. But that too, she knew, would be considered odd and she tried to ration her eccentricities because a surfeit of them would cause trouble.

Jim was a little bit dark, like her other boarders, but whereas they were dark from birth Jim had that healthy darkness all Americans seemed to have from spending the entire year pursuing vigorous outdoor sports and from having sun a great portion of the year. He had thick dark hair and thick strong bones. Really, he was a good-looking young man and friendly and appealing, too. Mrs Ward couldn't understand why such a fine young man wanted to live in dreary Ireland, but then she knew that others wondered the same about her.

Mrs Ward worried about Jim, and not just because he asked too many questions, had no reason to be in the town, had no religion, received no letters, offered no information about himself. She worried about him for another reason.

She had seen him on the beach the other day with silly little Cathy Mackie. Cathy was simple and everybody knew it. Only Jim didn't seem to know it. He walked with his arm around her, apparently enjoying her innocent conversation. Mrs Ward, watching the couple from high above on a cliff, had at first felt angry: she suspected that Jim intended to take advantage of the mindless girl. That didn't seem like the sort of thing he would do, though. Then she wondered if Jim did not know that Cathy Mackie was simple. Maybe he thought all Irish girls were equally silly. Americans were like that: they thought that everybody else, including Canadians, were inferior in every way. Whatever he was doing with Cathy Mackie, Mrs Ward thought at last, he was really courting trouble, and she feared for him.

Nobody else had ever walked on the beach with Cathy, although she was twenty-three, an age when most of the local girls had walked many a time on the beach with many young men and then married. She had not known the attentions of young men because she was so simple, of course, and also because she was her father's daughter. Her father was Bob Mackie, not the Bob Mackie who ran the Anchor Inn but the other one, the one who claimed never to have set foot inside a pub, the one who claimed that he spoke with God, the one who led the Temple of God in worship and from that position of authority denounced his cousin Bob Mackie the publican and everybody else in town as well, including Mrs Ward, for their sins. Bob Mackie the minister matched a sin to every name in town and then proceeded to prophesy proper punishment for every sinner, foretelling hellfire and damnation in every instance.

His congregation was small, comprised only of his immediate family and some distant relatives from nearby towns. Because the Temple of God afforded him such a limited audience he often took his message right to the streets. Nobody would have paid any attention to him in the streets, except that he demanded attention and people sometimes found it hard to get away from him. In fact, some people were afraid to move away from him because his evangelical style included physical persuasion, bullying and badgering by arm as well as by voice.

Mrs Ward generally avoided Bob Mackie and he avoided her in return, ever since the time he had brought his message right into her Bed-and-Breakfast, marching in uninvited to preach to her lodgers at breakfast-time. She had thrown a heavy metal teapot at him and then had graciously invited him out of her house. He had accepted the invitation. He still preached against her, finding plenty of material in her, for surely no Christian woman wore the clothes that she wore, gave lodging to heathens, drank in pubs and, worst of all, of course, had the bad judgement to have been born in Canada, a land that was full of pagan savages.

Mrs Ward knew that Jim could not know about Bob Mackie. He could not have been expected to avoid the man's daughter or the man himself. She should have warned Jim, about Bob Mackie and about many other things. Now she couldn't say anything to him because he was gone. He had not been home for three nights. He still had clothes in his room, she knew. She waited for him to come back for his clothes.

Mrs Ward feared that Jim had gone off somewhere with Cathy Mackie. Looking down on them that day on the beach, Mrs Ward had suspected that walks on the beach would not be enough for them in the near future. Now maybe they had gone off somewhere to do more than walk on the beach. She wondered if Cathy Mackie had run away with Jim. If only she could know! But nobody in town was likely to know or care about the Mackies. Gossip didn't touch them, not because they were blameless but because they were beyond belief, too bizarre to be considered for normal, uplifting gossip. Mrs Ward now wished that a whisper of gossip might reach her to provide some clues about her lodger.

Mrs Ward, lying in bed worrying, heard a noise at the front

door, far from her bedroom which stretched out under the
kitchen at the very back of the house. She roused herself from
the small bed and slipped into the solid wool bathrobe, which
was a man's because women's nightwear was too flimsy and
small. She brushed her hand through her hair and prepared to
go to the door. Jim had come back, she hoped. If somebody else
had come to the door, a transient looking for a place to stay, she
would cringe with embarrassment to be seen in her bathrobe and
looking so tired.

But she had no need to open the door or even get near it.
Instead of finding a shadow behind the door – Jim or another
man waiting to gain entrance – she found a flashing light already
inside the door, a blinding white fire burning with a sour
chemical smell which suffocated and shocked her. Even though
she and everyone else in town had learned to expect shocks
during the last decade, it was certainly shocking to see the front
hall in flames. Even when you expected the worst, flames were
frightening.

She rang the breakfast bell with a flourish, screamed 'fire' and
then ran up the stairs, screaming fire again and again. The
students were slugabeds, especially the Indian in number seven.
She pounded hard on his door. All the lodgers came trooping
downstairs soon enough and she herded them out the back
door, through the kitchen to the small garden.

A fire truck arrived, unsummoned, and the fire was doused
with little ado. It was not a particularly forceful fire, or so the
fireman said, and it had not worked its way much beyond the
front hall, since all the downstairs rooms were safe behind
tightly shut doors.

There was no question of the fire's origin.

'It was a bomb, you know, madam,' the policeman said. He
had come to question Mrs Ward or to interrogate her. He seemed
sure that she did know that it was a bomb; in fact seemed sure
that somehow she expected and deserved the bomb.

Mrs Ward did know, or suspected anyway, that Bob Mackie
had somehow created the fire in her front hall. She did not say so
to the constable because she knew that it just wasn't done, to
accuse a minister of arson, even if the minister and the church he
represented were peculiar. She would say nothing, just as those
bombed for other reasons said nothing. Bob Mackie probably

knew that she would say nothing; he knew that he could hide his evil act, an act of evil quite blatant and banal, under the more transcendent terror that had transformed the people of Ulster into spiritual deaf-mutes.

When the policeman had gone away, taking with him the boarders because they could not sleep in their smoke-filled rooms, Mrs Ward went to her own room which was not affected by the fire. She changed from her smoky bathrobe to her soiled jeans. She threw on several large sweaters and an anorak and went outside.

Somehow it wasn't raining. That was unusual and comforting. A moon shone at infrequent intervals through the ever-present haze of clouds. The air was cool and damp and moving through it was soothing, like a cool hand on a feverish head.

Mrs Ward walked past the tourist shops, past the tea-room, the game parlour, all closed for the season, and past the movie-house, which had been bombed five years before and never re-opened. She climbed down off the concrete esplanade and walked unsteadily in the soft sand. Soon she had gone beyond the weak light of the street lamps and stood in total darkness on the beach, which was illuminated only when the moon broke through.

The beach faced north, her favourite direction. To the north there was nothing, or at least nothing much, certainly nothing you could ever see. Some Scottish islands were out there, Iceland to the north-west, and the glacial islands of the north pole. Mostly there was only sky. Some liked to travel to Donegal and to look westward, but Mrs Ward thought that an anti-climax. The Americas lay to the west and although you couldn't see them you knew they were there, always knew that they were there. You could not pass a day, really, without hearing about somewhere in America or Canada on the news. But over there, Mrs Ward knew, many days went by without a whisper of Ireland, except when there was violence.

Now the violence had occurred in her own front hall, although it was not the kind of violence that they meant when they spoke of the violence in Ireland. True, it was the kind of thing that happened often in America: deranged cult leaders like Bob Mackie flourished over there and acts of family violence seemed to be the rule, not the exception, if what the papers said were true.

Deborah Moffatt

In Ireland, Mrs Ward thought, it was not the norm for such things to occur. Bob Mackie was not normal, neither was his daughter. Jim Clark was not a normal part of the Irish scene; he was foreign, and so was she, for that matter. It was a concatenation of oddities which had resulted in an odd event that had nothing to do with Ireland.

The moon ducked back behind a cloud one more time and Mrs Ward turned to go home. In the darkness she realized that nevertheless the whole mess could only have happened in Ireland. Only in Ireland, in Ulster, would nobody have said anything to prevent the violence, only here would nobody now say anything to explain it.

She went into her house. It was still smoky throughout and damp and ashy in the front hall. She prepared a cup of coffee and sat down in the cold kitchen to drink it. It was a strange time to drink coffee, nearly three in the morning. There was a strange feeling in her brain, as she felt words awakening so inappropriately in the late night, words long exiled. Words fled Ireland, like the constant flight of the natives. Words were abundant, on the one hand – there were plenty of cheap, common words, overused and undernourished by thought. But other words, words to express reflection, consideration, truth, were rare and dangerous.

Mrs Ward started to talk out loud, anxious to get words flowing. Her mind, like a pump, needed priming. 'I'll have to start to talk,' she said, hesitating, as if air bubbles held the words back. 'Have to start talking, we will, or die trying.' She muttered away for quite some time with nobody to hear her.

# KRISTIEN HEMMERECHTS

## The Sixth of the Sixth
## of the Year Nineteen Sixty-Six

Tania was a lovely child, with light blue eyes and soft brown curls. She lived in a house with her father and her mother. There were many rooms in this house but only one room was Tania's. This house also had a garden with flowers and grass and vegetables and a fishpond and a willow tree. The garden was bordered by a hedge. Beyond the hedge there were cornfields. Tania never went into these fields because the corn had to be left alone to grow, till it was time to reap it. Often Tania would stand and watch the cornfields from the window of her room and think about the corn growing in the fields.

One day Tania's father came home and said:
– Today is the sixth of the sixth of the year nineteen sixty-six. Later that night Tania repeated to her bear:
– Today is the sixth of the sixth of the year nineteen sixty-six. And she went and stood by the window and looked at the corn growing in the field, and said:
– Today is the sixth of the sixth of the year nineteen sixty-six. Tania tried to work out when the time would come that she would be able to say:
– Today is the seventh of the seventh of the year nineteen seventy-seven. But the thought was too big for her, and she went to sleep, whispering to her bear the magic words.

The next day, Tania's father did not come home and Tania's mother cried. They had strawberries with their dinner, but still Tania's mother cried and would not touch the strawberries. So Tania ate all the strawberries and was sick. That night Tania cried, not because her father had not come home, but because she would never again be able to say:
– Today is the sixth of the sixth of the year nineteen sixty-six. Nobody would ever be able to say so again. This was such a sad thought, Tania had to cry.

The next day Tania did not go to school, for her mother was

still crying. She wandered through the garden and looked at the flowers and the grass and the vegetables and the fish. She went and sat on her bed with her bear and the day was very long.

The next day Tania's father did come home. He brought flowers for Tania's mother and a bear for Tania. Tania thought this was very silly of her father. Surely he must know that she had already got a bear, and that she could not explain to him that from now on there would be another bear as well. So Tania politely thanked her father for the present. All the same, she could not accept this bear, for it would upset her own bear. Could he please take this bear back to the shop and get a warm jacket for her own bear instead. Tania's parents thought this was very funny and told her to go and play in the garden. Their eyes were shiny and they were sat close to one another. So Tania went out into the garden with this new bear and hid him behind the rocks that surrounded the fishpond. The fish would keep him company and he could always watch the flowers and the grass. For a long time, Tania went and visited this bear every day. She told him stories and sang songs for him. Once she tied a plastic bag over his head, so that he would not get so wet when it rained. Tania's father never asked her what had become of the bear that he had brought home for her, and Tania never told him. All this happened not long after people had said:

– Today is the sixth of the sixth of the year nineteen sixty-six.

Tania's father stayed away now regularly, and Tania's mother did not cry so much anymore when he was gone, nor did her eyes shine so much when he came back. Tania's father did not bring any more presents, and Tania was relieved. Sometimes now, when her father was gone, there came another man to the house, who made her mother's eyes shine. Every time he came to the house, he asked Tania what her name was, and how old she was, and whether she liked to go to school. He brought flowers for her mother and presents for Tania. Tania feared he might bring her yet another bear, but luckily he soon stopped bringing presents, and then he stopped coming to the house altogether. Other men came who brought flowers or who did not bring flowers. They asked Tania what her name was and then forgot.

One day Tania stopped visiting the bear who lived near the fishpond. It simply slipped her mind, just like it slipped her mind to pick up her own bear, who had rolled off her bed, and then

46

under it. There were other things now for Tania: dresses and parties and dances. Boys came to the house now, bringing flowers for Tania and chocolates for her mother. One day it so happened that her father was in the house when a boy came to visit her. When the boy was gone, Tania's father took the flowers that the boy had brought for Tania, and threw them in the bin. Tania cried that night but she did not hug her bear, for she had forgotten all about him.

One day it was the seventh of the seventh of the year nineteen seventy-seven, but nobody noticed and nobody said the magic formula. Tania was busy in her garden picking flowers to pin on her dress, and to put in her soft curly hair. Later that night, at the party, she would take the flowers out of her hair and pin them on Jonathan's shirt and he would look at her with shiny eyes and she would kiss him. That night, however, her father came to the house, and when he saw the flowers in her hair and on her dress, his eyes flashed with anger, and he tore the flowers off her dress and out of her hair and called her something she did not understand. That night Tania did not cry. She picked up the flowers and put them in a vase in her room. She did not go to the party nor did she go to any other party. In fact, after that night, she never again went out and her father never again came to the house. It was the seventh of the seventh of the year nineteen seventy-seven, but Tania had not noticed this, nor had her father.

One day, Tania's mother said she was getting married again and was moving out of the house. Now Tania lived on her own in the house. Once Jonathan visited her, but she had not put any flowers in her hair, and her eyes did not shine, so he left.

In the summer, Tania lived in the garden, and in the winter she sat by the fire inside the house. One summer's day, as she sat under the willow tree, she remembered the bear that her father had brought home for her. She searched behind the rocks of the fishpond and found the bear, ragged and dirty, with bits of plastic stuck to his head. Tania then remembered her own bear, who one day she had forgotten to pick up from the floor. When Tania saw both bears, dusty, worn and old, she cried, for she remembered that summer day long ago when her father had come home to say the magic words. She had two bears now, one for the winter and one for the summer, one for the house and one for the garden.

One day there was a letter. Tania noticed it as she came down the stairs and passed the front door. Soon she grew used to the white square on the green marble floor tiles. Dust collected on the letter, obscuring her father's handwriting.

The next summer, Tania decided to help the farmer reap the corn that grew in the field beyond the hedge. The farmer was pleased to have an extra hand, for the corn had grown plentiful that summer. Tania soon mastered the technique of reaping and for some weeks worked silently side by side with the farmer. At night she rested in the fields, wrapped in a blanket, and lay watchful listening to the sound of the fields until morning came. The smell of freshly reaped corn was in her clothes and in her skin, and her hair took on the colour of the corn. One day, all the corn was reaped, and it was made into flour. Tania asked the farmer could she have some of this flour and the farmer thought this was a fair settlement.

That winter, Tania sat by the fire and ate the bread that she had baked with this flour. One day she looked at herself in the mirror and thought it was time now for her to go. She went into the garden, took the garden bear and threw him into the fire. Then she went upstairs to fetch her house bear, and threw him into the fire, too. She went out into the corridor and picked up the grey square of dust lying on the green marble floor. This also Tania threw into the fire. When everything was burnt and nothing remained but ashes, Tania collected some clothes and the last of the bread that she had baked with the flour from the field. She then drew the curtains and left the house.

## Words

In the beginning was the Word,
and the Word was with God,
and the Word was God.

John, 1, 1.

My son does not speak. His is not a silent world, however. The sound of voices, cars, breaking glass or music reach his inner world, but are never relayed. There is a definite input. No output.

I like living with my son. We live in a spacious, old-fashioned house with many high-ceilinged, carpeted rooms, which are all empty now, except, of course, for our bedrooms, where we each have a mattress, and the living-room, where my son has put the table and the two chairs. Naturally we have no books. In all our house there is not a single printed or written word.

Occasionally we have a visitor, but visitors never stay long. Ours is not a house for conversational chats about the weather, the latest plane crash or the glamorous film star's suicide. Words move uneasily in the empty space, bounce painfully against the high ceiling and fall flat on the carpet. Most evenings my son and I draw our chairs in front of the window and watch the evening sun tint the world with rosy hues. At such moments I may choose to tell my son about my day's work. I speak softly and use my words sparingly. My son never makes any comment, but I can tell he is listening from the way he arches his eyebrows. When I stop talking, he turns his face towards me and smiles. My son is very beautiful when he smiles.

There was a time when my son used to speak.
There was a time when all the rooms were furnished and the house was filled with the clamour of voices, happy voices, angry voices, of the numerous guests who used to honour the house with their visit.

There was a time when all the walls were covered by bookcases, which sagged under the weight of the countless books.

There was a time when my husband was alive and we were a family with a father, a mother and a child.

Some of my husband's colleagues have written a book about that time. My husband had written many books himself and I guess it is by virtue of those books that they decided to round off the list with one more book. *Geoffrey James: A Complete Guide.* Sometimes I wish I had a copy of the book. Maybe if I looked at all the pictures long enough, maybe if I read all the footnotes and articles long enough, maybe some pattern would emerge, maybe all those words and phrases would combine to make sense of twenty-two years of wedded life.

I know the pictures in the book well. I mean, I was the one who selected them. One day Lionel, Geoffrey's former right-hand man and then chief editor of the book, visited me and explained the book's basic outline. Could they count on me for the pictures? Lionel phrased this simple request in his usual eloquent and elaborate manner, lacing his speech with as many 'my dear Hildas' as he could possibly fit in. As usual he was still explaining his request long after I had given my consent.

I felt I was facing an impossible task. How could I catch the essence of Geoffrey's life in fifty scenes, be they accidentally recorded by a cheeky camera, or especially performed for the camera's sake (Geoffrey proudly posing next to the statue of his favourite poet)? Which pictures could be said to be representative, significant, typical, momentous? Which pictures would Geoffrey have chosen himself? And what about the unrecorded, the hidden, the unrevealed?

'There is no picture of the breakfast table,' I said when Lionel came to collect the pictures.

I had offered Lionel my husband's seat and I watched him intently as he drank coffee out of my husband's cup and sipped my husband's favourite cognac, a combination Geoffrey could not resist after a good meal. It occurred to me that I might be able to conjure up my husband. Lionel would be the obvious medium. His students had nicknamed him 'his master's voice', because his manner of speaking, his opinions, the very inflexion of his voice, formed a perfect echo to my husband's.

'Pardon? Did you say the breakfast table? How delightfully

original, my dear Hilda, you are one of the truly original spirits of the age. You would be surprised how depressingly few genuinely original people one meets, even in a profession like mine.'

As Lionel rambled on about his frustrating experiences with the general drabness of the so-called creative set, I wondered whether I could possibly get him to sit at the head of the breakfast table as Geoffrey had done. I would have to starch and iron the white table-cloth, lay the table with the gold-rimmed white china, the silver cutlery and the white serviettes folded in the silver serviette rings. Then a freshly-cut red rose (still sprinkled with morning dew) in a crystal vase next to Geoffrey's plate, fresh orange juice, hot coffee, crisp rolls, creamy butter, rich cheese, home made jam, and milk. He would have to wear Geoffrey's dressing gown. The deep red dressing gown was an indispensable prop. I'd teach him how to wear it in Geoffrey's casual manner so that the silk lining showed with every movement. I smiled as I realized he would have to come straight out of Geoffrey's bed and bath, having used Geoffrey's bath oil, soap, talcum powder, aftershave lotion and thick soft towels. In fact, he would have to come out of bed with me, so the peculiar mixture of smells would be just right: the scent of soap and lotion, with a faint whiff of stale sex and sleep, which no quantity of lotion could dissipate. I would watch him attentively as he'd come down the stairs, open the door, walk over to me, kiss me on the cheek ('Good morning, my dear Hilda'), sit down at the head of the table, smell the rose and say: 'How perfectly considerate of you, my dear Hilda, to have thought of a rose. I think a red rose with breakfast makes the prospect of a new day quite bearable. Quite bearable.'

And while pouring him some coffee, still watching his every movement and facial expression, maybe it would all suddenly become clear to me, maybe I would suddenly grasp the meaning of the breakfast ritual, which had been performed without any change in the script, every morning for nearly twenty-two years.

'Would you like to see the bedroom?' I interrupted Lionel. He blushed. Clearly.

'Er, my dear Hilda, I am so sorry for keeping you. I know the book must put an awful strain on you. Those memories would try the strongest of us. Oh dear, is it already gone four? I must rush or I'll miss the meeting.' He quickly drank his cognac down and got ready to go. 'Oh dear! I almost forgot. My dear Hilda, can I ask you one more favour? It is dreadfully important. You see, the book would be incomplete, embarrassingly incomplete, if we did not include a chapter on Geoffrey's articles in newspapers and magazines. Damian was actually saying the other day that the very seeds of Geoffrey's most fundamental work lay scattered over the pages of the weekly and daily press. It just occurred to me that you might have kept some of the newspaper cuttings. Listen, I'll call round again next week, my dear Hilda, and we'll discuss it then.'

He planted the customary three kisses on my cheeks and dashed out of the house. As I watched him walk away, I noticed for the first time that he wore exactly the same cut of coat as Geoffrey used to wear, and that his walk was very much like Geoffrey's.

Well, naturally I had kept all the newspaper cuttings. Any piece that Geoffrey ever did for a newspaper or magazine, or any piece that had ever been done on him, had been cut out and carefully filed. While Geoffrey was out at the University, or at a conference or seminar, I stood watch at home, scanning the press for Geoffrey's name, and drawing a circle round it, in blue for the pieces by him, in red for the pieces on him. Geoffrey was especially sensitive to the latter. Over the years, I had gradually turned the sewing room into a filing room. In the first years of our marriage, I used to spend hours up there trying out patterns, colours and materials. I loved making patchwork wallhangings. A garden I'd create, or a farm, or a beach, out of myriad different rags. But as Geoffrey produced more and more words, and as those words generated yet more words, I needed every spare moment to keep this endless flow of words under control. Soon the filing cabinets started to overtake and finally the sewing machine had to be moved to the attic. Blue labels went on the cabinets that held Geoffrey's pieces: book reviews, critiques, gossip columns, philosophical essays, extracts from his novels, letters, lectures, conferences. Red labels for the pieces on him: on his book reviews, on his critiques, on his gossip columns, on his philosophical essays, on his novels, on his letters, on his lectures, on his conferences. Geoffrey produced the words. I filed them.

Exactly one week later Lionel called round again. He was sporting a white silk scarf as Geoffrey used to.

'Hello, Geoffrey,' I whispered, 'how was work?'

'My dear Hilda, so glad to see you! You look absolutely super in that cream outfit! How are you, dear? Aren't we having the most titillating weather? I mean, isn't it ghastly having to work on a day like this? Listen, my dear Hilda, I am in a most hellish hurry. I'm on my way to Damian to discuss the piece he's to do on the newspaper material. Do you recall me briefly mentioning it last week? Damian feels strongly about the idea of doing something which could be an important statement on, er, well . . .'

'Sure, Lionel, it is all up in my sewing room, I mean filing room, it's all there. I'll show you.'

I led the way. We passed between a double row of bookcases that lined the hall. I ran my finger over the backs of the books as we climbed the stairs.

'Do you know how long it takes to dust all the books in this house?' I asked.

'Pardon, Hilda, did you say dust? Oh no, no idea. Never gave the matter any thought, I must admit.'

'Three hours and forty-five minutes, not counting the ones that are up in the attic.'

I waited for a reply but could only hear Lionel panting behind me on the stairs.

'This way, Lionel.'

Lionel stopped short.

'You don't mean, my dear Hilda . . .'

He had obviously not been prepared for this. I guess he had expected a few crummy shoeboxes, not rows of filing cabinets reaching up to the high ceiling. His mouth fell open as his eyes wandered over the cabinets.

'But, my dear Hilda,' he finally said, 'Damian will be absolutely thrilled to bits. Let's say he wants to do something on the book reviews, so he simply opens this drawer here and . . . but, my dear Hilda, there is nothing there,' he said. 'Nor here,' he said opening another one, 'nor here, nor here . . .' He opened every single cabinet, but there was not one scrap of newspaper to be seen.

'But,' I said.

Lionel needed exactly thirty seconds to tune in to the new situation. He put his arm round me, brushed my hair away from my face, and started speaking in a soothing voice.

'There, there, dear, everything will be fine. Listen, I've got a plan. You forget all about the book, and I and Damian and the others will take care of everything, OK? Now listen, you have a lie down, promise? There's a good girl.'

He swept from the room and hurried down the stairs.

'He thinks I'm going mad.'

I lay down on the bed and concentrated on relaxing. It was no good. I kept imagining Lionel lying there, lecturing on Geoffrey's fundamental thought, Lionel in his tailor-made clothes and white silk scarf, Lionel brushing my hair out of my face. It was no good.

I got up and had another look in the filing room. The cabinets were still empty. I wandered into Stevie's room. Stevie only came home now at weekends, and I loved being in his room during the week. The bed looked strangely lumpy. 'Oh dear,' I thought, 'Maybe Lionel is right, maybe I am losing my grip on reality, maybe I am going round the bend. Cuckoo,' I giggled. I started prodding the bed. Something had been tucked under the mattress, there could be no doubt. I lifted the mattress a little, groped under it, and pulled out a little transparent plastic bag. I turned it round in the light. It seemed to hold newspaper print, torn up in minute particles. I lifted the mattress higher and found hundreds more of these bags. For a second I felt tempted to remake the bed and pretend I had never set eyes upon the bags. Then I forced myself to confirm my suspicion. I opened one of the bags, and examined the tiny shreds. On quite a few of them Geoffrey's name was partly or completely spelt out. I could no longer fool myself. These were the remains of the newspaper cuttings Lionel and Damian wanted so badly.

On Saturday, I spread all the bags out on the dining table and waited for Stevie to come home. Stevie kissed me hello as usual. When he saw the bags, he smiled and started throwing them in the bin.

I helped him.

I helped him throw the work of years into the bin.

When the last bag had been pushed into the bin, Stevie started on the bookcases. With the same methodical fervour he packed all the books in cardboard boxes, and carried the full boxes out on the pavement for the binmen to collect. He looked so peaceful and restful, I could not resist his smile, and again I helped him.

But Stevie hadn't finished yet. As soon as the last box was out on the pavement, he started hauling the furniture out of the house. Wardrobes, chests, stools, tables, desks, beds, seats and bookcases, were dragged out of the house into the garden. He only left the two chairs, the table and the mattresses. All the rest was set on fire.

We sat down by the fire and watched the flicker of the flames.

We sat down by the fire till daybreak.

At daybreak only ashes remained.

As we entered the empty house, I realized we hadn't said a word during the entire operation.

'Would you like to eat something, Stevie?' I asked.

Stevie nodded and I understood that he was not going to speak anymore. He had worked all night to move all the words out of the house and was careful not to let any new ones in. I made us both a cup of coffee and a piece of toast and we sat down on the kitchen doorstep and had our breakfast. I had never before in my life sat down with my son on the kitchen doorstep. It felt very good and peaceful.

When the sun was no longer a painfully delicate birth, we got up and went to sleep on our mattresses.

The following Thursday, Lionel called round.

'My dear Hilda, I happened to be in this part of town and . . .' He stopped. His mouth fell open. He took off his hat and wiped his brow.

'Where, where is everything?' he managed at last.

'Gone,' I said.

'Gone?'

'Yes, gone.'

We stood together in silence, and contemplated the bare walls and the naked floors. Lionel made no sound. The house had silenced him. Presently, he turned round and left the house.

Some months later, I received an invitation to the press reception of *Geoffrey James: A Complete Guide*. I attended and listened dutifully to the speeches praising Geoffrey's art and fundamental thought. Lionel expressed his regret at having been unable to get hold of Geoffrey's work for the daily and weekly press. Some people came up to me and hugged me. They talked about the book and I agreed it was indeed a marvellous book. Someone even asked me to sign her copy. I managed to slip away unnoticed, and casually left my copy of the book on the counter of the cloakroom. I hadn't had a look at it yet. There was, however, no point in taking it home. Stevie would only put it out for the binmen.

*A text for four voices:*

the wife: Jane
the husband: Neville
the daughter: Mary-Lou (a silent part)
the son: Ronny (a silent part)
the wife's friend: Joan
the painter: Max

Scene One

JOAN: They are dancing.
JANE: Oh yes, they always dance after dinner.
JOAN: They move in perfect harmony.
JANE: Oh yes, I know, one movement, one body, one swing.
    The ultimate father and daughter union.
Jane is washing the dishes. Her back is turned towards the
doorway. Her friend Joan is wiping the dishes. She stands in the
doorway of the kitchen and watches the couple dance in the
living-room. There is a dishwasher in the kitchen, that is not out
of order, but Jane prefers to wash the dishes by hand. She claims
she gets nervous watching Neville and Mary-Lou dance.
JOAN: Glenn Miller.
JANE: Always Glenn Miller.
JOAN: I can remember dancing to Glenn Miller, Jane. With
    Bobby. Remember Bobby? Long legs, crew cut, chewing-
    gum, and Camel cigarettes. He used to give me stockings.
    And chocolates. He could lift me up with one arm. He said it
    was the steaks. He said all Americans are strong and tall
    because they eat so much steak.
JANE: Did he really say that?

JOAN: Oh yes, he did. That. And other things.

Joan giggles. Her eyes twinkle. She is young again and is swaying languidly with the handsome GI. She remembers.

JANE: You and your GIs, Joan, you were incorrigible.

JOAN: Bobby asked me to go back with him, you know.

JANE: Really? And you refused?

JOAN: Well, it seemed such a long way at the time. But would you believe, Jane, that sometimes I almost regret having turned him down. He was not like the other GIs.

JANE: Well, you are the expert, Joan. I can't talk. I was already going steady with Neville. Nev wouldn't let me anywhere near the GIs. He'd dance with me all evening, so no GI would get a chance.

JOAN: Bobby would have liked to dance with you.

JANE: Really?

JOAN: Oh yes. He used to go on about your hair. About how beautiful it was and about how he would hold you and stroke your hair while dancing.

JANE: Oh dear, Neville would have had a fit.

JOAN: You shouldn't have had your hair cut, Jane.

JANE: No, I shouldn't have.

JOAN: Why did you, Jane?

JANE: Well, after I had the twins, it just kept falling out, handfuls at the time, and the shine went. I tried various shampoos and treatments, but to no avail. Besides I was married. It seemed the normal and proper thing to have done. Now, of course, it has turned grey.

JOAN: Didn't Neville mind?

Jane stops washing the dishes and turns round to look at her friend. Her eyes are narrowed to two thin slits.

JANE: I think he was pleased, Joan. I think he was pleased and relieved. But I kept it. Neville doesn't know.

JOAN: Did you? Can I see it?

JANE: Some other time, maybe. No one has ever seen it but me.

The two women continue their work in silence. When they have finished with the dishes, Jane wipes the cooker, while Joan stands in the doorway and watches Neville and Mary-Lou.

JOAN: You know, Jane, your hair isn't lost, whether you have kept it or not.

JANE: What do you mean?

JOAN: Just look at Mary-Lou, Jane. Just look at her.

Mary-Lou is wearing a tight skirt and flat shoes. Her thick curly hair falls in endless layers over her shoulders and reaches down to her waist. Jane does not look up from her work.

JANE: I know, Joan. Only hers is more curly than mine. I guess she's got that from her father.

JOAN: But it's the colour, Jane. I've never seen the like of that colour. It isn't blonde, nor ash, nor ginger, nor . . .

JANE: It's Venetian blonde.

JOAN: It's what?

JANE: Venetian blonde. From Venice. Neville says that is the proper name for it.

JOAN: I see.


Scene Two

Jane sits at the dressing-table and runs a comb through her short, grey hair. Neville is in the bathroom. The bedroom door is ajar. Jane gets up and closes the door furtively. Then she sits down again at her dressing-table, opens one of the drawers and takes a wooden box from underneath a pile of nighties. She opens the box and looks admiringly at the thick strands of golden hair. She takes the hair out of the box and feels it with her cheek. When she hears the light being turned off in the bathroom, she quickly replaces the hair and the box, and gets into bed. Neville enters the bedroom and gets into bed. He turns the light off.

NEVILLE: Are you asleep, Jane?

JANE: No, I'm not asleep yet.

NEVILLE: Jane, it's Mary-Lou's birthday soon.

JANE: Yes, I know. And Ronny's.

NEVILLE: She will be eighteen, Jane.

JANE: So will Ronny, Nev.

NEVILLE: Listen Jane, I have been thinking. I want to give Mary-Lou something special. Something which will be a lasting tribute to the splendour of her youth.

JANE: You're making me quite curious.

NEVILLE: Jane, listen. I want to have her portrait painted. I mentioned the matter to David the other day, and he suggested I have a word with the chap who's done his father-in-law's portrait. I phoned him yesterday, as a matter of fact. He seemed interested.

JANE: Oh, it's all settled, then.

NEVILLE: Well, nothing is definite. I mean, one word from you and the whole thing is off.

JANE: What about Ronny?

NEVILLE: Oh come off it, Jane. You know perfectly well Ronny would not want to sit for a painting. But Mary-Lou would love it.

JANE: When can he begin?

NEVILLE: When we're ready.

JANE: When is that?

NEVILLE: Well, we could ask him round for dinner tomorrow night, and discuss it.

JANE: On a Thursday?

NEVILLE: Why not?

JANE: All right. Tomorrow, then. I wonder what he's like.

NEVILLE: He sounds fine over the phone. You'll like him, Jane.

JANE: We'll see. Good night, Nev.

NEVILLE: Good night, Jane.


Scene Three

Dinner the next evening, with the painter.

NEVILLE: If you ask my opinion Mary-Lou's face is a painter's delight. Madonna and temptress all in one. I dare you to catch that expression on canvas. Of course, I intend to give you complete *carte blanche*, as the French say. My wife and myself love the arts. If you are interested, I will show you my collection of prints some time. I possess some fascinating items, I think you would be surprised. Anyway, as I said, we love the arts and we realize that the artistic genius should be given free rein in order to . . .

MAX: You shouldn't wear white.

NEVILLE: Pardon? Oh I see, Mary-Lou's dress. Yes, it is white. The appropriate colour for a young and innocent girl.

JANE: It was a present from her father. Quite exclusive, really.

MAX: Your skin is white. Your skin is milk.

JANE: (*coughs*) Mary-Lou has the most sensitive skin. She cannot stand the slightest exposure to the sun. We always spend the summer holidays . . .

MAX: Your colour is black. I will paint you in a black dress. No jewellery. Your skin will be your jewellery. Your hair will be your crown.

JANE: But Mary-Lou hasn't got anything black. Black is so gloomy.

MAX: I will start painting you now, if your parents will excuse me.

NEVILLE: Excuse me, sir, but Mary-Lou and myself always dance after dinner. It is a pleasure I will not easily forsake. May I have the honour, Mary-Lou?

Mary-Lou and Neville start dancing. Tonight, Mary-Lou moves haltingly. Suddenly, she trips and falls.

NEVILLE: Be careful, dear. Did you hurt yourself. Sit down. You look tired.

Max, who has been watching the couple attentively, stands up and takes Mary-Lou by the hand.

MAX: Come, Mary-Lou, let us dance.

The painter and Mary-Lou dance. Neville is fidgeting with his serviette. The painter holds Mary-Lou tightly and strokes her hair. Jane starts clearing the table. Neville turns the record-player off.

NEVILLE: Enough for tonight. We don't want to exhaust Mary-Lou, do we?

MAX: We start tomorrow at nine, Mary-Lou. Be ready. I will bring you a black dress. Good night.


Scene Four

Dinner, one month later.

NEVILLE: They are out.

JANE: Oh yes, they are always out at night.

NEVILLE: Mary-Lou hasn't had dinner with us for over three weeks now.

JANE: Max wants to spend as much time as possible with her. He says he wants to absorb her features.

NEVILLE: I wish you'd stop calling him Max.

Silence.

NEVILLE: Jane, tell me honestly, what do you think of the portrait? Do you think it's any good?

JANE: Well, he's only just started, really.

NEVILLE: He's done the dress. I mean, he's done a great job on the dress. You'd swear it was real cloth.

JANE: And he's done the face.

NEVILLE: Oh, that's the face. I thought it was just a white blob, you know, sort of background.

JANE: No, it's the face. He told me.

NEVILLE: Ah, he told you.

Silence.

NEVILLE: Shall we do the washing-up, Jane?

JANE: We've got a dishwasher, Nev.

NEVILLE: Anything on telly?

JANE: Some programme or other about D-day.

NEVILLE: Oh, D-day.

JANE: I was eighteen then.

NEVILLE: Were you?


Scene Five

Two weeks later, one evening, just before dinner. Neville stops Max and Mary-Lou in the corridor as they are on their way out.

NEVILLE: Excuse me, do you have a minute? I had a look at your work last night. As a matter of fact, I have a look at your work every night. On my way to bed, I walk into Mary-Lou's room and spend a couple of minutes in front of the easel. I hope you don't mind my saying so, but I find the progress you're making not in the least satisfactory. I am especially wondering about the hair. Am I correct in presuming that the patch of bare canvas is where the hair should be?

MAX: That is correct, sir.

NEVILLE: And may I ask you when you intend to start working on the hair?

MAX: I won't. Your daughter's hair cannot be painted.

NEVILLE: I don't think I quite understand you.

MAX: I said that your daughter's hair cannot be painted. As far as I am concerned, my work is finished. Will you kindly excuse us now? We will be late for dinner.

Mary-Lou and Max leave the house together. Neville watches them, dumbfounded.

Scene Six

Two weeks later. Dinner.
JANE: They are in the South of France. Ronny had a letter from Mary-Lou this morning.
NEVILLE: Please, Jane, I told you, I don't want to hear another word about it. I don't care whether they are in Hong Kong or on the moon.
JANE: Tell me, then, Neville, why do you spend every night up in her room staring at that portrait? Don't imagine I don't know! You can't fool me!
Neville looks up at Jane. He opens his mouth, ready to speak, but closes it again. Then he pushes his plate away and leaves the room. Jane picks up the serviette Neville has dropped.

Scene Seven

Jane is in bed. Neville enters the bedroom quietly and lies down next to her. Jane pretends to be asleep and waits for Neville to fall asleep. Presently she gets out of bed, takes the box of hair out of its hiding place and steals out of the room. She fetches some glue downstairs and enters Mary-Lou's room. She turns the lights on and sits down in front of the unfinished painting. She opens the box and sighs. She picks up the hair and holds it against the patch of bare canvas. She smiles. Then she starts gluing the strands of hair meticulously onto the canvas.

Scene Eight

The next day. Dinner is just over. Jane settles down in a comfortable chair with a magazine. Neville disappears upstairs. Less than a minute later he comes haring down.
NEVILLE: Jane, Jane, the portrait. Come and have a look. You won't believe your eyes!

JANE: I know. The hair.

NEVILLE: Mary-Lou's hair, Jane!

JANE: My hair, Neville.

NEVILLE: Your hair, Jane?

JANE: My hair, Neville.

NEVILLE: Oh, my God, Jane! Your beautiful hair! I didn't know you had kept it! We must celebrate. Hang on. Let me turn the record-player on. We will dance, you and I, to Glenn Miller! Just like old times!

JANE: One moment, Neville. I must fetch something from upstairs. It won't take a minute.

Presently Jane returns with the portrait and places it in Neville's arms.

JANE: Here, Neville, you dance with her.

For a moment, Neville is taken aback. Then he puts his arms fondly round the canvas and starts moving in time to the music. In the kitchen, Jane starts washing the dishes noisily. Meanwhile, hair falls sultrily against Neville's cheeks.

DOUGLAS GLOVER

# Fire Drill

The bentwood rocker in our living-room belonged to Aunt Maggie. Jack refinished it, glued the joints solid and had the wicker seat re-woven for our third anniversary. But Aunt Maggie died of Alzheimer's Disease, and sitting in her chair always gives me the creepy feeling I'll turn out the same. 'You're weirder than I thought,' says Jack, eyeing me as if my worst fears have already been realized.

Also in the living-room we have an iron wood-burning stove of the kind Jack sells out of his bicycle shop over the winter lull and a giant aquarium which I gave him as a graduation present. The aquarium is full of greenish water, plastic plants and coloured pebbles, but the last Black Molly vanished six years ago when we moved to Aurora from the city. For a while, it housed a goldfish Erin won at the county fair, but no one has seen 'Gilda' for months. Now Erin perches on the landing above the tank and throws in pennies for wishes. We're the only family I know with a private wishing well in the living-room. I tell Jack he's pretty weird himself.

On Erin's first day of kindergarten, I forget what I'm doing and sit in Aunt Maggie's chair by mistake. Erin huddles in my lap, pale as death, unwilling to cry, taut as piano wire. I don't know which of us is freaked out the most. Erin is freaked out because they pulled a surprise fire drill on her bus on the way home and it terrified her. I'm freaked out because Erin is freaked out. But, except for landing in Aunt Maggie's rocker, I am maintaining control.

I am waiting for Jack to get home from the shop before I break down completely. This is as per my instructions from our therapist, who has deduced that I am unable to cope well in crisis situations. Now, if anything happens to Erin, I keep my lips zipped up, calmly hand her over to her father, and leave the room. Later, when the cut is cleaned and bandaged, when the bruise is kissed and the tears wiped away, she can come to me for a hug. The therapist says this way I won't turn my daughter into a basket case before she gets to high school.

Naturally, I have already phoned Jack.

'Come right home,' I say. 'I can't handle it. She won't say a word. They stopped the bus in the middle of the road and made all the kids climb out the back. She didn't know what was happening.'

'She'll be OK,' says Jack. He is altogether too cool in a crisis. A year ago, I nearly died haemorrhaging from an ectopic pregnancy. The orderlies were wheeling me into the operating room, my abdomen full of blood, tubes sprouting from my arms and nose, and someone whispers, 'Has the husband seen her? Make sure she sees her husband before she goes under.' I know this is the end. I know I'm going to check out on the table. Jack bends over me, and I realize we have to make the most of this last moment together. He says, 'How does it feel to have one of those things down your nose?' I say, 'Well, it's not as bad as you might think.' Those were my last words. At least, they could have been my last words. As I say, Jack is altogether too cool.

'How do you know she'll be OK? You can't see her. Why would they scare a kid like that?'

'It's the law,' he says. 'They do it for their own protection.'

'It's a dumb law.'

Jack doesn't drive home early. He refuses to be rattled. I phone my best friend, Peggy, who has a little boy Erin's age who also started kindergarten today. Mike takes a different bus, but Peggy has a horror story just the same. No fire drill, but they switched bus routes on Mike halfway through the morning. His bus missed its normal turn and took the long way around to Mike's stop, Mike weeping quietly till he got safely into his mother's arms. Peggy is not as upset as I am, but we are both unnerved at the way the world is mauling our babies.

This is the first time I have put Erin in the hands of an institution, except for the dismal two months she spent in hospital when she was three. On that occasion we rushed her to Emergency with an acute asthma attack. The doctors had to do a tracheotomy, then misplaced and fouled the hole, scarring her throat. For a while we thought we were going to lose her. I even told Jack to call a priest. We were waiting outside surgery, expecting the worst, and no priest showed up. I was sobbing, trembling, leaning on Jack to stay upright, when finally a nurse appeared and said Erin was all right. 'Where's the damn priest?' I asked Jack. That was the first thing I thought of. 'You didn't call the priest, did you?' Jack just looked sheepish.

After that experience, I can't stand the thought of anything happening to Erin. I won't let anyone but Jack or my mother touch her. I write down the licence numbers of speeding cars and phone the police. I keep my eye on suspicious-looking strangers, noting significant physical characteristics, in case I have to give a description. My ears are tuned to the sound of her voice when she rides her bicycle down the block out of sight. And in my nightmares, I have saved her from drowning, from blazing buildings, from bullies and from embarrassment.

'I think I'll stay home from school tomorrow,' she says, echoing my thoughts. She utters the words in a matter-of-fact, adult manner.

'We'll see what Daddy says,' I reply. Despite a flurry of broody emotions, I am able to think clearly that the therapist would not want me to make a decision on this without consulting my husband.

Later, when he reaches home, we're calmer.

'There,' he says, 'Erin's okay. You're the one who gets upset.'

'We thought there was a real fire on the bus,' I say. 'We don't want to go to school tomorrow.'

Jack shakes his head. He feels as if he has to take responsibility for the whole family. Sometimes he feels as though he's got two kids and no wife. And I have to say there is some truth to that, though it wasn't always so. It is just that after Erin's hospital fiasco and my bad pregnancy, I've never had a chance to catch up. 'You're afraid of taking action,' says our therapist, with her usual flare for the obvious. 'You're afraid of the consequences of taking steps.'

Jack and I stopped having sex three months ago and started counselling. For Jack, this is no substitute. When I turned thirty in July, he told our bowling buddies, 'She's hitting her prime now. I don't know how long I'll be able to keep up the outside activities now that Jenny's past the big three-oh.' He said it nicely; Jack loves me. But his voice had a sad ring to it which made me want to cry.

After supper, notable only for the over-cooked cauliflower and our silence, he takes Erin upstairs to her bedroom to have one of their heart-to-hearts. She has always told Jack more than she tells me. I interrupt and give advice. I try to tell her how to handle situations. When she tells me about the fire drill, I immediately empathize. 'Were you scared, honey? You shouldn't have been scared. It was only a drill.' She stops talking and looks depressed. I have failed to say the right words.

My husband never falls into that trap. He just lets her talk. He says, 'Is that right?' or, 'And then what happened?' And after a while she's explained things to herself and becomes quiet. Then he says, 'Well, that's the way the world works, Erin.' It's a little infuriating. I try and screw up; Jack does nothing and has a somewhat mature relationship with our daughter. After they have had one of these talks, they both look at me as if I were the witless child caught up in a whirl of infantile fears and feelings.

On this particular night, they come solemnly down the stairs to the landing and Jack pulls a penny out of his pocket and hands it to Erin.

'Here we go,' he says. 'You remember the words?'

'I wish I wouldn't be afraid of that pesky old fire drill again,' she says, enunciating slowly, then tossing the coppery penny into the aquarium.

I glare at Jack. He gets away with cheap tricks like that because he doesn't get excited. Sometimes, I tell the therapist, I think he doesn't care as much as I do. If he cared, he wouldn't be able to think clearly either, right?

Erin and I are alike in this: we both believe in magic doors, talking animals and rewards for the virtuous. When Peter Pan saves Tinker Bell by asking the audience if it believes in fairies, I nod my head just as vigorously as Erin does, shaking the tears out of my eyes. We are dreamers, we like to sift amongst the possibilities.

The next day, on her way out the door to catch her bus, she asks, 'What are you going to do all morning without me?'

'Oh, I'll make out,' I say. 'I'll find something.'

She's wearing a dress she picked out herself. It has a white skirt with black piping, a gray bodice and a white Dutch collar. It's a little formal for kindergarten, I think, but this is her way of establishing distance from me. As she disappears into the yellow and black bus, as the doors accordion shut behind her, all I can think of is how I used to fan her butt with my hair dryer because of her diaper rash. Frankly, I don't know what I'll do all morning.

Then Jack calls. He's phoning from the shop, which is called The Bike Garrett, Garrett being a pun on our name. He sells Motobecane, Peugeot, Fuji and Univega, as well as building his own specialty frames. In the winter, as I say, he sells stoves. One winter he sold and installed fifty stoves in welfare homes for the province, but other winters we've had to eat a lot of macaroni.

He's decided we're out of shape, he says. Now that Erin's in school and we have all this free time, he has signed us up for a course at the Nautilus spa. What he really means is that I'm out of shape. Through the summer Jack has been riding his bicycle twenty miles every morning. I've been raising happy little fat cells and cellulite. He also doesn't want me to turn neurotic on him, sitting around the house thinking about fire drills.

'Price-Mart is hiring sales clerks,' I say. 'Peggy and I were thinking of getting jobs.'

'We'll go together,' he says, cheerfully ignoring me. 'The only time we get out of the house without Erin is when we bowl Sunday nights. This'll be good for us.'

I know the way Jack thinks. He likes to try new things; he loves the idea of living dangerously. Once he came home and asked me, if I could do anything, where in the world I'd like to live. He said he was willing to sell the shop, pack up the house and move wherever I wanted. 'Are you crazy?' I said. 'I want to stay right here. My baby is going to go to school here.' Or he'd like me to bleach my hair and do myself up like Angie Dickinson playing yet another fallen woman on the Late Show. I can just imagine shaking my ass with a dozen or so sexy female weightlifters while my husband watches and laughs, but I tell him yes anyway. It's a no-win situation for me. I have to keep my eye on him while giving the impression of psychological normalcy.

After I hang up, I drive into town and buy myself a work-out suit, dance slippers, sweat socks, a sport bra and a pralines-and-peach cone at Baskin-Robbins. Then I break the speed limit twice on the way home to be there when Erin arrives. I am sitting on the steps in my new outfit when she alights from the bus.

Grim. I say to myself, 'Children are not supposed to look this unhappy.' As she drags across the street, I jog out to the picket fence to meet her. I made Jack build this fence to keep Erin in and protect her from dogs and perverts. My fingers are in my mouth, and for a brief, paranoiac moment, I tell myself she is blaming all this on me. Kindergarten was invented by mothers who want to get rid of their babies, right?

'How was school?' I ask, brightly.

'Okay,' says Erin, without looking at me. She trudges wearily into the yard, lugging her school bag like a ball and chain.

'Was the bus ride okay?' I ask. I want a conversation here. I want her to know I care. But somehow I feel like the Wicked Witch of the North harassing Judy Garland along the Yellow Brick Road.

'Yes,' she moans.

I know something has happened. Right away I want to pry it out of her.

'What's the matter, sweetheart?' I ask like a fool, scrunching down on the cement walk so that our faces are on the same level. Why does it seem to stab me that she will not make eye contact? I fight the hysteria rising in my chest like water in a clogged sink, feeling as though any move I might make will only increase her burden.

'We had a pretend fire drill at school,' she says, adding quickly, 'I wasn't afraid as much as yesterday. They didn't ring the fire thing.'

'The siren,' I say.

She ignores me.

'Tomorrow we're going to have a real fire drill and the teacher will time us with a real watch. The teacher said we have to be fast because slowpokes can die in a fire.'

I don't know what to say. I send my child to kindergarten and right off the bat they are instilling a morbid and abnormal obsession with fire hazards. Two days ago she was a carefree urchin with a tracheotomy scar in her throat to remind me of her utter fragility, and this morning she's a short adult striving to deal with the stress of unpredictable and incomprehensible death threats. Twenty years from now, she'll have cancer from this.

'Twenty years from now she'll have cancer,' I tell Jack over the phone. 'I don't think our child will ever laugh again.'

'It seems a little excessive,' says Jack. 'But they probably know what they're doing. What if there really was a fire?'

'Jack,' I say, 'have you ever heard of a child dying in a school fire? The school is built of bricks. It can't burn. They are doing this to break her spirit. They don't have to scare the hell out of her the first week.'

As usual, Jack refuses to become excited. He refuses to leave the shop early. He claims he has a customer waiting. When I get off the phone, Erin is slumped in Aunt Maggie's chair, her skirt rucked up to her hips, staring at the aquarium.

I am uncomfortably reminded of my own childhood as she tips the rocker back and forth awkwardly with the toe of her shoe. Aunt Maggie came to live with us when I was eight, after Uncle Bart was killed in a car accident. She was already a little bughouse even then, though she lived another fifteen years, rocking away, always moving, never getting anywhere. At first I had thought she was kindly disposed toward me because she was always taking my hands, kissing them, holding them against her cheek and saying, 'Poor little Jenny. Poor little Jenny.' But then one day she lifted two of my playmates onto her lap as she rocked and whispered into their ears, thanking them for coming around to visit me so often. 'Why are you thanking us?' Michelle Laforte asked. 'Well, you know,' said Aunt Maggie, conspiratorially, 'poor Jenny's a little retarded.' Even after I went to university, Aunt Maggie couldn't shake the notion that I was mentally deficient.

'You want to go shopping?' I ask Erin. I have a ton of laundry to do, dinner to fix, the logistics of a weekend trip to a Montreal bicycle trade fair to plan, but it seems important that my daughter and I do something to re-establish the routine of her life.

Thirty minutes later, we are zipping down Highway 11 to Eaton's. Erin, now cheerful, relieved, tells me she wants jeans; she wants the Jordache look she's seen on TV commercials. I am willing to fall in with her whims until the moment when we enter the designer jeans department and discover that the Jordache look is going to cost me $25 for a pair of pants that will last about two months at the rate she is growing.

I quickly steer her down the aisle and find something in a price range that will not bankrupt us but also with a designer-like patch on the rear pocket. Erin tries these on and waltzes around, pleased with herself, preening in the mirrors next to the change room. But craning her neck to check the fit over her behind, she makes an alarming discovery.

'These don't say Jordache,' she says, eyeing me darkly.

'Well, they're not exactly Jordache,' I say. Soon she will really be able to read, and then a whole era of our lives together will have ended.

'Well, what does it say?' she asks.

'It says they're just like Jordache. They're just as good.'

'What does it say, Mommy?'

'Health-Tex,' I say. 'Now let's look at something else.'

Soon she has forgotten about the designer patch anomaly and is prancing around in a baggy, pleated minidress of the kind young women have been wearing in Toronto this summer. She's twirling and watching the way the skirt follows her in the mirror. She looks like a midget street-walker. I mentally add the punk make-up and haircut. The truth is, my daughter has terrible taste. In this she takes after me. When I was five, I thought I had the cruellest mother on earth because she refused to buy me a pair of white leatherette go-go boots with pom-poms.

'We've got your jeans, sweetheart,' I say. 'That's enough for one day.'

'You just want me to look awful, don't you, Mother?' she says.

'Yes, Erin, I want you to look awful.'

We drive home in a sulk.

When she has gone to bed, Jack pushes me gently onto the living-room couch and says, 'Let's talk about it.' Jack has really gotten into this therapy stuff. He loves the ritualized conversations. Mostly because he always comes off so well. I'm the one who goes ape when Erin scrapes her elbow. I'm the one who refuses to have sex. During one session with the therapist, I exploded. 'You don't care, you bastard. When our daughter was dying, you read back issues of *Maclean's*.' He looked at me. 'That's not true,' he said. 'When I went outside, when I went to meet your mother at the airport, I cried so hard I couldn't stand up.' 'Well, why didn't you do that in front of me?' I asked. 'Jack realizes he has to take charge,' said the therapist. 'He has to set an example.'

This time, as Jack pushes me down on the couch (he

generally sits in Aunt Maggie's rocker), I say, 'I don't want to talk. I want to be alone. I want to go to the basement to do my laundry, and I don't want you interrupting me.'

Jack takes this in his stride. He understands that we both need alone time. According to Peggy, who has a crush on him, Jack is the Perfect Husband. This is in contrast to Vinnie, her husband, who sleeps around and embarrasses her at parties. Jack is unfailingly loyal, polite and considerate. The harshest thing he's ever said about our lack of a sex life is, 'This is your only time around, Jenny. In twenty years you may regret that you wasted it.'

While I separate the clothes and start the wash cycle, I think things over. I do not understand why I have lost my sense of proportion. It has something to do with seeing my baby suffering, sinking toward death, butchered by a surgeon who didn't even know her name. (Jack held her in his arms for six straight hours the night she was not supposed to pull through. I was too hysterical to do anything but sob and moan at the foot of her hospital crib.) Now everything that goes wrong immediately escalates in my head to that level of disaster. I am always expecting the worst, believing that things will not turn out well.

We have a storeroom next to the laundry, and for a while I rummage in there, examining the leftover paraphernalia of Erin's babyhood. We have kept everything so that we could use it for her brothers and sisters. The automatic swing no longer works when I wind it up. The Big Bird doll we bought when she was three months old is losing its stuffing. In a box in the corner, I find the shipment of baby clothes my sister sent only to have them arrive after Erin had already outgrown them. Her own things are as good as new, neatly folded away in a trunk that smells of mothballs and cedar. Unaccountably, the mothball smell makes me start to cry. Even as I stand here, it says, everything is moving backward and away from me. I am powerless to stop the flow. I realize suddenly that I am terrified and don't know where to turn.

The next morning Erin has a difficult time waking up. She dips her elbow in her Fruit & Fibre, throws a tantrum when I put on her green corduroy jumper, and kicks me in the chin by accident as I buckle her shoes. I shove her out the door as fast as I can, suppressing the urge to motivate her with a hard slap on the butt. Then I peep out the window while she waits, both hands clasped on her school bag, eyes downcast, examining the crumbling edge of the pavement.

Her first day of school already seems a decade away, I think, as I recall Jack posing us for the camera. Snapping shots of Erin and me on the porch, Erin halfway to the gate, three-quarters of the way, Erin slipping through the gate, her hand waving like a flag above the shut gate, me gazing after her, hugging myself in the morning chill. The last photo, when it comes back from the developer, will be a shot of the bus with two tiny feet waiting patiently on the other side for the doors to open.

And it is the same now. The last thing I see of Erin is her feet. Then I am alone in the living-room, Jack having gone off early to take his free one-day trial at Nautilus. I look around at the sparse furnishings: Jack's stereo, the heavy Victorian couch, the stove on its brick pedestal, Aunt Maggie's rocker, the aquarium. It is austere, a room of relics. The real life of the house has moved to the back, where Jack built a two-storey passive solar family room with a dining nook, chests for Erin's toys and a view of our birch woods.

When I was a kid, I lived in a smaller house with five sisters and brothers, my parents and Aunt Maggie. My mother's living-room had cheap shag wall-to-wall broadloom and was over-populated with deep, lumpy, threadbare chairs and sofas. Mother was always sighing, 'Someday these floors will be uncovered and we'll have Persian rugs and antique end-tables and a china cabinet in the corner.' For years I thought we were just too poor to afford these luxuries. It wasn't until the last child moved away that I began to see how Mother's decor was really an act of love. She didn't want fine things if it meant having to nag, 'Don't scuff up the floors!' or, 'Be careful of Mommy's lamps!' She wanted her living-room to be a place where the family congregated; she adored cats, dogs, children and chaos, preferably in as small an area as possible. And when we were gone, the broadloom disappeared, the floors were refinished, and she moved in a lovely beige sofa, a love-seat and an intricately woven Oriental rug. It seems to me, sitting across from Aunt Maggie's ghost, that my mother has had everything.

'We were not happy this morning,' I tell Jack when he comes home from his work-out. His hair is hanging over his forehead, making him look a little like Bobby Kennedy. I'd like him to give me a hug, but from previous experience I know that any move in that direction can lead to trouble. Jack will think I want to make love and, when I tell him I won't, his feelings will be hurt.

'We weren't aware that school would be every day,' I say. 'We thought we could just go when we felt like it.'

Jack is eating granola out of the box with his fingers, which I hate because he leaves little granola crumbs wherever he's been.

'Why do you always say "we" when you talk about Erin?' he asks. He sounds exactly like the therapist, neither aggressive nor critical, merely curious.

'It's so that, if she happens to overhear, she won't think I'm talking about her behind her back,' I say, my cheeks beginning to burn.

'Oh,' he says, flipping the radio dial to a country-and-western station he likes. Usually he's already gone to the shop this time of day, but the bicycle business takes a seasonal slump as soon as school starts, so he's not that worried about opening early. 'But she's not in the house.'

I feel as if he's trying to get at me now. Using 'we' when I talk about Erin is just a habit, I think. It grew out of consideration for her. But Jack is making a big deal out of it, while pretending not to.

Willie Nelson comes on singing the theme music for *The Electric Cowboy*, which is Jack's favourite movie, and when it's over Jack wanders out the door and heads for work, humming to himself. I am furious with him, but there seems to be no logical way to engage him. Sometimes I just want to throw plates. But Jack never gets mad, so throwing plates would only make me look silly. The fact that I can't make Jack angry almost drives me crazy.

I run upstairs to our bedroom, yank open the bottom drawer of our communal chest and rummage around till I find his holey old University of Toronto sweatshirt, the one he wears on drinking expeditions with his college buddies or on field trips to watch the Maple Leafs. Then I take it to the kitchen and shove it into the garbage bag.

I call information and ask for the Price-Mart number. I dial the number, bringing myself slowly under control. I don't really want a job, at least not one that goes on. But I'd like one for a week just to show Jack.

'So you've worked at your husband's bicycle shop,' says the manager. He has the voice of a man born to wear polyester checks. 'You know bicycles. That's good, Jenny. What about cosmetics?'

'I wear make-up,' I say. 'I used to belong to a cosmetics club.'

'Well, do you know anything about jewellery?'

'I like jewellery,' I say. 'My husband gives it to me when we can afford it. I know good stuff from bad stuff.'

'Guns, Jenny? You ever sell guns?'

'Listen,' I say, 'who are you going to find who knows all this and will work for $3.65 an hour?'

'Well, thanks for calling, Jenny,' says the manager, sounding as if he's already three steps away from the phone. 'What we really want is someone who can walk right into the job. I know that doesn't make you feel better.'

I run upstairs and curl up on the bed with a pillow over my face. What I really want is to call the school and ask them to cancel the fire drill, maybe even excuse Erin so she can come home and play with me. I imagine her rushing terrified for the exit, the warning bells clanging, sirens whooping, her head full of nameless fears, dreaming the smell of smoke, the dart of flames, the screams of other children, while her teacher remorselessly counts off the seconds on her wrist watch. I imagine my baby tripping, stumbling under the hurrying feet, coming to in a hospital, her tiny body making barely a dent in the tight white bedsheets. I feel weak, quivery, yet strangely full of energy.

I head back downstairs to the kitchen, retrieve Jack's sweatshirt and toss it into a laundry bag. I pick up the phone again.

'I'd like to place a classified ad,' I say to the person at the other end. 'One large, freshwater aquarium,' I say. 'Completely equipped. Cheap. Just put that in.'

In the distance, I hear the wails of fire-engine sirens. I dial the shop, hang up. 'Do you love me, Jack?' I ask myself.

I remember the house off-campus where Jack lived in his senior year and the year after graduation. It contained a half-dozen boys, almost indistinguishable at first, with their long hair and racing bikes, a glade of thriving marijuana plants, a Nixon

poster taped to the toilet lid, and eight aquariums. The one I gave
Jack was the biggest. Nights they'd turn off the lights and get
stoned watching the fish in the green glow of the tanks. I
remember the green glow and the bubble patterns on my skin the
first time we made love. Day-dreaming, I plug in the aquarium
and switch on the air pump and underwater light. I am relieved to
see that everything is still in working condition.

Watching the slow rise of bubbles, I think how empty the tank is
without a live fish fanning its tail among the fake water weeds.
There is never enough life, I think, and I feel a sudden urge to fill
aquariums with minnows, houses with children. When I get
down in the dumps, as likely as not Jack will say something pithy
such as: 'Life is crap – and then you die.' He thinks he's a realist;
he scored an A in Atheism in his junior year. But, secretly, I
believe, he too is aware of the sad mystery of existence, this brief
haunting like the flash of light on a fin or the accelerating rise of a
bubble that can't seem to wait to crash to the surface and disappear.

Outside, I hear the metallic screech of the bus brakes. I reach to
switch off the aquarium, then decide to leave it. I wait on the
couch, bracing myself for what's to come. The gate swings and
creaks on its hinges. Erin's feet thud on the steps. My heart is
heavy. If one child can make you feel this helpless, I ask myself,
how in heaven's name did my mother survive with six?

'Hi,' I say. 'Howdy, stranger.' I wave my hand, feel silly. Why
do I act like such a kid with my kid?

'Hi,' she says. She slumps down next to me, then falls sideways
and nestles her head on my lap.

'Did you have fire drill?' I ask, aiming to sound light and
conversational.

She nods, her chin gouging my stomach.

'How did it go?'

'OK,' she says. 'I'm tired out. We had to do it two times.'

'Well, a real fire will be no problem after this.'

'Mommy, there was a real fire,' she says patiently. 'A bad boy
set fire to the dumpster when we were lining up to go back in.'

I am staring at my daughter, unable to speak. It occurs to me
that I have just discovered a new natural law: things always get
worse. I resist a wild impulse to call Jack so that he can
participate in this conversation. Since I am holding her and she is
talking and her limbs are moving, I know she is unhurt.

Physically. But one by one my nightmares are coming true. In kindergarten, my baby is falling under an evil sign. She is consorting with sadists and pyromaniacs. And if she survives, people will be falling over themselves to ply her with drugs, paw at her clothes, and break her heart.

'I closed my eyes in the smoke,' she adds. She measures her words as if she is not quite sure how much to tell me. In her face I read the message: Don't fall apart, Mommy. Listen. Let me rest. 'A little girl started to cry, and I held her hand. I told her, "You'll be safe if we hold hands." But I was scared.'

I bite my lip and pull her tight against my chest. 'That was very brave of you,' I say, though I have a lump in my throat. I find it difficult to imagine anyone being little in relation to Erin, this pint-sized shadow self I created. But she has surprised me.

She's weeping now, letting go after the tension and fatigue of the morning, her tiny hands clasping my waist, her blue-veined throat pulsing next to the shiny tracheotomy scar. To me she still smells like a baby.

'I think she's going to be my best friend,' says Erin, drowsily. 'Her name is Sue.'

In my mind's eye, I picture the two children, hand in hand, standing to one side as the fire trucks spin out their hoses and men deal with the smouldering dumpster. Other children clot together in fear and confusion or race up and down, shrieking in mock panic. Teachers pace, smoking cigarettes, making jokes and checking their watches. Erin and her friend bend together, whispering over their knuckle-white hands. Already, I think, she is bringing new life into her world.

I am weeping a little, too, now. Letting go. Weeping for my mother's chaotic love, for Aunt Maggie's unwitting cruelty, for Peggy, who is stuck with Vinnie while dumb Jenny lucked into a man like Jack, for Jack holding Erin in the oxygen tent, for Jack crying alone in the car. And for my daughter, who has instinctively reached out and offered the only comfort we can expect in this life, the presence of another.

At length, I realize that I am the only one crying and that Erin is breathing quietly, dozing. I wake her slipping off her shoes, stretching her out on the couch.

She says, 'I'm all right, Mommy. The teacher said we would be on TV. Wake me up when it's time, OK?'

I drape a blanket over her, then go to the kitchen extension. I call the newspaper and cancel my aquarium ad. Then dictate another: 'One antique bentwood rocker. Extremely cheap.'

I dial the shop. I say, 'Sweetheart, the baby's asleep. She's taking a nap. If you come right home, we can get in a quickie before she wakes up. I can't promise . . .'

'I'll be right there,' says Jack, hanging up before I have a chance to reconsider.

Retracing my steps, I kiss Erin's forehead. Asleep, she is rebuilding her defences, growing stronger. But she will always have a good heart. There will always be this little girl inside.

Heading upstairs to take a shower, I pause on the landing and fish a pocketful of change out of my pants. I toss it into Jack's aquarium, splashing drops of water onto the hardwood floor. As I watch the shoal of pennies, nickels, dimes and quarters slice haphazardly towards the pebble bottom, I cross my fingers. I make a wish.

# Dog Attempts to Drown Man in Saskatoon

My wife and I decide to separate, and then suddenly we are almost happy together. The pathos of our situation, our private and unique tragedy, lends romance to each small act. We see everything in the round, the facets as opposed to the flat banality that was wedging us apart. When she asks me to go to the Mendel Art Gallery Sunday afternoon, I do not say no with the usual mounting irritation that drives me into myself. I say yes and some hardness within me seems to melt into a pleasant sadness. We look into each other's eyes and realize with a start that we are looking for the first time because it is the last. We are both thinking, 'Who is this person to whom I have been married? What has been the meaning of our relationship?' These are questions we have never asked ourselves; we have been a blind couple groping with each other in the dark. Instead of saying to myself, 'Not the art gallery again! What does she care about art? She has no education. She's merely bored and on Sunday afternoon in Saskatoon the only place you can go is the old sausage-maker's mausoleum of art!' instead of putting up arguments, I think, 'Poor Lucy, pursued by the assassins of her past, unable to be still. Perhaps if I had her memories I also would be unable to stay in on a Sunday afternoon.' Somewhere that cretin Pascal says that all our problems stem from not being able to sit quietly in a room alone. If Pascal had had Lucy's mother, he would never have written anything so foolish. Also, at the age of nine, she saw her younger brother run over and killed by a highway roller. Faced with that would Pascal have written anything? (Now I am defending my wife against Pascal! A month ago I would have used the same passage to bludgeon her.)

Note. Already this is not the story I wanted to tell. That is buried, gone, lost – its action fragmented and distorted by

inexact recollection. Directly it was completed, it had disappeared, gone with the past into that strange realm of suspended
animation, that coatrack of despair, wherein all our completed
acts await, gathering dust, until we come for them again. I am
trying to give you the truth, though I could try harder, only
refrain because I know that that way leads to madness. So I offer
an approximation, a shadow play, such as would excite children,
full of blind spots and irrelevant adumbrations, too little in parts;
elsewhere too much. Alternately I will frustrate you and lead
you astray. I can only say that, at the outset, my intention was
otherwise; I sought only clarity and simple conclusions. Now I
know the worst – that reasons are out of joint with actions, that
my best explanation will be obscure, subtle and unsatisfying,
and that the human mind is a tangle of unexplored pathways.

'My wife and I decide to separate, and then suddenly we are
almost happy together.' This is a sentence full of ironies and lies.
For example, I call her my wife. Technically, this is true. But now
that I am leaving, the thought is in both our hearts: 'Can a
marriage of eleven months really be called a marriage?'
Moreover, it was only a civil ceremony, a ten-minute formality
performed at the City Hall by a man who, one could tell, had
been drinking heavily over lunch. Perhaps if we had done it in a
cathedral, surrounded by robed priests intoning Latin benedic-
tions, we would not now be falling apart. As we put on our coats
to go to the art gallery, I mention this idea to Lucy. 'A year,' she
says. 'With Latin we might have lasted a year.' We laugh. This is
the most courageous statement she has made since we became
aware of our defeat, better than all her sour tears. Usually she is
too self-conscious to make jokes. Seeing me smile, she blushes
and becomes confused, happy to have pleased me, happy to be
happy, in the final analysis, happy to be sad because the sadness
frees her to be what she could never be before. Like many
people, we are both masters of beginnings and endings but
founder in the middle of things. It takes a wise and mature
individual to manage that which intervenes, the duration which
is a necessary part of life and marriage. So there is a sense in
which we are not married, though something *is* ending. And
therein lies the greater irony. For in ending, in separating, we
are finally and ineluctably together, locked as it were in a ritual

recantation. We are going to the art gallery (I am guilty of over-determining the symbol) together.

It is winter in Saskatoon, to my mind the best of seasons, because it is the most inimical to human existence. The weather forecaster gives the temperature, the wind chill factor and the number of seconds it takes to freeze exposed skin. Driving between towns, one remembers to pack a winter survival kit (matches, candle, chocolate, flares, down sleeping-bag) in case of a breakdown. Earlier in the week, just outside the city limits, a man disappeared after setting out to walk a quarter of a mile from one farmhouse to another, swallowed up by the cold prairie night. (This is, I believe, a not unpleasant way to die once the initial period of discomfort has been passed.) Summer in Saskatoon is a collection of minor irritants: heat and dust, blackflies and tent caterpillars, the night-time electrical storms that leave the unpaved concession roads impassable troughs of gumbo mud. But winter has the beauty of a plausible finality. I drive out to the airport early in the morning to watch jets land in a pink haze of ice crystals. During the long nights the *aurora borealis* seems to touch the rooftops. But best of all is the city itself, which takes on a kind of ghostliness, a dreamlike quality that combines emptiness (there seem to be so few people) and the mists rising from the heated buildings to produce a mystery. Daily I tramp the paths along the riverbank, crossing and re-crossing the bridges, watching the way the city changes in the pale winter light. Beneath me the unfrozen parts of the river smoke and boil, raging to become still. Winter in Saskatoon is a time of anxious waiting and endurance; all that beauty is alien, a constant threat. Many things do not endure. Our marriage, for example, was vernal, a product of the brief, sweet, prairie spring.

Neither Lucy nor I were born here; Mendel came from Russia. In fact there is feeling of the camp about Saskatoon, the temporary abode. At the university there are photographs of the town – in 1905 there were three frame buildings and a tent. In a bar I nearly came to blows with a man campaigning to preserve a movie theatre built in 1934. In Saskatoon that is ancient history, that is the cave painting at Lascaux. Lucy hails from an even newer settlement in the wild Peace River country, where her father went to raise cattle and ended up a truck mechanic. Seven years ago she came to Saskatoon to work in a garment factory (her left hand bears a burn scar from a clothes press). Next fall she begins law school. Despite this evidence of intelligence, determination and ability, Lucy has no confidence in herself. In her mother's eyes she will never measure up and that is all that is important. I myself am a proud man and a gutter snob. I wear a ring in my left ear and my hair long. My parents migrated from a farm in Wisconsin to a farm in Saskatchewan in 1952 and still drive back every year to see the trees. I am two courses short of a degree in philosophy which I will never receive. I make my living at what comes to hand, house painting when I am wandering; since I settled with Lucy, I've worked as the lone overnight editor at the local newspaper. Against the bosses, I am a union man; against the union, I am an independent. When the publisher asked me to work days, I quit. That was a month ago. That was when Lucy knew I was leaving. Deep down she understands my nature. Mendel is another case: he was a butcher and a man who left traces. Now on the north bank of the river there are giant meat-packing plants spilling forth the odours of death, guts and excrement. Across the street are the holding pens for the cattle and the rail lines that bring them to slaughter. Before building his art gallery, Mendel actually kept his paintings in this sprawling complex of buildings, inside the slaughterhouse. If you went to his office you would sit in a waiting-room with a Picasso or a Roualt on the wall. Perhaps even a van Gogh. The gallery is downriver at the opposite end of the city, very clean and modern. But whenever I go there I hear the panicky bellowing of the death-driven steers and see the streams of blood and the carcasses and smell the stench and imagine the poor beasts rolling their eyes at Gauguin's green and luscious leaves as the bolt enters their brains.

We have decided to separate. It is a wintry Sunday afternoon. We are going to the Mendel Art Gallery. Watching Lucy shake her hair out and tuck it into her knitted hat, I suddenly feel close to tears. Behind her are the framed photographs of weathered prairie farmhouses, the vigorous spider plants, the scarred child's school desk where she does her studying, the brick-and-board bookshelf with her meagre library. (After eleven months, there is still nothing of me that will remain.) This is an old song; there is no gesture of Lucy's that does not fill me instantly with pity, the child's hand held up to deflect the blow, her desperate attempts to conceal unworthiness. For her part, she naturally sees me as the father who, in that earlier existence, proved so practised in evasion and flight. The fact that I am now leaving her only reinforces her intuition – it is as if she has expected it all along, almost as if she has been working toward it. This goes to show the force of initial impressions. For example, I will never forget the first time I saw Lucy. She was limping across Broadway, her feet swathed in bandages and jammed into her pumps, her face alternately distorted with agony and composed in dignity. I followed her for blocks – she was beautiful and wounded, the kind of woman I am always looking for to redeem me. Similarly, what she will always remember is that first night we spent together, when all I did was hold her while she slept because, taking the bus home, she had seen a naked man masturbating in a window. Thus she had arrived at my door, laughing hysterically, afraid to stay at her own place alone, completely undone. At first she had played the temptress because she thought that was what I wanted. She kissed me hungrily and unfastened my shirt buttons. Then she ran into the bathroom and came out crying because she had dropped and broken the soap dish. That was when I put my arms around her and comforted her, which was what she had wanted from the beginning.

An apology for my style: I am not so much apologizing as invoking a tradition. Heraclitus, whose philosophy may not have been written in fragments but certainly comes to us in that form. Kierkegaard, who mocked Hegel's system-building by writing everything as if it were an afterthought, *The Unscientific Postscript*. Nietzsche, who wrote in aphorisms, or what he called 'attempts', dry runs at the subject matter, even arguing contradictory points of view in order to see all sides. Wittgenstein's *Investigations*, his fragmentary response to the architectonic of the earlier *Tractatus*. Traditional story writers compose a beginning, a middle and an end, stringing these together in continuity as if there was some whole which they represented. Whereas I am writing fragments and discursive circumlocutions about an object that may not be complete or may be infinite. 'Dog Attempts to Drown Man in Saskatoon' is my title, cribbed from a facetious newspaper headline. Lucy and I were married because of her feet and because she glimpsed a man masturbating in a window as her bus took her home from work. I feel that in discussing these occurrences, these facts (our separation, the dog, the city, the weather, a trip to the art gallery) as constitutive of a non-system, I am peeling away some of the mystery of human life. I am also of the opinion that Mendel should have left the paintings in the slaughterhouse.

The discerning reader will by now have trapped me in a number of inconsistencies and doubtful statements. For example, we are not separating – I am leaving my wife and she has accepted that fact because it reaffirms her sense of herself as a person worthy of being left. Moreover, it was wrong of me to pity her. Lucy is a quietly capable woman about to embark on what will inevitably be a successful career. She is not a waif nor could she ever redeem me with her suffering. Likewise, she was wrong to view me as forever gentle and forbearing in the sexual department. And finally, I suspect that there was more than coincidence in the fact that she spotted the man in his window on my night off from the newspaper. I do not doubt that she saw the man; he is a recurring nightmare of Lucy's. But whether she saw him that particular night, or some night in the past, or whether she made him up out of whole cloth and came to believe in him, I cannot say. About her feet, however, I have been truthful. That day she had just come from her doctor after having the stitches removed.

Lucy's clumsiness. Her clumsiness stems from the fact that she was born with six toes on each foot. This defect, I'm sure, had something to do with the way her mother mistreated her. Among uneducated folk there is often a feeling that physical anomalies reflect mental flaws. And as a kind of punishment for being born (and afterwards because her brother had died), Lucy's feet were never looked at by a competent doctor. It wasn't until she was twenty-six and beginning to enjoy a new life that she underwent a painful operation to have the vestigial digits excised. This surgery left her big toes all but powerless; now they flop like stubby, white worms at the ends of her feet. Where she had been a schoolgirl athlete with six toes, she became awkward and ungainly with five.

Her mother, Celeste, is one of those women who make feminism a *cause célèbre* – no, that is being glib. Truthfully, she was never any man's slave. I have the impression that after the first realization, the first inkling that she had married the wrong man, she entered into the role of submissive female with a strange, destructive gusto. She seems to have had an immoderate amount of hate in her, enough to spread its poison among many people who touched her in a kind of negative of the parable of loaves and fishes. And the man, the father, was not so far as I can tell cruel, merely ineffectual, just the wrong man. Once, years later, Lucy and Celeste were riding on a bus together when Celeste pointed to a man sitting a few seats ahead and said, 'That is the one I loved.' That was all she ever said on the topic and the man himself was a balding, petty functionary type, completely uninteresting except in terms of the exaggerated passion Celeste had invested in him over the years. Soon after Lucy's father married Celeste, he realized he would never be able to live with her – he absconded for the army, abandoning her with the first child in a drover's shack on a cattle baron's estate. (From time to time Lucy attempts to write about her childhood – her stories always seem unbelievable – a world of infanticide, blood feuds and brutality. I can barely credit these tales, seeing her so prim and composed, not prim, but you know how she sits very straight in her chair and her hair is always in place and her clothes are expensive if not quite stylish and her manners are correct without being at all natural; Lucy is composed in the sense of being made up or put together out of pieces, not in the sense of being tranquil. But nevertheless she carries these *cauchemars* in her head: the dead babies found beneath the fencerow, blood on sheets, shotgun blasts in the night, her brother going under the highway roller, her mother's cruel silence.) The father fled, as I say. He sent them money orders, three-quarters of his pay, to that point he was responsible. Celeste never spoke of him and his infrequent visits home were always a surprise to the children; his visits and the locked bedroom door and the hot, breathy silence of what went on behind the door; Celeste's rising vexation and hysteria; the new pregnancy; the postmarks on the money orders. Then the boy died. Perhaps he was Celeste's favourite, a perfect one to hold over the tall, already beautiful, monster with six toes and (I conjecture again) her father's look. The boy died and the house went silent – Celeste had forbidden a word to be spoken – and this was the worst for Lucy, the cold parlour circumspection of Protestant mourning. They did not utter a redeeming sound, only replayed the image of the boy running, laughing, racing the machine, then tripping and going under, being sucked under – Lucy did not even see the body, and in an access of delayed grief almost two decades later she would tell me she had always assumed he just flattened out like a cartoon character. Celeste refused to weep; only her hatred grew like a heavy weight against her children. And in that vacuum, that terrible silence accorded all feeling and especially the mysteries of sex and death, the locked door of the bedroom and the shut coffin lid, the absent father and the absent brother, somehow became inextricably entwined in Lucy's mind; she was only nine, a most beautiful monster, surrounded by absent gods and a bitter worship. So that when she saw the naked man calmly masturbating in the upper-storey window from her bus, framed as it were under the cornice of a Saskatoon rooming-house, it was for her like a vision of the centre of the mystery, the scene behind the locked door, the corpse in its coffin, God, and she immediately imagined her mother waiting irritably in the shadow just out of sight with a towel to wipe the sperm from the windowpane, aroused, yet almost fainting at the grotesque denial of her female passion.

Do not, if you wish, believe any of the above. It is psychological jazz written *en marge*; I am a poet of marginalia. Some of what I write is utter crap and wishful thinking. Lucy is not 'happy to be sad'; she is seething inside because I am betraying her. Her anger gives her the courage to make jokes; she blushes when I laugh because she still hopes that I will stay. Of course, my willingness to accompany her to the art gallery is inspired by guilt. She is completely aware of this fact. Her invitation is premeditated, manipulative. No gesture is lost; all our acts are linked and repeated. She is, after all, Celeste's daughter. Also, do not believe for a moment that I hate that woman for what she was. That instant on the bus in a distant town when she pointed out the man she truly loved, she somehow redeemed herself for Lucy and for me, showing herself receptive of forgiveness and pity. Nor do I hate Lucy, though I am leaving her.

My wife and I decide to separate, and then suddenly we are almost happy together. I repeat this crucial opening sentence for the purpose of reminding myself of my general intention. In a separate notebook next to me (vodka on ice sweating onto and blurring the ruled pages), I have a list of subjects to cover: 1) blindness (the man the dog led into the river was blind); 2) a man I know who was gored by a bison (real name to be withheld); 3) Susan the weaver and her little girl and the plan for us to live in Pelican Narrows; 4) the wolves at the city zoo; 5) the battlefields of Batoche and Duck Lake; 6) bridge symbolism; 7) a fuller description of the death of Lucy's brother; 8) three photographs of Lucy in my possession; 9) my wish to have met Mendel (he is dead) and be his friend; 10) the story of the story or how the dog tried to drown the man in Saskatoon.

Call this a play. Call me Orestes. Call her mother Clytemnestra. Her father, the wandering warrior king. (When he died accidentally a year ago, they sent Lucy his diary. Every day of his life he had recorded the weather; that was all.) Like everyone else, we married because we thought we could change one another. I was the brother-friend come to slay the tyrant Celeste; Lucy was to teach me the meaning of suffering. But there is no meaning and in the labyrinth of Lucy's mind the spirit of her past eluded me. Take sex, for instance. She is taller than I am; people sometimes think she must be a model. She is without a doubt the most beautiful woman I have been to bed with. Yet there is no passion, no arousal. Between the legs she is as dry as a prairie summer. I am tender, but tenderness is no substitute for biology. Penetration is always painful. She gasps, winces. She will not perform oral sex, though sometimes she likes having it done to her, providing she can overcome her embarrassment. What she does love is for me to wrestle her to the living-room carpet and strip her clothes off in a mock rape. She squeals and protests and then scampers naked to the bedroom, where she waits impatiently while I get undressed. Only once have I detected her orgasm – this while she sat on my lap fully clothed and I manipulated her with my fingers. It goes without saying she will not talk about these things. She protects herself from herself and there is never any feeling that we are together. When Lucy's periods began, Celeste told her she had cancer. More than once she was forced to eat garbage from a dog's dish. Sometimes her mother would simply lock her out of the house for the night. These stories are shocking; Celeste was undoubtedly mad. By hatred, mother and daughter are manacled together for eternity. 'You can change,' I say with all my heart. 'A woman who only sees herself as a victim never gets wise to herself.' 'No,' she says, touching my hand sadly. 'Ah! Ah!' I think, between weeping and words. Nostalgia is form; hope is content. Lucy is an empty building, a frenzy of restlessness, a soul without a future. And I fling out in desperation, Orestes-like, seeking my own Athens and release.

More bunk! I'll let you know now that we are not going to the art gallery as I write this. Everything happened some time ago and I am living far away in another country. (Structuralists would characterize my style as 'robbing the signifier of the signified'. My opening sentence, my premise, is now practically destitute of meaning, or it means everything. Really, this is what happens when you try to tell the truth about something; you end up like the snake biting its own tail. There are a hundred reasons why I left Lucy. I don't want to seem shallow. I don't want to say, well, I was a meat-and-potatoes person and she was a vegetarian, or that I sometimes believe she simply orchestrated the whole fiasco, seduced me, married me, and then refused to be a wife – yes, I would prefer to think that I was guiltless, that I didn't just wander off fecklessly, like her father. To explain this, or for that matter to explain why the dog led the man into the river, you have to explain the world, even God – if we accept Gödel's theorem regarding the unjustifiability of systems from within. Everything is a symbol of everything else. Or everything is a symbol of death, as Lévi-Strauss says. In other words there is no signified and life is nothing but a long haunting. Perhaps that is all that I am trying to say . . .) However, we *did* visit the art gallery one winter Sunday near the end of our eleven-month marriage. There were two temporary exhibitions and all of

Mendel's slaughterhouse pictures had been stored in the basement. One wing was devoted to photographs of grain elevators, very phallic with their little overhanging roofs. We laughed about this together; Lucy was kittenish, pretending to be shocked. Then she walked across the hall alone to contemplate the acrylic prairie-scapes by local artists. I descended the stairs to drink coffee and watch the frozen river. This was downstream from the Idylwyld Bridge where the fellow went in (there is an open stretch of two or three hundred yards where a hotwater outlet prevents the river from freezing over completely) and it occurred to me that if he had actually drowned, if the current had dragged him under the ice, they wouldn't have found his body until the spring breakup. And probably they would have discovered it hung up on the weir which I could see from the gallery window.

Forget it. A bad picture: Lucy upstairs 'appreciating' art, me downstairs thinking of bodies under the ice. Any moment now she will come skipping toward me flushed with excitement after a successful cultural adventure. That is not what I meant to show you. That Lucy is not a person, she is a caricature. When legends are born, people die. Rather let us look at the place where all reasons converge. No. Let me tell you how Lucy is redeemed: preamble and anecdote. Her greatest fear is that she will turn into Celeste. Naturally, she is becoming more and more like her mother every day, without noticing it. She has the financial independence Celeste no doubt craved, and she has been disappointed in love. Three times. The first man made himself into a wandering rage with drugs. The second was an adulterer. Now me. Already she is acquiring an edge of bitterness, of why-me-ness. But, and this is an Everest of a but, the woman can dance! I don't mean at the disco or in a ballroom; I don't mean she studied ballet. We were strolling in Diefenbaker Park one summer day shortly after our wedding (this is on the bluffs overlooking Mendel's meatpacking plant) when we came upon a puppet show. It was some sort of children's fair: there were petting zoos, pony rides, candy stands, bicycles being given away as prizes, all that kind of thing, in addition to the puppets. It was a famous troupe which had started in the sixties as part of the counter-culture movement – I need not mention the name.

The climax of the performance was a stately dance by two giant puppets, perhaps thirty feet tall, a man and a woman, backwoods types. We arrived just in time to see the woman rise from the ground, supported by three puppeteers. She rises from the grass stiffly then spreads her massive arms toward the man and an orchestra begins a reel. It is an astounding sight. I notice that the children in the audience are rapt. And suddenly I am aware of Lucy, her face aflame, this crazy grin and her eyes dazzled. She is looking straight up at the giant woman. The music, as I say, begins and the puppet sways and opens her arms towards her partner (they are both very stern, very grave) and Lucy begins to sway and spread her arms. She lifts her feet gently, one after the other, begins to turn, then swings back. She doesn't know what she is doing; this is completely unselfconscious. There is only Lucy and the puppets and the dance. She is a child again and I am in awe of her innocence. It is a scene that brings a lump to my throat: the high, hot, summer sun, the children's faces like flowers in a sea of grass, the towering, swaying puppets, and Lucy lost in herself. Lucy, dancing. Probably she no longer remembers this incident. At the time, or shortly after, she said, 'Oh no! Did I really? Tell me I didn't do that!' She was laughing, not really embarrassed. 'Did anyone see me?' And when the puppeteers passed the hat at the end of their show, I turned out my pockets, I gave them everything I had.

I smoke Gitanes. I like to drink in an Indian bar on 20th Street, near Eaton's. My nose was broken in a car accident when I was eighteen; it grew back crooked. I speak softly; sometimes I stutter. I don't like crowds. In my spare time, I paint large pictures of the city. Photographic realism is my style. I work on a pencil grid, using egg tempera, because it's better for detail. I do shopping centres, old movie theatres that are about to be torn down, slaughterhouses. While everyone else is looking out at the prairie, I peer inward and record what is merely transitory, what is human. Artifice. Nature defeats me. I cannot paint ripples on a lake, or the movement of leaves, or a woman's face. Like most people, I suppose, my heart is broken because I cannot be what I wish to be. On the day in question, one of the coldest of the year, I hike down from the university along Saskatchewan Drive, overlooking the old railway hotel, the modest office blocks, the ice-shrouded gardens of the city. I carry a camera, snapping end-of-the-world photos for a future canvas. At the Third Avenue Bridge, I pause to admire the lattice of I-beams, black against the frozen mist swirling up from the river and the translucent exhaust plumes of the ghostly cars shuttling to and fro. Crossing the street, I descend the wooden steps into Rotary Park, taking two more shots of the bridge at a close angle before the film breaks from the cold. I swing round, focusing on the squat ugliness of the Idylwyld Bridge, with its fat concrete piers obscuring the view upriver, and then suddenly an icy finger seems to touch my heart: out on the river, on the very edge of the snowy crust where the turbid waters from the outlet pipe churn and steam, a black dog is playing. I refocus. The dog scampers in a tight circle, races towards the brink, skids to a stop, barks furiously at something in the grey water. I stumble forward a step or two. Then I see the man, swept downstream, bobbing in the current, his arms flailing stiffly. In another instant, the dog leaps after him, disappears, almost as if I had dreamed it. I don't quite know what I am doing, you understand. The river is no man's land. First I am plunging through the knee-deep snow of the park. Then I lose my footing on the bank and find myself sliding on my seat onto the river ice. Before I have time to think, 'There is a man in the river,' I am sprinting to intercept him, struggling to untangle the camera from around my neck, stripping off my coat. I have forgotten momentarily how long it takes exposed skin to freeze and am lost in a frenzy of speculation upon the impossibility of existence in the river, the horror of the current dragging you under the ice at the end of the open water, the creeping numbness, again the impossibility, the alienness of the idea itself, the dog and the man immersed. I feel the ice rolling under me, throw myself flat, wrapped in a gentle terror, then inch forward again, spread-eagled, throwing my coat by a sleeve, screaming, 'Catch it! Catch it!' to the man whirling toward me, scrabbling with bloody hands at the crumbling ledge. All this occupies less time than it takes to tell. He is a strange, bear-like creature, huge in an old duffel coat with its hood up, steam rising around him, his face bloated and purple, his red hands clawing at the ice shelf, an inhuman 'awing' sound emanating from his throat, his eyes rolling upwards. He makes no effort to reach the coat sleeve trailed before him as the current carries him by. Then the dog appears, paddling toward the man, straining to keep its head above the choppy surface. The dog barks, rests a paw on the man's shoulder, seems to drag him under a little, and then the man is striking out wildly, fighting the dog off, being twisted out into the open water by the eddies. I see the leather hand harness flapping from the dog's neck and suddenly the full horror of the situation assails me: the man is blind. Perhaps he understands nothing of what is happening to him, the world gone mad, this freezing hell. At the same moment, I feel strong hands grip my ankles and hear another's laboured breathing. I look over my shoulder. There is a pink-cheeked policeman with a thin yellow moustache stretched on the ice behind me. Behind him, two teenage boys are in the act of dropping to all fours, making a chain of bodies. A fifth person, a young woman, is running towards us. 'He's blind,' I shout. The policeman nods: he seems to comprehend everything in an instant. The man in the water has come to rest against a jutting point of ice a few yards away. The dog is much nearer, but I make for the man, crawling on my hands and knees, forgetting my coat. There seems nothing to fear now. Our little chain of life reaching toward the blind, drowning man seems sufficient against the infinity of forces which have culminated in this moment. The crust is rolling and bucking beneath us as I take his wrists. His fingers, hard as talons, lock into mine. Immediately he ceases to utter that terrible, unearthly bawling sound. Inching backward, I some-how contrive to lever the dead weight of his body over the ice lip, then drag him on his belly like a sack away from the water. The cop turns him gently on his back; he is breathing in gasps, his eyes rolling frantically. 'Tank you. Tank you,' he whispers, his strength gone. The others quickly remove their coats and tuck them around the man, who now looks like some strange, beached fish, puffing and muttering in the snow. Then, in the eery silence that follows, broken only by the shushing sound of traffic on the bridges, the distant whine of a siren coming nearer, the hissing river and my heart beating, I look into the smokey water once more and see that the dog is gone. I am dazed; I watch a drop of sweat freezing on the policeman's moustache. I stare into the grey flux where it slips quietly under the ice and disappears. One of the boys offers me a cigarette. The blind man moans; he says, 'I go home now. Dog good. I all right. I walk home.' The boys glance at each other. The woman is shivering. Everything seems empty and anticlimactic. We are shrouded in enigma. The policeman takes out a notebook, a tiny symbol of rationality, scribbled words against the void. As an ambulance crew skates a stretcher down the river bank, he begins to ask the usual questions, the usual, unanswerable questions.

This is not the story I wanted to tell. I repeat this *caveat* as a reminder that I am willful and wayward as a story-teller, not a good story-teller at all. The right story, the true story, had I been able to tell it, would have changed your life – but it is buried, gone, lost. The next day Lucy and I drive to the spot where I first saw the dog. The river is once more sanely empty and the water boils quietly where it has not yet frozen. Once more I tell her how it happened, but she prefers the public version, what she hears on the radio or reads in the newspaper, to my disjointed impressions. It is also true that she knows she is losing me and she is at the stage where it is necessary to deny strenuously all my values and perceptions. She wants to think that I am just like her father or that I always intended to humiliate her. The facts of the case are that the man and dog apparently set out to cross the Idylwyld Bridge but turned off along the approach and walked into the water, the man a little ahead of the dog. In the news account, the dog is accused of insanity, dereliction of duty and a strangely uncanine malevolence. 'Dog Attempts to Drown Man', the headline reads. Libel law prevents speculation on the human victim's mental state, his intentions. The dog is dead, but the tone is jocular. *Dog Attempts to Drown Man*. All of which means that no one knows what happened from the time the man stumbled off the sidewalk on Idylwyld to the time he fell into the river and we are free to invent structures and symbols as we see fit. The man survives, it seems, his strange baptism, his trial by cold and water. I know in my own mind that he appeared exhausted, not merely from the experience of near-drowning, but from before, in spirit, while the dog seemed eager and alert. We know, or at least we can all agree to theorize, that a bridge is a symbol of change (one side to the other, hence death), of connection (the marriage of opposites), but also of separation from the river of life, a bridge is an object of culture. Perhaps man and dog chose together to walk through the pathless snows to the water's edge and throw themselves into uncertainty. The man was blind, as are we all; perhaps he sought illumination in the frothing waste. Perhaps they went as old friends. Or perhaps the dog accompanied the man only reluctantly, the man forcing the dog to lead him across the ice. I saw the dog swim to him, saw the man fending the dog off. Perhaps the dog was trying to save its master, or perhaps it was only playing, not understanding in the least what was happening. Whatever is the case, my allegiance is with the dog; the man is too human, too predictable. But man and dog together are emblematic – that is my impression, at any rate – they are the mind and spirit, the one blind, the other dumb; one defeated, the other naive and hopeful, both forever going out. And I submit that after all the simplified explanations and crude jokes about the blind man and his dog, the act is full of a strange and terrible mystery, of beauty.

My wife and I decide to separate, and then suddenly we are almost happy together. But this was long ago, as was the visit to the Mendel Art Gallery and my time in Saskatoon. And though the moment when Lucy is shaking down her hair and tucking it into her knitted cap goes on endlessly in my head, as does the reverberation of that other moment when the dog disappears under the ice, there is much that I have already forgotten. I left Lucy because she was too real, too hungry for love, while I am a dreamer. There are two kinds of courage: the courage that holds things together and the courage that throws them away. The first is more common; it is the cement of civilization; it is Lucy's. The second is the courage of drunks and suicides and mystics. My sign is impurity. By leaving, you understand, I proved that I was unworthy. I have tried to write Lucy since that winter – her only response has been to return my letters unopened. This is appropriate. She means for me to read them myself, those tired, clotted apologies. I am the writer of the words; she knows well enough they are not meant for her. But my words are sad companions and sometimes I remember ... well ... the icy water is up to my neck and I hear the ghost dog barking, she tried to warn me; yes, yes, I say, but I was blind.

I have hair like Ethel Kennedy's. I am about her age too. Around the compound I wear chinos and T-shirts without a bra. People say that from ten yards away I look half as old. Up close they can see the broken veins and alligator skin from too much New Mexico sun. Red doesn't like me to wear a bra. 'Let 'em hang,' he says. 'I like to see 'em swing and bounce.' It doesn't matter who hears as far as he's concerned. 'Large and useful, that's what I like. Don't give me any of those teeny twenty-year-old titties.' Red's from Texas. As Sylvie says, Red's a trip.

I also have long, thoroughbred legs and a high ass from playing field hockey at Smith. I married an Amherst boy out of college when we were both still virgins. He was a tall blond dream from Missouri who wore specs instead of glasses, played a mean banjo and walked with a limp from a riding injury. His name was Jack Titus. He gave me three children: Sylvie, Francine and Pierre. All three are, to use Sylvie's words, fucked up, a condition for which, they claim, I am mostly to blame. Sylvie has as much as said, 'If you hadn't left Jack, I'd never have gotten mixed up with Leo.' Leo is a pill-popping, glue-sniffing loser who has put her in the hospital twice from car accidents. Franky and Pierre, 26 and 24 respectively, still haven't managed to leave home. They sit around watching me, trying to make me feel guilty. Red calls them 'the yard birds'.

When I met Red, I was getting ready to die in Kansas City. This was ten years ago. I had given up the kids to various branches of the family, and I was down to my last $38 and no job. I went to a K-mart and bought a cheap bikini to die in, then checked into the downtown Holiday Inn and parked myself beside the pool. My plan was to lie there in the sun, buying drinks on a tab until the management asked for money. Then I would suck in my cheeks, assume an air of impregnable Smithy hauteur, stride to the elevator and throw myself out an upper-storey window. It would have worked, too, except on the second day I met Red.

It was about 11.00 a.m. and I was already smashed. He was wearing lime green Bermuda shorts, a Hawaiian shirt out of a Douanier-Rousseau jungle, and flip-flops. His skin was the colour of boiled lobster; his hair looked as if it had been dipped in red ink. When I first saw him, his face was set in a fierce, creased expression that made me think he was mad at me for something. And when he spoke, he stood so close that the ashes from his cigar fell on my bare stomach.

'You wanna hold my cucumber, honey?' he said, snatching the cigar out of his mouth to take a long pull on his highball glass. I pushed my sunglasses down my nose and examined him over the lenses. He was over six feet tall. His head was in the sun. All I could see was a gut like a basketball jutting from under his shirt. I started to giggle.

'Hey lady, it's pay or play,' he said. 'In Mexico I've had women fight for what I got. I've had prima donnas like you beg for it. Name your price, sweetheart.'

His shirt was streaked with sweat where it hung over his belly. As he spoke, a drop slipped from his nose and fell on my chin. I stuck out my tongue and tasted it. I saw his eyes follow my tongue. I started to laugh and couldn't stop until I got the hiccups. He was grinning; he liked making me laugh.

'Name's Red Mulvaney,' he said, gesturing with his cigar. 'I build shopping centres, drink and whore all the time, and if I keep it up, the doctors say I'll live another five years – tops. Hell, I got a lotta living to do!'

He took another drink and shoved the cigar between his teeth. His eyes were sparkling. They were honest eyes. He was vulgar and crude, but after Jack I'd had enough of nice and evasive. I was ready for vulgar and crude. Hell, I had about five days left and a lot of living to do, too.

'I've only slept with two men in my life,' I said, adjusting my straps so he'd stop looking down my chest. 'One was my husband, the other was my divorce lawyer. I only did it once with the lawyer because he was a pervert. I'm telling you this so you won't be disappointed.'

He dropped down on his haunches so that his face was even with mine. His eyes were leaf green with red flecks, like pimento.

'I've been watching you since you checked in,' he said. 'I say you're sad and you don't give a shit who you disappoint. I say something's snapped inside and you don't care what anyone thinks. We've got a lot in common. I'll never be disappointed.'

Unaccountably, I started to cry. Twenty years with Jack and we had never been this intimate. I felt as if Red had ripped open my chest and left my heart beating in the air. Suddenly I knew how lonely I had been. I wept and wept. People were staring; the waiters looked as if they were afraid I'd clear the pool deck. But Red didn't try to stop me. He let me blow my nose on his shirttail, then ambled off to buy me lunch, my first square meal in a week. Afterward, up in his room, I talked for eight hours straight, then fell over asleep on his bed. He hadn't touched me and the last thing I remember him saying was, 'You get some sleep, Flo. You need it. You can hold my cucumber in the morning.'

Franky went to law school in Boulder, but she's failed her bar admission exams three years running. Pierre is gay; he works as a waiter at the Gold Bar in Santa Fe. Six months ago, Franky got pulled over for speeding on the interstate and gave the cop a blow-job to let her go. 'And I paid for four years of law school,' says Red. Though he's not mad. He laughs. It has been ten good years and he's not dead yet. As far as I know, he's never been unfaithful, and he's only hit me once. The worst thing that's happened was when he took Pierre hunting quail in the Jornada one winter and Pierre shot him in the back with a 12-gauge by accident. Even then, Pierre fainted and Red had to carry him back to the truck.

We were married in his room at the Holiday Inn about a week after I discovered sex. Red was right: I didn't care. I tried everything, and everything was just great. Red wired money and plane tickets to each of the kids, but only Sylvie showed up in time. When she came through the door, we were getting dressed for the wedding. Red was in his bathrobe; I had on my bikini bottoms and one of his Hawaiian shirts. She came through the door objecting: 'Mother, this isn't like you. Are you out of your ever-loving, fucking mind?' When she saw Red, she started to cry. She sat out the ceremony in the bathroom, sniffling behind her dark glasses and popping downers. By the end of the day she was so stoned we left her in our bed and rented another room down the hall. When we made love it was like hot steel running through my body, and when we slept, I held Red's face tight to my breasts to stop the ache.

A week later Red flew us all from K.C. to Roswell, where his company was building a shopping centre. We were living in a mobile home on the site, and the kids were almost comatose. There was nothing for miles around but mesquite, creosote and wandering steers. The three of them sat in front of the TV from noon till dawn, watching the soaps, the weather forecasts, the late-night movies and *M.A.S.H.* repeats, smoking dope they had bought from the Mexican labourers. At night they'd call Jack to tell him what Red had done that day. I understood. Red was hard to love and easy to hate, just the opposite of Jack. 'You wouldn't believe it,' they'd whisper into the receiver. 'We're living in a mall that's not even built yet. It's a forest of I-beams. He took her bowling. *Bowling*, Daddy. And yesterday they were shooting beer cans in the desert. Daddy, you've just got to save us!' It was in Roswell that they began trying to bring Jack and me together. And Jack egged them on, said he wanted to re-marry. That was the meanest thing he ever did, making his kids believe in him like that.

Weekends we drove into the mountains to explore the Spanish and Indian villages, hunting up secluded Penitente chapels, buying blankets in Chimayo or pots in San Ildefonso, watching the Pueblo sacred dances as the calendar turned.

One day Red said he had something special to show me and we drove up to Santa Fe, then east along the highway to Pecos. Just outside the town, he pulled off onto a dirt lane that led into a small, V-shaped valley with pines climbing up its slopes and a stream running down from the Blood of Christ Mountains. Below us stretched the flood plain of the Pecos River, and the ruins of an old Spanish mission, like the hulk of a ship at sea. 'This is home,' he said. 'I bought this for you and the kids. I know you all hate that itty-bitty trailer back there. We need something that's just for us.'

He meant that – literally. The house we live in, the compound, nobody touched but Red and I. We lived in a tent that summer while building our first adobe room. Sylvie came out to visit; she was with Leo by then. Leo stayed in the car while Sylvie walked up the hill in her dark glasses, sweat pants and Christian Dior sailor shirt. 'Mother, I can't believe you're doing this to us,' she said. I was mixing mortar; Red was shovelling it into a wheelbarow and manhandling it up a ramp to the top of our wall. His face was sunburned and peeling. He had a cigar in his mouth. There was a cooler of Dos Equis beside the mortarbox. I don't think we had seen another human being for a week.

'Pierre is suicidal, Franky is fucking a Mexican chilli cook named Felipe, and every man I go out with is a jerk,' said Sylvie. 'And all you do is play in the mud with this over-sexed, macho, crypto-fascist pig.' She took off her sunglasses and said, almost in a whisper, 'Jack is in the hospital again. I think you should go and see him.'

As the years passed, we added to the house: five rooms, a solarium, a sauna and a stable. When things got comfortable enough, the kids moved back. I discovered a talent for potting; Red helped me build a studio and kiln. For a whole year we spent every spare moment wandering across the state, learning everything we could from the Indians about the old ways of turning and firing and applying glaze. I made friends with the museum administrators in Santa Fe. One day I woke up and found I was a local expert who could sell my pots, sometimes for as much as a thousand dollars. Red was proud, but he never said a word.

Instead, he hit me. This happened about a year ago. He had flown in that morning from a construction site in Silver City. He came barging into the studio about mid-afternoon after stopping at a couple of bars to find the mood, gruff as usual, drunk as per same, saying nothing, just wanting to see me. I was finishing a storage pot in the Mimbres style, large as a bushel basket. It had taken me two months from scratch. Red hefted it in his muscular hands; he likes to fondle the things I make almost as much as he likes to fondle the maker. Somehow he lost his grip and the pot slipped, first to the work table, then to the floor where it broke. I went down on my knees without a word, and when I looked up, he was gone. I wanted to run after him then, but I held back. I knew he hated pity and condescension.

At dinner, he made up a fight over the posole. When I argued back, he slapped me good and hard across the face. Franky and Pierre were goggle-eyed, straining their necks like turtles on the other side of the table. I was crying and they were staring, and Red took a bottle from the cabinet with him down to the creek. I wanted to explain how badly Red felt that he had broken my pot. I wanted to tell them how I would hug him in bed that night even when he tried to turn away. How I would hug him till he knew he was forgiven. But I knew they wouldn't understand. For some reason they are afraid of life and take it out on me.

Red never said he loved me; nor I him. At the Holiday Inn in Kansas City we had struck a deal. I told him I had three children I wanted to keep with me and support through college. I was being blunt; I was also holding his cucumber. 'I love children,' he said. I have to say he didn't bat an eye. But then, unlike Jack, who hyperventilated and had to breathe into a paper bag every time anyone so much as mentioned getting a job, Red never had trouble with money. He spent it as fast as he made it, but he was always making it.

For his part, Red admitted it wasn't quite true what he had said about all the drinking and whoring. Until a year and a half before we met, he had been married to a Mexican woman called Patrice, an abstract expressionist painter in the style of Ruffino Tamayo, who had died of a stroke. They had run into each other in Upper Volta one year while he was building the sluice gates on a power dam for the government; Patrice was backpacking, studying African primitives. When she failed to conceive, she 'went Catholic' instead of going to see a doctor, according to Red. She even got him to go to mass, praying for a child that never came. 'She was a difficult woman,' he said, shaking his head. 'But I can't forget her. Take me, and you'll just have to put up with her like a ghost in a house.' I cried all the time he was telling me the story. I had never met a man so romantic. Sometimes I think I had just never met a man.

Jack was just the opposite. Jack lied every time he opened his mouth. He lied when he said 'good morning' or 'how are you?' It wasn't that he was trying to be cruel; he would always explain his prevarication by saying he only wanted to make me happy. I didn't know until the second year of our marriage that he was an alcoholic. I didn't know until he went into the hospital with acute alcohol poisoning and the doctor told me himself. 'But Jack doesn't drink,' I said, all innocence and wounded pride. 'Lady, when your husband came in here, he had more bourbon than blood in his veins.'

Jack's mother never gave me any help. She said the same thing every time it happened: 'He is such a sensitive boy. He always gets like this when he's tired and drinks too much coffee. I think he's allergic to coffee.' I went a whole year saying, 'Jack, maybe you should lay off the coffee this morning.' Jack just looked at me as if I were a loon.

If Jack was allergic to anything, it was to work. First he wanted to be a writer. So I bought him a typewriter with money left over from the wedding. When he decided to be a drummer in a band, I became suspicious. We moved to Florida and had Sylvie. Jack panicked; he was in the hospital seeing rats before I took the baby home. He was 'on the wagon' when Franky was born. Every morning he went straight to the kitchen for a large glass of fresh-squeezed orange juice – which was mostly vodka. He got a job in a bank owned by some relative, stole $8,000 in American Express travellers' cheques and left a trail of bad paper that led the police to the Bide-A-Wee Motel in Lincoln, Nebraska, where he was living with a college girl. He had told her he was a writer. For a couple of years after Pierre was born, Jack seemed to pull himself together. He picked his banjo, read books about Jesse James, and stopped robbing the kids' piggy banks. He went back to being the charming, urbane, affectionate boy I'd met at the Amherst mixer. That was about as close as he ever got to being a responsible father.

My family was floating loans to support us. I had a part-time job as a representative for a tea company. I drove around to sports events, fairs and public meetings in a van that opened up at the back to serve free samples. My boss liked to tell me that if Smith had taught me anything it had taught me how to pour tea. Jack stayed with the kids; he was a kid himself. He always had a grin on his face when I came through the door, always had a wisecrack or a funny story and a pair of idle hands to help with the groceries.

We were living in K.C. then, though his parents had ceased to give us any money. And it was while I was working on the tea wagon and Jack was being so nice that he was also having an affair with our dentist's wife, who met him mornings at the Muehlebach Hotel. He panicked when I caught on. I wasn't mad. I was willing to let things go. But Jack ran off with a go-go dancer he was convinced needed protection from the mob. She called me from Fargo. He'd told her he was a drummer in a band and that he limped because he'd been shot robbing a bank. That was when I left him.

Sylvie and I have had many heart-to-hearts about this. She believes she speaks for the family. And maybe she does. Sylvie says she is caught between two worlds and doesn't know where to turn. She wants to be an artist, and Red pays for her to study printmaking with Lazansky in Iowa. But she claims she can't commit herself as deeply as she must because of the divorce. She can't build a life on shifting sands, she says. Everything vanishes. No one can be trusted. She is afraid of failure because she thinks I failed.

Once in a while, when she has been staying with Red and me for a few weeks and has settled down, she gets as far as saying, 'But Daddy was always nice to us. He couldn't have been that bad, could he?' I never say anything, nor does Red. This was something I decided early on, this silence, though I knew Jack would be telling his side of the story to anybody who would listen until the day he died.

Sometimes, when Sylvie has been especially hard on me, Red cannot restrain himself. 'You kids sure have been dealt a bad hand,' he'll say. 'You got the best mother in the world, all the money you could ever want, a home you can come to in God's own country – shit, you got every reason to take a gun off that wall there and put yourselves out of your misery.' He'll poke the fire, muttering to himself for a while, then add: 'Shells are in the top right-hand drawer.'

They're like their father; they've decided to be unhappy.

One night Red and I are alone, lying naked in front of the fireplace in our bedroom, with a tripod of piñon logs spitting and throwing our shadows on the white-washed walls that surround us. We are listening to Lotta Lenya singing songs from *The Threepenny Opera*, from an old album of Red's. He's got an original 1930s recording made in Berlin and a 1950s version cut during a performance at the Théâtre de Lys in New York. Patrice had taken Red to see the show on their honeymoon, and the album has a skip where they knocked a candle on it while making love. Somehow I never feel jealous of Patrice. I can tell

Red loved her so much that my jealousy would be next to blasphemy.

Around us are the trophies of our ten-year marriage: Kachina dolls, the drawings I copied from potsherds, framed and mounted on the walls we built with our own hands. Next to the chimney hangs Patrice's last painting, a crimson figure with his arms outflung, shining like the sun. There are also photographs of the children and me that Red took. The kids are shy and crabby in front of the lens, but we crowd together as if seeking that family feeling we all miss.

We are lying together when the telephone rings. It's Sylvie, sounding desperate. Leo's been arrested in Stone City, Iowa, wasted on coke, after sideswiping five parked cars outside an all-night roadhouse. She loves him, she feels sorry for him, but she wants to leave him. Maybe she will kill herself. She has decided she will never be able to lead a normal life unless she is somehow sure Jack and I were never meant for each other. Her voice, thin and weary at the other end of the line, is like a knife in my ribs. My firstborn is 28, confused, and trapped in events that took place over a decade ago. In a moment of weakness, I tell her I'll do anything to make her happy, though I know what's to come. She wants me to meet Jack, whom I have not laid eyes on since the divorce. I know this is her fantasy quest, her dream reunion. She wants the clock turned back.

I have overheard the three of them, Sylvie, Franky and Pierre, discussing this when they think I am out of the house. They imagine us appearing to each other out of the gloom in a darkened bar. They see our eyes meet with a look of startled recognition, then we approach each other timidly, warily, like wild animals. Suddenly our love is rekindled: we talk in the old, bantering way they remember; we sip our drinks; we share one chaste kiss and part, forever. Even in their ideal visions, the kids cannot get Jack out of a bar or force us to remarry. But they think they could live with the divorce if I would admit it was a mistake.

According to Sylvie, Jack is living in Aspen now, where he runs a service station with a woman named Marge. She says he is willing to come down if I agree to see him. Her voice is breaking; I know she may never speak to me again if I don't say yes. I tip-toe back to the fireplace to tell Red the arrangements. Jack will take a cottage at La Posada for the weekend at the kids' (meaning Red's) expense. I am to rendezvous with him in the courtyard Saturday afternoon. I tell Red we are just going to talk for my children's benefit, but as I say the words, I am conscious of my own ambiguity. Sylvie has planted the words 'what if' in my head, though I am only doing it for her sake. Red has never said 'what if' in his life. That is why it's so easy for me to bear his love for the dead Patrice. He mourns, but he never regrets. And now he says nothing. Just grunts. Which is Texan for 'Do whatever you like.'

Red cannot speak of things that are close to his heart, and because of that people like Sylvie often think he doesn't have one. She also thinks that the way he has of remembering Patrice is a kind of infidelity. She does not want complexity and refuses to see that Red is an ugly, gentle man who grew up in a place where gentleness was hidden out of necessity. When Red starts playing his albums, Sylvie will recall that Jack used to own every record Bob Dylan ever made. But she has never felt Red's body stiffen with pain and longing when Lotta beings to sing *The Black Ship*. She will never know.

On Saturday Red drops me at the plaza in front of the Palace of Governors and heads for his dermatologist. Once a year he has the skin cancers removed from his face. With his complexion, he was never meant to live in the south, but, like me, he loves the sun. Red's been good about this get-together with Jack. He hasn't said a word, treating it like another lunch with one of my museum pals. As far as I can tell, he doesn't have a jealous bone in his body. He says he'll pick me up in a couple of hours.

I stroll lazily up San Francisco toward Archbishop Lamy's Gothic revival cathedral. I stop to watch a juggler, a child on roller skates, a Pueblo woman selling turquoise. I idle along because I do not know where I am going. I know La Posada, of course, but I do not know where I am going in my mind. I recall Jack during our courtship, his corny, winning ways, his slightly Edwardian air, the nights he serenaded me, strumming his banjo and singing Missouri ballads beneath my bedroom window. Whenever I dated another boy, Jack tailed us in his battered Hudson. He wrote love letters every day, left messages for me in classrooms, at the dry cleaners, at the café where I went evenings, at the residence desk. 'Save a sigh for a drowning man,' he wrote, seeing himself always as the underdog. When it came time for me to make a decision, Jack had simply outlasted his competition.

Stepping through the adobe arch, I find him watching the street with an anxious expression that alters suddenly into that pleased, boyish grin I remember so well. Only now I see that one of his front teeth has been capped and the enamel is discoloured. He's wearing jeans, a Levi's work shirt and moccasins. His hair still falls over his forehead, but his eyes are lined, darker. Still slim and tall, he is no longer ageless, though ageing gracefully. I am aware, as I always was before, that we are a striking couple. He clutches a red rose, long-stemmed, in his hand, which looks silly, and when he passes it to me, I feel silly. All of a sudden I see what I never noticed before, that Jack does everything a beat off, like an actor missing his cue; that his gestures and protestations are always slightly marred, hypocritical, sheepish, embarrassing. But he always means well, I think to myself. The old apologetic refrain.

As he escorts me through the vestibule, past the desk clerk and into the bar, I note that his collar and cuffs are comfortably worn, that his jeans bag a little in the ass. Actually, he's slimmer than I recall, too thin. He waits for me to decide where we will sit, a bar stool or an armchair by the unused fireplace. I choose the deep, threadbare comfort of a sofa by the window, and catch Jack winking at the bartender, a man with whom I am sure he has been holding intimate colloquy since long before my arrival. I place the rose on the floor with my bag, thankful to be able to get it out of sight. Jack orders a bourbon on the rocks, a double, and a Mexican beer for me. His hand shakes as he reaches for the glass. Above the wrist, his arm is pale. Crossing his legs, he leans back, languid and graceful, yet in a way exhausted. He has had a hard life keeping up with himself.

So far we have spoken very little beyond the usual pleasantries. I realize that I want Jack to be bowled over by me. In spite of myself, I have spent a good two hours getting ready for this, and I am dressed to kill. That's why I am suddenly angry, angry with myself. The whole modus operandi of our marriage was me trying to make an impression on Jack, trying to make him see what his drinking did to us, trying to make him happy to keep him from drinking, just trying to make him notice. But after being hopelessly infatuated with me for six months leading up to the wedding, his ego has remained impervious to mortal wiles ever since. Worst of all, I liked him being infatuated. It appealed to my lowest instincts, but I liked it. So wanting him to be bowled over now is a kind of revenge I have been planning; but as usual, Jack is unreachable. He has given me a rose.

'How's Red?' he asks slyly. His smile is not quite a smirk.

'How's Marge?' I ask back. I know he wants to put me on the defensive, and I don't care so long as we don't discuss Red. Red saved me from dying because of this man. After a decade, Red is still sacred. I will not have him spoken of in ways that diminish him.

'Marge is a good friend,' he says, laughing. Jack will run anybody down behind their back. 'She's good-hearted.'

Interpreting what Sylvie says I gather that Marge is an overweight, depressed woman who also drinks too much but manages to keep food on the table by pumping gas twelve hours a day when she's sober. I hope she gives him a sharp knee in the balls if he ever calls her 'good-hearted' within earshot.

Aware that his charm is ineffective, Jack makes an effort to be frank and affectionate. This is his second line of defence; after the rifle pits and forward trenches have fallen, he becomes frank and affectionate.

'Well, it's good to see you. It was worth the trip. The kids have been working their darned little butts off to get us together,' he says. He rattles on about what good kids they are. Jesus, I don't like this man. I wasted twenty years on him, and it only makes me mad to think I am washing yet another afternoon of my life down the same drain.

'Our kids are just like you,' I say. 'They haven't come to grips with the difference between the way the world works and their daydreams. For the time being, they're blaming this disparity on our divorce. It's not pleasant to watch. But I keep telling myself I had to stagger through a bad marriage into middle age before I grew up.'

I order another beer because I see that I am talking too much. That's always a bad thing to do with Jack. He's the white hunter of the conversational jungle: he sets traps. Red wouldn't have put up with this for thirty seconds. Red would have taken advantage of one of Jack's nerve-racking silences to walk out of the bar and into another one farther down the street.

'We all have to learn to accept ourselves, the good and the bad,' says Jack, who accepts himself by signalling for a triple.

'I feel out-manoeuvred,' I say, and he smiles. 'Sylvie's been after me for ages to give you another chance. Now I see that talking is never going to decide anything.'

'It's just nice to be together again,' he asserts blandly, ignoring what I have just said. 'It's been a long time.'

I am practically blind with anger now. I know I am over-reacting; I haven't resolved all my self-hatred and disgust for the years I spent hoping Jack would miraculously reform, thinking somehow that I could perform the functions of mother, wife and redeeming angel all at once. 'Sylvie means well,' I catch myself thinking. And then, out of the corner of my eye, I see Red in the doorway, a bandage patched over the bridge of his nose, his eyes hunting for me. He's wearing pale blue shorts, an amazing, ruby-coloured V-neck sweater and sneakers with the toes cut out. In the normal run of events, Red can carry off this costume up to and including formal dinner parties. But today he suddenly looks out of place, frail and a little afraid.

I check my watch; he's early. He catches my eye, nods, then heads over to the bar, out of sight. Jack has been staring wistfully out the window and hasn't noticed. I'm not sure he would even recognize Red. But it's a mess anyway, because the bartender knows us by name and he'll guess that something funny is going on. It's not like Red to put himself in that kind of position. In my mind there is a stampede of images: the rose, the bandage on Red's face, my divorce lawyer prancing around in lace undies, Sylvie crying in her chair, Franky and Pierre huddled in silent conspiracy.

I know Red likes people to be decisive. I retrieve Jack's rose and hand it back to him, bloom first, like a sword. Then I grab my bag and say, 'Would you excuse me, please?' I can see he's puzzled. I am probably going to the bathroom, he thinks. But why give him the rose?

I am slipping up to the bar before he can wipe that smirk off his face and utter a word. I am nudging Red's elbow, saying softly, 'Buy me a drink, sweetheart.' Then he turns to me and gives me a shock. A patch of blood has seeped through the gauze on his nose, tiny pinheads of sweat are running together over his brow, and there are tears sliding down his cheeks.

I take his hand and give it a squeeze.

'I love you, Flo,' he says. 'If you leave me, I'll blow my brains out.'

That's Red, I think. When you need him, he's there. He lets you know where you stand. He takes your breath away.

'I love you, Red,' I say in a strong voice. 'One day we'll die together – it's the only way.' And having said this, I am suddenly sure that we will live forever.

## The Seeker, the Snake and the Baba

As a snake perceived in the twilight may prove to be a rope (merely a harmless rope, yet it was taken for a snake and inspired fear), even so the world, which inspires fear and desire, may be caused to vanish.

Hindu Proverb

The heat stunned him. In the square outside Puri Station, beggars swarmed like maggots, brandishing their stumps. A pyre smouldered by the river as kites swung back and forth expectantly on the thermals. Bearded mystics, caked in blood and ashes, skewered with nails, staggered in ecstasy. By the taxi stand, a slender youth, naked, his eyes hooded, teased a pair of snakes with a bulbous flute. Malory shuddered. After an hour's drive, the cabman announced, 'The ashram of Sri Govinda Baba. Very famous place. Many Americans are coming.' 'I am English,' said Malory. 'Also many English,' said the cabman. 'See, master, the river is almost dry here. The birds drop out of the trees. The Baba is expecting you?' 'I think not.'

*During the day the cobras slept . . .*

It was not his fault; the woman had put a spell on him with her love. Women. Jody, Ursula, Andrea. Though he perceived that they were all aspects of one woman: his mistresses, his muses, his graces, his fates, his victims. Of the three, Ursula was the key. Jody was the practical one. Independent. She wanted no ties. When she became pregnant, she moved in with him so that he could support her confinement. Then she fled. Andrea was Dutch and placid; he married her. It was Ursula, the middle one, who caused the trouble. She had an abortion; the baby was sacrificed so as not to chain him down. He didn't exactly tell her to do it. He disappeared (with Andrea) when she went to the clinic, so that he would not be there to influence her at the last. Then she seemed to think she had a hold on him, as though their love had a name now she had christened it with blood. He had a friend relay the news that he would be married. It had to be quick; Andrea was pregnant by this time. The night before the wedding, he went to Ursula. Her eyes accused him, but her words were soft and resigned. She said, 'It's not me I pity. It's you. You have to live with her.' And she wept tears like petals on their pillow when they made love. (No fear this time. Her wise doctor said, 'A healthy young woman like you ought to be on the pill.') The tuft of hair between her legs had not grown back from the operation, it all happened so fast. After the wedding she went away, though he had wanted her to stay near him. She went away not to be free, as Jody had done, but to give him a chance to make a marriage. She knew he would never settle down as long as she was around. She had her nose straightened and murdered love with work and light diversion. But something remained amiss; the doctor diagnosed a malignancy and operated. He telephoned when he heard. 'My seed is bad.' 'Nonsense,' she said. 'I've lost my hair.' 'If it doesn't work, how long?' he asked 'Two years,' she said. 'You can have a lot of fun in two years,' he said. Her friends had wept when she told them. 'That's just Kenneth Malory,' she said, 'inept and cruel.' She loved him still.

*During the day the cobras slept in the river-bank gardens of the ashram, where the gravel was cool and moist. At night, they came into the houses to hunt for mice.*

It was not his fault; his father had made him in his image. The two of them. For there was a sister, and with her he sometimes thought he could truly love. ('You had better go, Malory,' said Ursula's stepfather. 'Her mother is frail and I'm not up to the journey myself. Besides, the telegram is meant for you. It's addressed to us, but it's meant for you. I'll pay, of course. We should like her buried here.') She had been engaged four times and each time had broken it off just before the wedding. She was a small, pretty woman who worked in a travel agency. (Practice in evasion and flight, he thought.) She was open and kind, but when a man pushed her too far she would tighten up and hurl him back. He said, 'We are the same, you and I. We cannot commit ourselves to love.' And this once she defied him. 'Not true, Kenny. We are not the same. I can love, believe me I can love, but I will never let a man rule me. You are like Daddy, you prove yourself by getting babies.' Ursula had said, 'You don't know what you want. But I think you are afraid of hurting women. It's the guilt that drives you on.' (Too true, he thought. The guilt for Ursula's baby made him marry poor Andrea. Though Andrea was an afterthought, a mistake. He had intended to stop with Ursula.) Jody said he was a misogynist. 'Maybe you're gay underneath,' she said. 'I think you hate us, try to drive us down into the earth, the blood and the pain. It's the sadism of childbirth that excites you.' It was not his fault; his father was a drunk and a wife-beater who lived mostly away from home. He had been home the day Malory's mother was sent to the hospital with a 'female complaint'. The old man refused to sign the papers for an operation. He refused on the grounds that it would make him less of a man in bed with her. So she died. ('KENNETH, COME QUICKLY,' said the telegram, like a revelation.)

*He was not sure there was a snake in the hut. Other nights he had heard rustling in the kra logs and bamboo of the walls. He held his terror, fluttering like a moth against his ribs, his teeth chattering a travesty of castanets. The night sucked up his breath.*

'They came by bus from Kabul after the rains,' said the German woman who had looked after Ursula. 'She was already sick.' At first, Malory had been angry. He had sent the German woman away and ordered the taxi to Puri to fetch fresh food and a doctor. By the time the doctor arrived, he had managed to clean the worst of the filth from the hut and air the blankets Ursula was using. She was emaciated, her hair hung in rat-tails, she could not close her lips over her teeth, she was incontinent. He found needle tracks on her arms and legs, erupted, almost gangrenous, like snake bites. The doctor, who spoke little English, pointed to the punctures and shrugged his shoulders. 'Kaput,' he said. 'Poison.' When he washed her, Malory had to steel himself to touch the strange, waxy skin and bend the flaccid joints. He did not understand how a white woman could be allowed to languish in such misery. The ashram disgusted him: the rag-tag huts where the European disciples lived, the crowd of followers milling at the gate, the white-clad attendants with their buttery cheeks, the stench, the heat. He couldn't even find water clean enough to rinse the fouled bed-clothes, but had to buy a kettle and firewood for boiling. Once, briefly, while he was moistening her lips with a rag, her eyes opened and she saw him. Her look was cold; it seemed to pierce him with the iciness of remorse. As he dried her belly he touched her sex experimentally. 'The doctor scraped me out like a cream carton,' she had said. 'No more baby panics for me.' In the evening, the German woman returned. 'I lied,' she said. 'There was no other, no man. She . . . she took care of me.' 'You were lovers,' he said. 'No. No, you misunderstand. I am a sinful person.' She showed him the marks on her arms. 'Ursula helped me to stop.' 'But she took drugs as well,' he said. 'Yes, after. We went to Afghanistan for the drugs. When the Russians invaded, we came south. When she took the drugs she would sigh and whisper, "Shiva, Lord of Sleep." We came here to find peace.'

*On the cot in the night, he sweated with fever. He had forgotten to mix purification tablets in his drinking water. He was afraid to leave the cot to go to the humid ditch which served as a latrine for the foreigners' compound. The pain of cramps, dehydration and his enforced stillness had driven him nearly delirious. He imagined the black swaying body, the spectacle patterns on its hood peering at him, just there beyond his feet. The void enclosed him at the point of contact. He was enveloped in an emptiness that moved like the body of a snake.*

The ashram was made dangerous by the proximity of migrating elephant herds. For Malory it was a nightmare of heat, death pyres and bearded ascetics drinking their own urine by the gates. He watched Ursula, her face made beautiful by suffering, and told himself that character is fate, that every human being is treacherous to another, that men only dream of union. 'She is happy,' said the German woman. 'Memory was such a torture to her.' She did not die; she merely continued. He rose late each day because it disgusted him to go to the ditch which served as a toilet when the Indians were there. Most of the foreigners arrived after mid-morning, unless they were ill, and squatted at decent intervals staring tactfully ahead. After visiting the ditch he would wash carefully, despite the trouble of preparing the water, before attending to Ursula. Twice a day, in the morning and the afternoon, the Baba would appear at the gates of the ashram with his closest disciples. The pilgrims, who at times mustered in the thousands, would rush to the spot in an uproar of devotion. Around the gate was a low hill which served as an amphitheatre. The crowds would settle on the incline and the Baba would begin to meditate. No one had ever heard him speak to the pilgrims, though sometimes he searched among them with eyes that were at once alarmingly direct and peacefully muddy. Here and there he would transfix a visitor with his stare. This happened to Malory, the second day, as he stood upon the hill near the back of the multitude. The Baba's gaze, placid yet peremptory, even insolent, chilled him and filled him with anger. It seemed to him that the holy man was contemptible in his detachment, that he fed on the suffering endured in his name, that all India was suffering to earn his redemption. After the observances, the crowd had dispersed in search of food. This was a constant preoccupation since, with native impracticality, the ashram had been built miles from any town. There were no stores, no sewage facilities, and, except for the river, in which the bodies of men and animals mixed indiscriminately, only a few wells for water. There were several carts at the gate which sold Indian food, but the foreigners generally did not trust the sanitation. They traded and horded amongst themselves in an atmosphere of despair and suspicion. In the evening, returning to the hut with some cans of American soup, Malory had found Eva murmuring to herself at the foot of Ursula's cot, the air heavy with the smell of burning joss. 'You must be mad to be taken in by this fraud,' he said. 'He is a saint,' she said. 'He can foretell the future.' 'She wanted to live her life in a dream,' he said, looking down at the dying woman. 'She wanted you to come,' said Eva, 'to rescue her from this. She never accepted separation. But she understood that one must relinquish to truly love.' 'Ursula was a masochist,' said Malory. 'A woman's masochism comes from her maternal instinct,' said Eva. 'It is not a perversion. A mother suffers, gives, feeds . . .'

After a few days at the ashram, no one was completely well.

Women missed their periods; men shook with fever. Malory watched the Indians burning their dead on pyres by the river, with bodies and logs piled neatly in alternating layers. When the ashes were cool, the remains were pushed over the bank. There were always more dead. Sometimes it seemed as though there were more bodies than living people, so that he assumed the corpses were brought from far away for cremation at the holy place. Everywhere there was a stench of human excrement, saffron, burning bodies, ghee butter used in sacrifice; and unwashed humanity. In the afternoons, after the meditation, the Baba performed the ceremony of the holy ashes. He would walk to the edge of the crowd and, twirling his hand in the air above his head, would materialize a pinkish, fine-grained ash, almost like smoke as it fell from his palm. The devout held up their arms to receive the mysterious gift. It was said to cure illness if eaten or procure great spiritual benefit if retained in a charm pouch around the neck. The Baba's inner circle was in the business of selling the ashes to pilgrims in tiny, folded envelopes. The holy one could change the weather, bring rain, Malory was told. One day he had walked in the sea and a necklace of precious stones had miraculously appeared about his ankle, the waves' offering to God incarnate. The previous year he had levitated at the prime minister's swearing-in. Evenings he could sometimes be seen driving golf balls toward the river from the temple roof, his whispy beard floating about his cheeks, his white robes hiked up on his shoulders. Malory found many men willing to help him achieve an audience with Sri Govinda Baba. They took his money, as alms, and like attorneys proceeded to put the machinery in motion. In Malory's case, the machinery appeared to be perpetual and circular, for the Baba would not see him.

*It was worse when he could detect no sound at all. It meant that the snake was coiled quite near, waiting. If he but swung his hand out to touch the table by the bed, it would strike. A dart of fangs in the night. He dared not put his foot to the floor, lest the snake be there.*

In a dream the Baba appeared to him. 'What is it you seek?' the holy man asked. 'Release, master.' 'You know the Bhu-vaneshvara?' asked Baba. 'It is not far from here.' 'I have seen it on the map,' Malory replied. 'There is a temple called the Rajrani, built in ancient times by a wealthy courtesan for her king. If you go, Englishman, into the lightless holy of holies in the Rajrani you will find no image or symbol whatsoever. The people say that when the king entered the sanctuary the presence there found was the courtesan herself.' Baba began to giggle at the conclusion of his tale. 'I don't understand,' said Malory. At this, the saint began to laugh heartily.

The next day, leaving Eva to watch over Ursula, Malory hiked to the Rajrani of Bhuvaneshvara to see the whore's temple. A crowd had gathered at the entrance to the sanctuary, where a group of ascetics and fakirs were performing. There was a man with a basket of cobras. He had laid the snakes out on a hemp mat and was serenading them with a flute. Some of the snakes had coiled and spread their hoods and were swaying back and forth in time to the music. Others lay in the sunlight, flicking their tongues, oozing off the mat in sluggish attempts at escape. Without halting his playing, the fakir would reach down with one hand and return the snake to his mat. From time to time one of the coiled cobras would dart its head forward in a strike, but the blow was awkward and easily avoided by the man with the flute. 'You are fascinated by the snakes?' asked a man in a white dhoti among the spectators. 'It is like bull-fighting, really.' The speaker was not one of the ascetics. He had an accent that was very correct, very English. 'The cobra is rather slow and dull- witted and cannot hear at all. The music is for our benefit, not the snake's. He only watches the motion of the flute. That is what he strikes at. And of course he is not a quick snake, like the viper.' 'But surely their fangs are pulled,' said Malory. 'No. No. It is quite real. I dare say he has been bitten. One develops an immunity, I'm told. But there are so many snakes and they come into the houses. Many people die each year. It's horrible, they say, pain, numbness, loss of coordination, incontinence, convulsions.' 'They aren't extermin- ated?' Malory interrupted. 'Heavens, no! Life is sacred to us. Also, the snakes help keep down pests. Why look so disgusted? I am told that Americans have ophitic cults where the devout handle rattlesnakes. The snake is a very old, very revered symbol in all cultures.' Malory entered the sanctuary haunted by the image of the black, wriggling bodies on the hemp mat. Inside, the temple was dark. He could not see to place his feet. The feeling of apprehension grew as he shuffled down a row of bare stone steps. Something rustled beneath him. Perhaps he had dislodged a pebble. He could see nothing. His heart raced. He found that he could not move his feet forward. Abruptly, he turned and fled, rushing up the steps, to the delight of the man in the dhoti, who had waited by the entrance. 'What are you afraid of?' he shouted. 'The dark! The king's whore! You see it is not walls that hinder us. It is the power of our own thoughts. These spikes,' he said, indicating a holy man covered in ashes and blood, steel spikes driven through his thighs, 'these spikes are no bother when one knows the power of the human soul. Neuroses, all those so-called psychological illnesses of the West, however sad they may seem, are but acts of belief.'

*What sound did the snake make dragging its heaviness across the sand? What sound did Death make? What sound the Holy Ghost? He was certain of a presence that was not a presence so much as a void, an emptiness, just beyond his ability to sense in the darkness. He imagined again the black, weaving body, the eyes of its hood staring. I have a visitor, he thought, covering his face. He cried out. And the void sucked up his cries.*

For a week Ursula declined, yet lingered, muffled in coma. Malory discovered his clothing infested with body lice. One day he neglected to mix purification tablets with the water he drank. 'You were delirious last night,' said the German woman. 'I dreamed about snakes,' he said. She nodded. 'I also when I close my eyes. Once I desired nothing more than to live the life she led. Now Shiva has come to me in my sleep.' It was on his return from Rajrani that he had discovered the first penitents before the hut, the first saucers of burning ghee set near the door. Now there were fifty or more every day, beggars, invalids, the self-tortured. They had festooned the lintel with garlands of flowers. They had brought food, which he would not eat. While they demanded nothing, they persisted, quietly, amid the flies and dust. Their presence was a mystery only Eva dared to interpret. 'They worship her,' she said. 'She was the innocent who was always offering.' To Malory, they seemed only to be waiting. Shuddering inwardly, he told himself he was disgusted and no longer cared. It seemed to him that India was wearing away his civilizing resolve. He felt himself slipping into a form of madness that was simultaneously frightening and seductive. His anger and discomfort had become his justification.

The Baba woke him coming to speak with Ursula. 'She will die before morning,' he said. At first, Malory could not understand. The hut was full of retainers wearing bells and chanting mantras. They bore oil lamps, held high, and peeked fearfully into corners as though looking for ghosts. Sri Govinda Baba walked directly to Ursula's cot, knelt and began an ecstatic prayer. A young man followed, carrying a framed painting of the holy man's annun-ciation: the boy, Govinda, asleep on his bed with a large cobra watching over him, just as his mother had found them that holy morning. Now past sixty, the Baba looked fat and healthy. His cunning eyes devoured the sleeping Ursula. He snapped his fingers. A bowl was provided. And he dabbed her face with a paste of ashes and butter. Malory tried to protest. 'She had pain in here,' said the Baba, pointing to her heart. 'Now it has vanished. Her illness was but a candle in the sun of Shiva.' To Malory, the Indian seemed to embody the split nature of the androgyne, male and female, father and mother. 'She is the goddess of all things which the vigour of living destroys. She is Shakti.' Malory wanted to reply but the old man imposed respect. He continued, pointing to the open door where the worshippers had gathered in silence. 'They understand. It is the bhairava, the terror, the cult name of Shiva.' He fingered the infected wounds on her arms. He gazed at Malory. 'She came to find peace and discovered the power of Shiva. She gave herself to him, Shakti the divine, the fecundating force. She gave herself.' 'She took drugs,' said Malory bitterly. 'She let the cobra strike her,' said the Baba. Malory felt the hair at the back of his neck rise. His throat spasmed, making a dry clicking sound, like a rattle. 'It came in the night. There! There!' cried the Baba, gesturing at the walls. 'Mahadeva of the thousand names, Shiva, the void, the eternal corpse, the terrible destroyer; Shiva, Lord of Sleep.'

It was not his fault. Nothing had ever been his fault. Driven from the hut by the press of believers, the drone of prayers, and the sickening sweetness of the joss, he had spent the night on his feet in the open. Before sunrise, he found a man with a car who could drive him to Puri. The doctor who had treated Ursula at the beginning was a Moslem. He was up early, performing his ritual ablutions, when Malory knocked on his door. 'She lives?' he asked, with disbelief. Malory shook the doctor by his shoulders. 'Poison! You said poison! My God, it was the drugs, the needles. Another boy died while I was there. Hepatitis. He had hepatitis from the needles.' The doctor backed away, brushing down his sleeves. 'No, poison,' he said. His hand darted, the first and second fingers extended like fangs. 'Ssst! Ssst! Naja . . . cobra.' 'What about her cancer?' cried Malory in desperation. The doctor shrugged. Malory slumped in a chair. 'I want to move the body,' he said. 'I must return it to England.' 'A month,' said the doctor. 'Papers, police, the government.' He shrugged once more. Returning to the ashram, Malory found the area around the hut deserted. Eva met him at the door, weeping. The odour of death and putrefaction was heavy in the air. Inside, the hut was empty. 'Was it true?' he asked, his voice taut with horror. 'Did she do what he said?' Eva nodded. 'Where have they taken her?' The German woman extended her hand towards the river. A pyre was being erected. The bank was teeming with Indians, looking like brown insects in the harsh sunlight. A little to one side, surrounded by his retinue, Sri Govinda Baba sat erect in a jeep, painted pink and covered in flowers. 'You can't,' shouted Malory when he reached the jeep. 'She must go back to England with me.' The Baba, his eyes closed in meditation, took no notice. But a middle-aged man touched Malory gently on the arm and said, 'It is better this way, master. She had begun to decay even before she ceased to breath.' He pointed towards the sun. 'It is hot. A policeman has ordered the cremation as a sanitary measure.' The man's voice was soft and reassuring. What he said seemed reasonable, especially when he mentioned the policeman, although Malory had not seen a policeman since his arrival at the ashram. Yet he wanted to protest. Something needed to be said. He shook off the speaker's hand angrily. The man stepped back. 'Men die because they cannot join the beginning and the end,' he said. Immediately a second voice behind Malory repeated the words. 'Men die because they cannot join the beginning and the end.' A mournful sigh, the totality of a thousand exhalations, emanated from the river bank. As Malory turned, the flames roared upward. The Baba's jeep coughed into life and turned toward the ashram gate, where the line of food carts stood waiting. Even at a distance, Malory could feel the heat of the pyre. He felt its radiance on his chest and his forehead. The flames danced in his eyes. He held up his hands, feeling the warmth on his palms stretched toward the flames, and in the pit of his belly he felt a knot. His mouth opened as if to vomit, and all the breath that was in him seemed to rush out in one mad cry.

*During the day the cobras slept in the river-bank gardens of the ashram, where the gravel was cool and moist. At night, they came into the houses to hunt for mice.*

*He was not sure there was a snake in the hut. Other nights he had heard rustling in the kra logs and bamboo of the walls. He held his terror, fluttering against his ribs, his teeth chattering a travesty of castanets. The night sucked up his breath.*

*He thought it must be the fever that made him so sensitive to the presence and the sound that was almost a negative as though it sucked up and annihilated every other sound. He lay awake, absorbed in listening for the undulating black body dragging itself across the sandy floor. He should not have forgotten the purification tablets. He had to go to the ditch. What sound did the snake make oozing across the sand? What sound did Death make? What sound the Holy Ghost? He imagined the snake emerging downward from the wattles of the roof, lengthening in the emptiness of night, then sagging with the weight of its body and dropping with a lush heaviness to his bed.*

*Something touches his foot.*
*Malory screams.*
*The snake sucks up his screams.*

# DOROTHY NIMMO

# The Healing

We were messing about, which we shouldn't have been doing, but there you are. We should have been outside, but it was freezing out. Karen was showing off doing this flip thing she's just learnt. I don't mind Karen showing off because she's been my friend since the Junior and she's really good, anyway. Then she sort of slipped and she just lay there on the floor.

'Oh Lord,' she said. 'That's torn it!'

And we remembered about the competition.

You might think we were making a big thing about it but there wasn't much you could do around our school that made people think anything of you. Everyone wants to be someone, I mean everyone wants to be special. Don't they? Look at all the people who go on the prize shows on the telly, they'd rather look like prize wallies and be able to say they've been on the telly than spend their whole lives never doing anything.

At our school you do all right if you play football. If you get in the team you do all right. And the big boys have their bikes. They start with the mopeds and then they get the big Hondas, with the fairings and that. They're really big deal on those bikes, with their leathers and boots and their heads twice the proper size in the helmets. You can't see the spots under the visors. And the girls hang round them. There isn't much for the girls. You get noticed if you go around, you know, if you're easy, and if you get pregnant they talk about you but they don't admire you. There isn't much a girl can do apart from swimming and gymnastics.

They put us all in for the competitions, that's the way they have. They think there's no point in anything unless there's a competition and a prize. They mean well, they think we're losers so they'll give us a chance at something, even if it's something really diddy, like cookery. They had a cookery competition one time, it was some custard-powder company, they all had to think up different things you could make with custard powder. Sandra went in for that because there was a prize, twenty pounds. She made this cake with custard powder and then custard on top, you know, and then all different fruit; it was a lovely colour, really bright yellow, but she didn't win. My Mum does flower arrangements. Honestly, she spends hours finding this stuff, dried flowers and leaves, and she has all these different baskets and bits of log hollowed out. I think it looks terrible. It looks dead and it stands around the house all winter getting deader and deader. But she puts these things in the Flower Show and gets prizes; she gets a real kick out of the prizes. So she says to me, 'Why don't you make a sponge cake, Marty, there's a class here for a sponge? Or scones, that's easy, go on. Just for fun. It doesn't matter if you win or not, that's not the point. It's the competition is the fun!'

I don't understand her. What's the point of going in for it if you know you're going to lose? It isn't fun, it's bloody murder, I think.

Karen used to go in for swimming. She said it was boring pounding up and down the pool. When they get keen they really drive you. It must do something for them, I suppose it would, for the teachers, if they can get a winner out of all of us losers. Karen was good at the swimming, but then she got something wrong with her ears and even old Evans thought it was a bit much to go deaf just so the school could get into the area championships. So then she took up the gymnastics.

Ever since I've known her she's been doing things like the crab, going round the playground all bent over backwards, and cartwheels and that, so she'd got the talent and she really took to it. Everyone was doing it that year, it was all on the telly and the girls were really keen, but it was Karen they kept on at to do the competitions. And there was Karen on the floor. The Championship was the next day.

Someone said she ought to go to the nurse and someone else said, try a hot-water bottle. Sandra said, 'What about an iron?' And we said, 'What do you mean, an iron?'

'You iron her back,' said Sandra, 'I've seen it done.'

'You're having me on,' I said.

'It's the heat,' said Sandra.

'Honestly?' said Pam. Pam believes anything, always has. One time I told her if she put her fingers down her throat she could touch her toes. She believed me. She was sick, you can imagine, all on her shoes.

'What about a rolling-pin?' I said, 'we could roll her out.' I didn't think they'd take that seriously.

'I think we ought to go and tell Mr Evans,' said Jenny.

'How are you feeling?' I asked Karen.

'Not bad,' she said. So I knew she felt bad.

'We'd better sort it out for ourselves if we can,' I said.

So then Sandra went and got in at the window of the Home Economics, which is easy for her. I reckon she can get into anything, it's a knack, she says. It'll get her into trouble. She got in at the window and then she got another window open and we all climbed in. Karen said it was easing up a bit, but we made her lie down on one of the tables. First we found the rolling pin and rolled it up and down. You wouldn't think that would do any good; it didn't.

'Roll on a floured board,' said Nell. 'That's what it says in the cookery books!' She thought that was such a good joke she was no help at all for a bit.

'Is that what it means?' said Pam, 'Honestly?'

'Oh Pam!' said Sandra.

Then we got out the iron, Sandra got the cupboard open, and we plugged it in and started ironing Karen's back through her vest until it got too hot and she yelled. And we'd had it on the lowest setting.

Then it was Nell said, 'Let's try the laying-on of hands.'

'Go on,' said Karen, 'what's that?'

'It's what Jesus did, what the healing people do, you know, like in the Bible.'

'I never get in in time for Assembly,' I said.

'We don't have Bible in Assembly any more,' said Pam.

'We always have sex in R.E.,' said Jenny.

'But we had it in the Junior,' said Nell, 'Jesus was always at it, putting his hands on people. And they do it up at the Pentecostal. There's a man used to come to the shop ever so lame and now he doesn't.'

'Go on Karen, let's have a go,' said Sandra.

'Do you have to say anything?'

'Pick up your bed and walk,' suggested Nell.

'I'm not on my bed,' said Karen.

'In the name of the Father and the Son and the Holy Ghost, amen?'

'I don't know,' said Sandra. 'You go first.'

Nell put her hands on Karen's back and said, 'Get thee behind me, Satan!'

I don't know where she got that from.

Nothing happened. We didn't expect anything to happen, we were just trying it on. Then Pam put her hands on and began stroking and squeezing like the massage people do in the films, but Karen said that made it worse. And then I did it. I put my hands on Karen's back and I could feel the warmth going on down my arm and running into her back. I felt like it was my blood running into her and if I didn't take my hands away I wouldn't have any blood left any more. It was quite hard, taking my hands away. I felt quite weak, honestly.

Karen lay there for a bit. Then she got up.

'How does it feel?' I said.

'It's fine,' she said. 'That's fixed it.'

Then they all started to go on at me.

'What did you do, Mart?' said Sandra.

'I didn't do anything.'

'You must have done something.'

'Try it on me,' said Nell.

'I've got this dirty great spot on my chin,' said Sandra.

'I've got warts,' said Jenny.

But Karen said to leave me alone, we'd better get out before someone caught us.

Karen was third in the competition. Mr Evans said it wasn't good enough.

Sometimes Nell or Sandra get at me about it. If they have a headache or a period pain they say, 'What about a bit of the old laying-on of hands, Mart?' But I don't take any notice. They'll forget about it.

I wouldn't like to do it again.

They probably have competitions for that, too. If they knew about it, they'd probably put me in for them. I can just imagine all the sick, lame people laid out on the floor and everyone having a go who can make them get up fastest. With stop-watches and numbers, like they do in competitions. And prizes. I know they don't really. I don't expect I'd win if they did.

The motorway goes on and on. Birmingham in the distance looks like a celestial city; then they are slicing through above the factory roofs and a tangle of transformers and out again on the other side. The soil turns red in Staffordshire, there is the place where they are reclaiming the spoil-heaps, there is the Ship Canal snaking pewter across the industrial plain, then there is the first sight of the hills, the first glimpse of the sea.

'Next turn-off,' said Barney.

'I know,' says Eleanor, turning the car on to the slip-road.

'Well, we had to come,' says Barney.

'It'll be all right,' she says.

'I'm not frightened.'

'Nothing to be frightened of. Just be patient.'

'Aren't I always?'

'You know you aren't.'

'It's only for a couple of days.'

Eleanor pulls up in front of the house. As they wait by the front door, they can hear the barking of dogs and cries of 'I'm coming, I'm coming! Don't bark, good dogs!'

Cynthia gets the door open at last and, 'Oh, what a journey!' she says, 'What a journey you must have had! Come you in, I've been quite worried about you. You must be tired out. Are you tired out, Elly love?'

'I'm fine, mother. It's nothing now, with the motorway.'

'All the same, it's a long journey. I heard the weather on the wireless, I do hope you didn't have any of the fog? They said something about an accident just north of Wigan, you didn't have any trouble, did you? Oh, it's lovely to have you here!'

'This is Barney, Mother.'

Barney shakes Cynthia's hand. She leans a thin cheek at an angle but he thinks it is too soon to kiss her.

'How nice to meet you,' says Cynthia. 'I've been looking forward to meeting you for so long!'

Barney has been with Nell for more than a year now; this is the first time he has come home with her. Nell has never suggested it before, he cannot be said to be responsible for the lapse, but somehow Cynthia's inflexion makes him feel guilty. Or rather, he feels uncomfortable. He does not yet recognize the source of his discomfort.

'Come in, come in!' says Cynthia. 'Come in to the warm, you must be frozen. It's bitterly cold out!'

Barney begins to feel quite proud of himself for having come so far in such terrible conditions.

'Nell drove,' he says.

'Oh, darling! In this weather! Come in, sit you down, let's get you warmed up! Elly, you look pale, you look tired, you've been working too hard. It's more than time you came home!'

They settle in front of the fire. The room is full of furniture, embroidered cushions, pictures of the family. The old family is in silhouette or stippled on ivory and framed in gold; the new family smiles widely in front of the school photographer's blue backing, hair sleeked, pigtails lying neatly on their school blouses. Barney has never seen so much family displayed on walls, treasured behind glass. Eleanor takes a chair a little way from the fire.

'Sit you down, Barney,' says Cynthia. 'Yes, take that one, take Daddy's chair. That was always Daddy's chair, it's very comfortable.'

Barney sits, disturbing an old dog, who groans and shifts further back in the seat. He feels he is displacing not only the dog but the spirit of Daddy. There is scarcely enough room for him in the chair.

'Now,' says Cynthia, settling herself, 'tell me all about it!'

Eleanor says everything is fine, the job is going well, the weather hasn't been too bad in London.

Cynthia tells them about the rest of the family. Cara, who has gone back to work now the children are all at school; Jessica, who is still house-bound but copes so well though James is away a lot. The children are all growing up.

'Amabel is getting quite a look of you, Elly. Those family likenesses crop up in the most unexpected places! I've a photo here, she looks just like you did at her age.'

Cynthia sorts through a pile of letters on the shelf by her chair. She finds the photograph. 'Look, Elly, don't you see a likeness? Wasn't there a snap of you looking just like that? It used to be in the drawer over there, see if you can find it.'

Eleanor opens a drawer in the heavy, carved sideboard. The glass-fronted cupboard above is full of china, a silver teapot and jug, several strange objects made of clay.

'Did you see the cow Selena made? Oh, you must look at Selena's cow, it's a hoot! That one, yes, the black-and-white one, lying down because Selena said she couldn't get the legs to stick on, bless her. I think it shows promise, don't you? I think she's the one is going to take after Cara. Can you see the photographs? I had them out to show Jessica when she was here last. Bring them over, I'm sure Barney would like to see them. Look at this! This is Elly, I think this is Elly, or is it Cara? No, it's Elly because here's old Sam. Wasn't she a pretty baby, Barney?'

She was a pretty baby – a little peaky, his mother would have said, she wouldn't have won the prize at the Baby Show but her smile was confiding. 'Oh I'm sure we are boring you, all this talk about the family! You know how it is, Elly hasn't been up for so long!'

'Well!' says Barney and smiles and spreads his hands because he can't think what one should say at this point.

'I expect all families are the same,' says Cynthia, though she is convinced that this family is unique.

'I'm the only,' says Barney.

'Oh dear!' She is truly sorry for him and glad that now he can be admitted into Elly's family and enjoy the pleasures he must have missed so much.

Barney thinks of his family. How Dad would never let him speak at meals, how Dad went on about getting his hair cut. How Dad went on about Mum, how Dad left. So they went to live in Manchester and he goes to see Mum a couple of times a year and they look at each other. After they have asked each other how they are and they have both said as well as can be expected except that Mum isn't sleeping, and Mum has cooked him fish and chips and he has refused ice cream, they have nothing to say to each other, so they watch the telly until he can say goodbye.

Mrs Anderson has a lot to say.

'That was taken just after she had the croup. She was never very strong, one thing after another, you can see how delicate she looks. She was three weeks in the hospital, I'll never forget. I sat by her bed all night and there she was, my little Elly, with her thumb in her mouth and her copy of *Peter Rabbit*!'

Mother used to tell Eleanor she was ill, she used to believe her mother.

'You don't look well, Elly, have you got a temperature? I'll take your temperature, shall I? You'd better take a few days off school. I'll just give them a ring. A few days quiet and you'll be as right as rain!'

Mother said she was ill and the rain fell down the window-pane as she lay in bed with a hot-water bottle and her chest rubbed with Vick. Mother would bring her up some Bovril and dry toast for lunch, a light diet, she said, just until you're better, then you can come down and sit in front of the fire when the house warms up.

It had seemed worth while to be ill, being close and warm with the rain outside and missing school. When she got back, they would have done the subjunctive or something and though she would copy out the notes she never would get the subjunctive straight.

But in London, Barney's Nell is never ill. When he has a cold and likes to think he is coming down with 'flu, he wants her to look after him. He lies sweating in bed and says, 'You won't be late back, will you? Is there anything to eat? Will you make me a cup of coffee?' But she holds the door-handle, eager to be away.

'You'll be all right,' she says, determined.

'Pour Barney some more tea, darling,' says Cynthia. 'Another biscuit? Another scone? Nothing for me, thanks, but help yourself!'

Barney takes a scone.

'Take two! You must be hungry after that long journey!'

Barney takes another scone.

'Won't you have one, Elly?'

'No, no, thanks.'

'Oh, darling! She's too thin, don't you think so, Barney? I worry about her, all by herself in London, I don't think she looks after herself properly.'

'Nell?' says Barney, holding out the plate. Nell ignores it.

'She always was a bit picky,' says Cynthia confidingly. 'Don't you remember, Elly, I used to sit with you when you were small and feed you your mashed potato? You never did like it. I used to mush it all up with the gravy and feed you, spoonful by spoonful, it was the only way to get it down her, Barney! One for Mummy, I'd say, one for Daddy, one for Sam! Eat it all up or I'll give it to old Sam, I'd say. He'd sit under the chair and look up so hopefully! I'd get it all down you. Oh, what a game!'

Nell remembers the cold, slow, thick mouthfuls of mashed potato.

'She was never very strong, Barney. When she had appendicitis I thought we were going to lose her. We were always very careful of her after that. They said we were never to let her get over-tired. Early bed for Elly always and she was off games for years. But she never did like games, anyway.'

Barney thinks of his Nell, in London. How she gets up early to run in the park. She wears a scarlet tracksuit and runs further and faster than he can, though he doesn't like to notice this. He avoids it by saying no, he won't be running with her this morning, not this morning, he has had a bad night. And not this morning, either, he has a lot of work to get through. He says he thinks running is boring anyway and pretty pointless really and people take it all too seriously. There's only one sort of exercise I like he says, indoor games for me. Ha!

Nell runs.

Eleanor gets up and goes to the window.

'Is that Tom waiting to come in?' says Cynthia.

'No, I don't think so.'

Outside, the wind beats the bare branches of the roses. Eleanor brings her focus back from the shadowy wet tangle of the garden and sees herself reflected in the glass, ghostly against the branches of the banksia whipped by the wind.

'You should get the banksia pruned, Mother,' she says. 'I'll get the ladder out in the morning.'

'Oh, do you think you should, darling? It's so high up. Be very careful. Maybe Barney would do it for me? It's a man's job. Are you interested in gardening, Barney?'

'Well,' says Barney, 'I've never . . .'

'You're from Liverpool, aren't you?'

'Manchester.'

'Oh, Manchester, of course, Elly told me. Did you ever meet Dr Holdsworth, was it, or Harmondsworth? I'm so bad at names! Such a nice man, head of Music, I think, at the Grammar School?'

'I wasn't at the Grammar.'

'Is your family from Manchester?'

'Mum moved there a few years back. Dad came from Belfast originally.'

Cynthia makes no comment on Belfast. Somewhere out there is a cruel world which she prefers not to know about. She knows about roses.

'The banksia,' she says. 'Elly will show you in the morning, if you have time. I can always rely on James, that's Jessica's James, he comes and does the pruning for me, the gooseberries and all, such a nasty job! But he's away a lot. And oh, while I remember, Elly, there's that light bulb. It is electrical engineering isn't it, Barney, your line?'

'Chemical,' says Barney.

'Well I'm sure you are a practical man. There's a light bulb gone in the hall, Elly, I thought maybe Barney could put in a new one. I've got a new one but it seems to stick, that socket. Could you? Oh, no, not now, later. Don't disturb yourself just when you're getting warmed up!'

'No, that's fine, that's fine,' says Barney. He doesn't know what to call Cynthia. Not Mother, obviously. Not Mrs Anderson, surely? So he doesn't call her anything, but he smiles down at her, flattered somehow and willing to please.

'I'll get the steps,' she says, scattering letters and photos.

'No, no, just tell me where they are!'

Nell takes the tea-tray through to the kitchen and shows Barney where the steps are in the washroom. He hauls them awkwardly into the hall. He climbs up with the bulb, holding the edge of the cardboard cover in his teeth as he twists the old bulb. The glass splinters in his hand, leaving the metal base fixed in the socket. 'Nell!' he shouts, 'I've done it again.'

135

'You don't know your own strength,' she says, coming through, 'Did you turn the light off?'

'Was it on?'

'Better check.'

She has watched him going under in the flood of Cynthia's conversation, drawn by its sheer volume into her world. He hasn't seemed to struggle.

'I'll do it,' she says, 'I've got the pliers.' She grips, twists and pulls. 'It's a knack,' she says.

'Shall I get supper, Mother?'

'Oh, if you would, darling! She's such a good cook, much better than I am Barney!'

And yet in London he has not known her do much more than warm up a frozen pizza.

'Can you find everything, Elly? I've done the beds. I put Barney in the Blue Room, is that right? And you are in your room.'

Cynthia says this very clearly, so there can be no misunderstanding. She no longer knows quite what to expect from her girls; things have changed. She would prefer not to think about it. She certainly isn't going to encourage it. Not in her house. So Barney is in the Blue Room and Elly is up in the attic and it's up to them really, isn't it?

Barney takes the rucksack up the stairs.

'Shall I put your stuff in the bathroom, Nell?'

There are two beds in the Blue Room, both narrow. They have slept together on narrower beds but Barney would hesitate to suggest that they share one of these. Here in the family house where, as he has noticed already, the floorboards creak as you go along the landing and on the other side of the landing Mrs Anderson sleeps, probably lightly.

'She does go on a bit,' says Barney. They have gone down to the pub after supper. Cynthia said, 'Of course, darling, you go on out. I'll be perfectly all right, I thought I'd just watch the news and have an early night. Be sure to turn the hall light out, won't you? And if you turn the television on again would you make sure the plug is out when you go to bed? Because there was that case at Bayside where the telly blew up in the night and all the poor old souls were burnt, do you remember? And lock the door, won't you?'

'She's just trying to get you. To get . . .' Nell hears what she has said and adds quickly, 'To get you straight.'

'I expect her life is a bit . . . since your father?' He gestures and drinks and feels better.

'Oh, she keeps herself busy. She's into everything in the village and there's Cara and Jessica, she sees a lot of them and the children. She's busy. All the time.'

'Yes,' says Barney. They are quiet. They look round the bar. They drink their beer. They do not look at each other.

'It's not long,' says Barney. He reaches for her hand. He has not felt close to her since they arrived, he has hardly touched her. He wonders why he came. And he feels Nell watching him as if she expected something of him. He is taking some sort of examination, undergoing some sort of test, and he has no idea what kind of answer will count as right.

In the morning they prune the banksia. Nell goes up the ladder, Barney steadies the end.

'Oh, I'm so grateful to you, Barney,' says Cynthia. 'Such a big job! Now, if you can just get the clippings piled up, we can set a match to them later.'

'It was Nell,' says Barney.

'Oh, Elly!' says Cynthia. 'All that way up! You've no idea what a timid little thing she used to be! She was terrified of dogs, do you remember Elly? Once we met a chihuahua on a train, she must have been about three, perhaps, she held on to my legs, wanting to be picked up. It was such a small dog! I said, "But Elly, that's such a little dog! You can't be afraid of such a little dog. How small would a dog have to be for you not to be frightened of it?" And she put her little fingers maybe an inch apart and she said, "About that big!" Oh, we did laugh!'

Hauling the clippings to the bonfire, Barney thinks of how they have cycled in France and there have been big dogs in farmyards. As they passed in the mist and early light, the dogs have hurled themselves barking the lengths of their chains in every farmyard. One dog, loose in the yard, leapt the fence and snapped at their feet. Barney pedalled faster but Nell stopped, turned, threatened the dog. 'Get out of it!' she shouted, her voice harsh. 'Get the hell out of it, dog!' The dog backed and snarled. 'You have to face them,' said Nell. 'You mustn't let them think you are afraid.'

Later, when the bonfire was well alight, they went out. 'You'll want to go out,' says Cynthia. 'You won't want to waste such a lovely day! But sometime this evening, darling, there's still a whole lot of stuff in your room. I wondered if we could clear it out? While you're here?'

Eleanor drives fast and Cynthia, in the back seat, points out the countryside.

'Look at the sea! You can see the sea from here! Slow down, Elly love, let Barney see the view. It's one of the loveliest views in England, I always say!'

She presents the landscape to him as if it were something in her gift with which she can afford to be generous. As she also presents him with her daughter, Elly.

Back by the fireside, with tea and chocolate cake, Cynthia says, 'She drives well, doesn't she, Barney? You'd never think she used to be so timid. I remember one time there was a moth in her room, she must have been about eight, and she came flying down the stairs. "There's a moth, take it out, take it out!" And her Daddy went and caught it, he showed it to her. "It's only a moth," he said, and tried to show her the markings, how pretty they were. But she wouldn't look!'

In France, huge crickets have invaded their tent. In Spain, spiders have had to be removed from showers. Barney has been afraid from time to time, of strangers stalking them on deserted beaches, of gangs of youths in amusement arcades, but Nell has not shown any fear. Would he have liked her to be a little afraid, to have clung to him and hidden her eyes and cried, 'There's a moth, there's a moth in my room!' Yes, he would, he realizes as he thinks about it. He would have liked that.

'She's changed,' he says.

'Well, she's grown up,' says Cynthia. 'But she's still my little girl, she'll always be little Elly to me. I still keep Aggie upstairs, Elly, did you know? That was the last doll she had, Barney, with all the clothes Cara made for her. I thought I'd keep her for you, Elly, for when you . . . for if you ever . . .' Cynthia starts another ball of wool, twisting the ends of the threads together. 'I like best of all to knit for the babies, you get the thing finished. This is for Sam, Jessica's youngest. Have you seen little Sam yet, Elly? Oh, he's getting quite big now. I think he has quite a look of Daddy. I thought he would suit this colour, it's a good strong colour for a boy.'

There is a baby now in the room. It lies on the floor between them and looks reproachful. Nell has no babies. She is not married but she is nearly thirty. Cynthia thinks she ought to get married and have children before she is thirty, then she will settle down and they will talk together about labour pains and breast-feeding and teething. Cynthia will be very careful not to interfere, she hopes she has never done that.

'Do you remember, Elly, how you used to play with Mark? That's Cara's eldest, Barney. Cara got married when she was twenty and had her family straight away so they could all grow up together, that was what Cara said and I thought it was very sensible of her.'

(You don't want to wait too long, hears Nell, you don't want to put it off too long. Do you think it's wise, all these, these pills and things? Get your priorities straight. All this work, all the things you do, all the money you make, my dear! But what is the most important thing, for a woman? Cara and Mark, Selena, Amabel, and Jessica and Adelaide and Anthony and Sam. My jewels, all of them!)

'Elly is six years younger than Cara, so when Mark was born she was, what, only fifteen, that's right. Elly was so good with Mark, he thought the world of her. I remember him lying in that little sling thing he had, on the table, and Elly making faces at him. Laugh! I've never seen anything like it!'

But in London Nell has never talked about babies. She has never said she wanted children. She talks about her job, about her plans for the next few years and there are no children in her plans. She does not peer into prams, she does not seem much to enjoy their weekends with friends who have children. Now Barney looks into Cynthia's eyes and sees a tender Elly who loves babies and has this knack of making them laugh.

'Cara used to let you give him his bottle and you'd sit there on the sofa, didn't you have your hair long in those days, Elly? Up in a pony-tail? It was pretty like that. I've never interfered with how you did your hair, but I did use to like it like that, up in a pony- tail.'

Now Nell's hair is short, so that in some lights, at some angles with her strong nose and the modelling under the cheek-bones, she looks masculine. Or at least not feminine.

Nell gets up and picks up the tray.

'Let me help you,' says Barney. 'Let me carry it for you, let me open the door!'

'Stay and talk to Mother,' says Nell.

'Are you sure, dear?' says Cynthia. 'Are you sure you can manage? You must be tired out!'

Nell goes into the kitchen.

Barney watches her go. Cynthia's daughter, nervous, frail – he imagines the swing of the pony-tail. The Nell he knows is strong, opens the doors herself, shrugs away offers of help. But under the competence and courage he has felt there was something softer, more vulnerable. Perhaps he can waken the sleeping beauty with a kiss?

'There's still a lot of things in your bedroom, I wondered if we ought to clear them out? While you're here? There might be something you would find useful?'

'Oh, throw them out, Mother, you might as well.'

'Let's go through them, shall we? You don't mind, Barney? I've kept them just in case you wanted them but anything you don't want I'll put in the dressing-up drawer. Cara's family love going through the dressing-up drawer when they come!'

The attic bedroom is small and bare. There is a bed, a dolls' house against one wall, a bookcase full of children's books and a view over the valley. Barney thinks of little Elly waking in that bed with the sun coming through that window, getting up to draw back those flowered curtains and look out on those fields. He feels close to Elly, closer almost than he does to his Nell, by whose side he has woken for the past year on the third floor of the tall house behind Holland Park Road where the window frames only the blank wall of a garage. 'I put the dolls' house in your room, darling, I didn't think you would mind. Look, all the furniture is still here, and the lights Daddy rigged up and all the little people! Mother in the kitchen, Dad in the garage, and look at Grandma! I've still got your riding hat, would you have any use for that? No, not in London, I suppose. And your bridesmaid's dress from Jessica's wedding. There's quite a lot of stuff in the skirt, I thought it might make something for little Amabel if you didn't want it?'

Cynthia's hands keep busy folding and re-folding pink taffeta. 'There's a whole lot of stuff, I don't know what it is! There's your leotard, and the evening dress you had when you first went to university – that sort of thing fetches quite a good price, doesn't it? And, oh, look! The Bo-Peep dress! Oh, look at the hat, look at the flowers! They're still quite fresh! Oh, put it on, Elly, let Barney see the hat!'

Barney picks up the hat, balances it on his hand and places it on Nell's head. Under the hat her face is shadowed.

'Try on the dress, Elly, why don't you? I expect you still fit it, you haven't grown much since you were fourteen, you certainly haven't put on any weight. She was quite a roundy little thing then, Barney. We had the dress made, oh, I don't remember, something about a school pageant, wasn't it? And then she used to wear it for fancy-dress do's. Go on, Elly!'

'Go on, Elly!' says Barney.

Eleanor's head comes up quite sharply as she hears her name.

Cynthia says, 'Oh, darling, do just let Barney see you! I was so proud of you!'

And she lifts the dress. 'Quick, darling, take off your jeans – Barney will turn his head away, won't you?'

Has Eleanor forgotten how to deny her mother anything?

Barney has seen her in bra and pants and less, but never before tight-laced into black velvet, never with breasts swathed in white muslin, crushed but still gracefully framing her shoulders.

'And the hat!' says Cynthia. 'There you are! Turn round, darling. It still fits you. Perfectly. Don't you think she looks lovely, Barney?'

He puts his hands round the boned waist. His hands almost span it. The sprigged skirt makes a mystery of her legs. Cynthia is busy folding the scattered clothes. 'I'll just put these in the dressing-up drawer if you're sure there's nothing you want?'

She picks up a heap of clothes and goes downstairs.

Barney holds Eleanor.

'What is it?' he says.

'Don't hold me,' says Eleanor, muffled with her face against his jersey.

He continues to hold her, pressing his fingers against the tight velvet and the stiffeners in the bodice. He bends her backwards, the muslin slips from her shoulders. It is right, dressed like this, that he should lift her, though her hands beat against his back and her head turns from side to side to avoid his mouth.

'Darling!' he breathes in her ear.

'Don't!' she says.

As he lays her on the narrow bed she left ten years ago, she brings her knee up and twists over, down to the floor, tearing the dress.

'Elly, for God's sake!'

The velvet splits as she drags the dress up over head. She grasps the skirt with both hands and tears it, tears it again and hurls it into the corner. It catches on the dolls' house roof and hangs, ragged.

'Where's my sodding jeans?' she says. She pulls them on, pulls the zip tight over her crotch. She drags the jersey over her head; it falls to her hip-bone, covering her breasts, her waist.

'Why don't you go and play with yourself?' she says.

It is Sunday afternoon.

'Well, better be off now, Mother,' says Eleanor.

'Oh, darling,' says Cynthia, 'it seems as if you'd only just come! Such a short visit! You've got the apples in the car, haven't you? And the chutney? I've enjoyed meeting you so much, Barney, and thank you for all your help – the bulb you know, and the roses!'

'It's been great. Hearing all about Elly. Really great.'

Cynthia rests her hand confidingly on his jersey and raises her cheek for his kiss.

'Her roots are here Barney. Take care of her.'

'Shall I drive?' says Barney.

'No,' says Eleanor.

'Oh all right. I thought you might be tired.'

'What gave you that idea?'

Barney waves to Cynthia, who is standing by the front door to wave them off.

Eleanor keeps her eyes on the road.

'Oh, my old man's a dustman!' she sings raucously until they get on to the motorway, where she gets into the fast lane and touches eighty.

'What did you do with the dress, Elly?' he says.

'Don't call me that,' she says.

'You didn't leave it, did you?'

'It's in the rucksack. I'll get rid of it.'

There is a pause. Barney puts his hand on Eleanor's knee.

'You all right, Elly?'

'I told you. Don't ever call me that.'

They were in the orchard, under the apple trees, making tea-parties in the summer house. The little table was laid out with a tea-cloth; they had put buttercups in an egg cup and made brown bread and butter for a real tea-party. An uncle had given them each a china rabbit; the two rabbits were going to have tea. Kate's rabbit was blue, its features only lightly indented, its ears lying along its back in a smooth curve. Ellen's was a more naturalistic rabbit, the fur suggested by a slight roughness in the clay. The two rabbits sat side by side on the table.

'Oh I do love my rabbit,' said Kate, elder by two years. 'He is so smooth and shiny and such a beautiful blue. Come along, Rabbit, would you like some bread and butter, or would you rather have a buttercup for your tea?'

'I like my rabbit better,' said Ellen determinedly. She was a square child who fell over continually; her skinned knees never healed properly, so that she went through the summer patched with elastoplast. She admired Kate because Kate was older and braver and knew more than she did. Kate was lovable and talkative and naughty and pretty and Kate was older.

'I like my rabbit better. Really,' said Ellen.

'Do you?' said Kate. 'He's awfully ordinary, just brown and rabbitty. Mine is blue. Blue like the sea, blue like the sky and he's smooth, like those pebbles you get on the beach.'

Ellen was increasingly aware of the extraordinary charm of Kate's rabbit. Her own rabbit looked more and more mundane, boringly realistic. She was thoughtful.

She said, 'I think your rabbit is lovely, Kate. I think your rabbit is much nicer than mine. Oh, Kate, it isn't fair! I wish Uncle Tom had given me one like yours. I want a rabbit like yours!'

'All right,' said Kate carelessly, 'I don't mind. You can have mine and I'll have yours.'

Ellen could hardly believe she had got her own way so easily.

She suspected there must be a snag. But Kate smiled and held out the beautiful blue smooth-eared rabbit. Ellen took him. Kate got some biscuits out of the tin they had brought up the garden. They drank their orange juice out of the dolls' teacups with the strange taste from the not quite clean bottoms of the cups, and then they started to weed between the cracks of the summer-house terrace. The rabbits sat beside them.

'Oh, I do love my new rabbit,' said Kate, scraping away with a kitchen knife. 'Mind you get the roots out, Elly, they'll only grow again if you don't.'

'They'll grow again anyway, they always do,' said Ellen.

'Of course they grow again in the end, but if you don't get the roots out we might as well not be doing this job at all. Go down and get a brush, will you?'

Ellen went down the garden path to the shed. She picked a bunch of redcurrants from the bush and burst them, one by one, in her mouth, juicy and sour.

'I see you!' shouted Kate. 'You're eating redcurrants and there won't be any left for jelly. I'll tell. Mum thinks it's the birds, but it's you, you eat them all the time. No wonder you're fat!'

'I'm not fat. Redcurrants aren't fattening and, anyway, I'm not fat!'

But Ellen was in despair because she knew she was fat. When she got back with the brush, Kate had stopped weeding and was making her rabbit climb the cherry tree.

'Do you know why I love my rabbit?' said Kate. 'It's because he is so brown, and I love the way his nose looks real. I love the way his ears go along his back like a real rabbit and the little rough bits he has on his fur. I might call him Rough.'

'I'm going to call mine Blue,' said Ellen.

'That's a funny name for a rabbit!'

'Rough is a dog's name, anyway.'

'Look,' said Kate. 'If I hide him in the grass a bit and cover him with this bit of meadowsweet, it makes a house for him. He's just coming out to eat his dinner. Look, he looks as if he lives in this little hole!'

'I'm going to make a house for my rabbit,' said Ellen.

'Oh, no, that's no good,' said Kate. 'Your rabbit is so blue! You can see he isn't a real rabbit. He's the wrong colour for a garden rabbit, he's no good for outside. You'll have to keep him on your dressing-table for an ornament. I think I'll leave my rabbit out all night to live in this hole and in the morning maybe he'll have turned into a real rabbit and run away with all the other rabbits to live with them!'

'He'll get myxi!' said Ellen.

'Oh, don't be mean, Elly, of course he won't. If you left your rabbit out, all the others would mob him, like birds do owls in the daytime, you know because he'd be all the wrong colour. Anyway, he hasn't got proper legs!'

Ellen fought with herself but she could not resist the pictures Kate put into her mind.

'Oh Kate, I wish I hadn't given you my rabbit! It was mine in the first place, because Uncle Tom gave him to me. I've changed my mind, he's much the nicest rabbit and Uncle Tom meant me to have him, so he's mine really!'

Kate smiled, conscious of her power.

'All right,' she said. 'You can have your rabbit back if you like. I don't mind. If you're going to make a fuss.'

Ellen took the brown rabbit. She made a nest by the corner of the summerhouse steps and lined it with leaves. She decorated it with cranesbill and buttercups and laid her rabbit in the nest. And it did look almost real.

But Kate smoothed her hand over the blue rabbit and a smile turned up the corners of her mouth. She said, softly crooning, thoughtful, 'I do love my blue rabbit and Uncle Tom meant me to have him because he's special. He is smooth and shiny and blue like the sea. I could take him to Jenny Brown's Point and put him in the sea and the waves would wash over him. He'd go all lovely colours like the pebbles do and I expect he can swim, too. He's a sea-rabbit.'

'There's no such thing,' said Ellen.

'Yes, there is. There's sea-horses and sea-urchins and sea-dogs, so there is sea-rabbits and mine is. Mine is the best rabbit in the world!'

And it was the truth, and Ellen acknowledged it.

JACI STEPHEN

We'll try some simple relaxation exercises to start. Close your eyes and start to be conscious of your body. Relax your toes, your knees, your thighs. Feel the tips of your fingers getting warm. They tingle. Now your hands are numb. Your arms. Feel the muscles in your neck and head relax. Now I'm going to count to ten. You'll open your eyes, but after thirty seconds they'll begin to close again. On waking, you'll feel alert, but will not be able to resist the temptation to close your eyes. One, two, three, four – slowly becoming alert – five, six, seven, eight – eyes slowly opening – nine, ten.' I opened my eyes. 'How do you feel?'

I felt nothing.

'Alert.'

'Now you begin to feel sleepy. Your eyes are getting heavier. You start to blink more and more. You cannot resist. Now I'm going to count from fourteen down to one and I want you to imagine you're travelling down a spiral staircase. Fourteen, thirteen, twelve – oh, and that feels so good, you feel so relaxed – eleven, ten – deeper and deeper – nine, eight, seven, six, five – the whole of your body is relaxed and calm, so peaceful – four, three, two, one.'

I knew I had made a good job of the blinking. I started with a brief flutter and then made the two lids flap uncertainly, as if attempting to take off from each eyeball. So this was what they called 'being under'. I wondered if I allowed myself to scratch the itch on my nose he'd know that I was still very much above surface. I didn't like to hurt his feelings in showing that I had not 'gone'. Now that I'd reached the bottom of this staircase (a pretty monstrous thing, stuck in the middle of someone's living-room) I had to climb up again.

'I'm going to count from one to ten and when you wake we're going to talk about one of the dreams that particularly disturbs you. We're going to try and understand the symbols of the dream so that it no longer frightens you. One, two, three, four, five, six – you're becoming alert – seven, eight – your eyes are opening – nine, ten – how do you feel?'

Exactly the same. Sick of going up and down all those stairs. And why were there four less on the way back?

'I feel . . . very alert.'

He looked pleased.

'I want you to pick on one dream. Read it aloud to me. Preferably a recurring one.'

I opened my book.

'Well, there are a lot of water dreams.' I flicked over several pages and saw a variety of headings in the margins – swimming-pools, beaches, waves. 'A lot of water.'

'Just read one.' He closed his eyes and waited. I chose a fairly mild one.

'The family, including myself, were going to the beach on an "outing", like the ones we used to go on with my parents when we were younger. We reached a dead end where the tide came right up to the car. My father wanted us to go for a walk. I got very angry and said that we didn't want to. He looked very hurt and I felt a lot of guilt in the dream.' There was a long silence. 'That's it.'

'Hm.' He opened his eyes. 'It's not really of a nightmarish quality though, is it? Just an ordinary dream, really. Have you got one that has disturbed you deeply?'

Here goes.

'A dream I had recently was quite disturbing, actually.' He closed his eyes. At least I would be saved the embarrassment of his stare. 'There was a telephone box, and the man I was going out with at the time was standing in the doorway. He wouldn't allow me to enter and there was another woman inside. The man's trousers were open and his penis was menstruating. He told me he couldn't have sex because of this and I wrapped a towel around it. But the blood kept coming, soaking itself into the towel.' I had struck gold. My hypnoanalyst knew I was not a fake. I could see his eyes, as they opened, claw meaning from the air.

'Could this man be your father?'

'No . . . well, I mean I suppose he's like him in some ways.' They were both balding, at any rate.

'The first thing that springs to mind is, of course, the castration symbol. The anger is directed towards your father in the first dream – Freud's penis-envy – and you want to castrate him. The blood comes as a result of that castration. Telephone boxes are red, so that's also symbolic of the blood. He's keeping you out ... hm ... interesting. Now I want you to relax again and we'll look at the dreams more closely under hypnosis.'

Back down the spiral staircase. This time, when I reach the bottom, there is a family sitting in the room watching *Coronation Street*. The father gives a nod, indicating my presence to the rest of the family, who pretend not to notice. I apologize for disturbing them and explain that I won't be there for long.

'In this state of deep relaxation the dreams will become more meaningful.

'We'll go back to the beach and I want you to go to the edge of the water. You step in. The water covers your feet and then your ankles. Now it's up to your thighs and now your stomach. How do you feel?'

'Sick.'

Don't be ridiculous. How can you feel sick? You're sitting on a chair in a room. There's no water. THERE IS NO WATER. My guru must have had a momentary vision of my throwing up on his carpet because he told me to get out of the sea a lot quicker than I'd gone in. I was back on the sand.

'Now I want you to think of being a man.' I became a bronze Mr Universe-type figure – muscular, dark and handsome. 'Now walk into the sea again.' I wondered if all hypnotists made their clients walk around so much. Anyway, I went back in. This time I felt OK. Deeper and deeper. He made the water come up to my chest. Deeper again. Up to my neck. Until only my head was above water, bobbing around in the liquid silence like a buoy. I was brought back to shore.

'Now I want you to stay as that man. You're on the beach and your penis starts bleeding. What do you think?'

What a relief, I'm not pregnant.

'I don't think much about it. It seems perfectly normal.'

'OK. Now look at the sand. Clean, golden sand. An image begins to appear on the sand. Can you see what it is?'

Please, please, image, come.

'No.'

'OK. There's a blank screen. You're watching a film in which there's a man coming out of a telephone box. As he comes out you see that his penis is bleeding . . .' Why, why, had I chosen that one? 'Then that image disappears and another one comes in its place. Can you see what it is?' It's the Treorchy Male Voice Choir, singing in the nude, their bloody penises (or is it penii?) painting the valleys red.

'Trees.'

'What sort of trees?'

'Tall trees. I can't see the sky through them.'

'Is there anything being done to the trees?'

'No.'

'Think of one of those trees in particular. It's being cut down by an axe.' What on earth had possessed me to pick trees? Now this huge, erect trunk was being castrated from its Mother Earth. But by whom? 'I want you to imagine your father walking through those trees . . .' Literally, did he mean? 'You're following him and you've got a knife . . . you want to kill him, murder him, you feel very angry towards him . . . you want to CASTRATE him!' My hypnotist was breathless. My father came towards me, smiling.

'Now, when I bring you round you will remember all these details and will be able to discuss your dreams and understand their symbolic meaning. I will make suggestions, not all of which will be true. But you will know instinctively when I make a correct interpretation. One . . . two . . .' The signature tune of *Coronation Street* serenaded my departure up the staircase. I had to step over a cat who was stretched out on the fifth step, licking her paws.

'How do you feel?'

'Alert.'

'Good. It's clear that you're repressing anger. Because you are unable to express anger, or feel guilty when you do, your murderous impulses are exceptionally strong in dreams. Your father is a passive figure and you spite him without really intending to hurt. But because you *do* hurt, you feel guilty. I suspect that that's how you are with men in general.'

Here was a fine grey hair pulled from a mass of black matter.

'Let's try some word association. I'm going to say some words and I want you to tell me the images that come into your mind. Father.'

'Mother.'

'Sea.'

'Boats.'

'Anything else?'

'Islands.'

'Penis.'

'Sex.'

'Anything else?'

'No.'

'Menstruation.'

'Vulnerability.'

'That's an interesting one. Telephone box.'

'Trapped.'

'Very interesting, because you were, in actual fact, outside it and therefore vulnerable. Anger.'

'Jealousy.'

My hypnotist started as if he had been pin-pricked. Here was an untouched area.

'Have you a younger brother or sister?'

'Yes, a younger brother.'

'Have you ever felt jealous of him?'

'Uh, no, not really.'

'Ah-ha!' He had hit the jackpot. 'I'm interested in the way you paused then. *Have* you ever felt jealous of him?'

'No, I just joke about it sometimes with my mother.'

'Does she pay more attention to your brother?'

'No.'

'Are there any similarities between the man in the telephone box and your brother?'

By now, the head of most men I knew had been attached to the body of the menstruating penis. It was causing quite a stir in the street where the box was situated. My brother's didn't fit.

'No.'

'So you've never felt jealous enough of your brother to want to spite or hurt him?'

I used to scare him with bath oils when my parents left us to play in the bath. I hid them until I heard the receding footsteps on the stairs and then slowly moved the round jelly through the water, ignoring my brother's tears and squeals. At the last moment I'd squeeze the rubbery outside and the fluid would spurt all over his pale, white flesh and he would cry, defeated.

Or there was the time I sang the same song, over and over again, when my mother locked us in the car while she went to a shop. I had learnt it in Sunday-school:

> Harvest-time is here again,
> Thanks to God for sun and rain,
> Harvest-time is here again,
> Give thanks for harvest home.

Two hundred times I counted. My brother was sobbing almost to the point of hysteria. Three weeks later he said, 'Hello, you bitch,' to the Sunday-school superintendent. She was sixty-five years old.

'No, I don't think I've ever been spiteful towards him, either.'

'I'm just trying to work out why you should have this sub-conscious desire to hurt and yet not be able to. Has your father ever attacked you?'

'No.'

'Have you ever been raped?'

'No.'

'Dreamt of being raped?'

'Yes. Once by a wolf and once by a bull.'

'Are you a lesbian?'

'No.'

'Uneasy with men?'

'No, more at ease.'

'You associate with them, perhaps?'

'Maybe.'

'Have you ever wanted to be a man?'

'I had an alter-ego as a child. He was a man.' Come to think of it, he was the bronze Mr Universe on my beach.

'I want you to pretend that the dream was mine and you tell me what you think it means.'

'Uh . . . pregnancy envy?'

'Anything else?'

'That you're frightened of having sex with a woman in the middle of her period.'

'Has a man ever tried to have sex with you during menstruation?'

Unfair, this was my analysis.

'Yes.'

'By force?'

'No.'

'Can you recall any other dreams associated with blood?'

I opened my book again and turned the pages – anger, water, possession, jealousy, blood.

'Here's one.' Oh, no. I read it to myself and took a deep breath. The dream came out quickly. 'I dreamt that I went to bed with someone who used a contraceptive sheath and afterwards I drank the contents but it was blood.'

'VAMPIRISM!' My hypnotist jumped in his chair. 'Have you ever had dreams about someone biting your neck?'

'No.'

'I have.' He looked as if he'd enjoyed it as well. 'Blood. So much blood. Fascinating. Very violent images, you see. Any others?'

'Well, this isn't really the same sort of thing, but I had a dream in which I went to a fortune-teller. When I arrived there, she was a nun. She put a reddish-brown dye on my palms.'

'That could possibly be a guilt symbol – blood on the hands, Lady Macbeth, can't clean the blood from the hands. Do you mind if I ask you if you have any religious complexes?'

'No, I uh . . .'

'You see, my interpretation would be that the nun is putting blood on your hands – the guilt for something you've done. Have you done anything you feel would be strongly against your religious principles? Take your time to think about it. Close your eyes. Think carefully. Whose blood do you feel on your hands?'

The hypnotist's voice had softened. When I closed my eyes I felt balanced at the end of each word that lengthened like a raindrop on a telegraph wire. As one word dropped, I fell with it. But it was not a feeling of falling *to* something; rather a feeling of falling from, with no place to land.

'Can you think of anything?'

The drops began to surface, this time in my own voice. Words coming from an uncontrollable source.

'Yes.'

'Go on.'

'I became involved with a teacher from my school. He was married. I used to baby-sit for him and his wife and then became

friendly with her. She didn't know anything about my relationship with him, though.'

Raindrops running the length of a wire, intercepting each
other's movements, growing heavy as udders.

'The relationship with the man finished, but my friendship
with his wife seemed to deepen, almost as a result of the split.'

Raindrops hanging stiff as icicles.

'Then very suddenly she was killed.'

Raindrops like tears, falling from a wire.

'Did you feel guilty for her death?'

'Yes.'

'Do you still feel guilty?'

'Sometimes.'

'Did your family know?'

'No. My mother was jealous of the friendship because I spent
so much time at their house.'

'Do you resent that feeling on your mother's part?'

'I suppose I do, really.'

'It's strange, then, that your mother doesn't feature more
strongly in your dreams. Now I want you to keep your eyes
closed and I'm going to take you back down the spiral staircase,
deeper and deeper into the unconscious. Fourteen, thirteen,
twelve – deeper and deeper.'

Deeper and deeper, spiralling the length of this long, fleshy
tube, each step stiffer than the last and meeting, travelling from
the root, a red lava that lifts me up, buoyant, and takes me to the
top. Spills me out with the hot flow of its blood at the soft,
circumcised rim and carries me down, swimming, to a red sea,
where my mother kneels, eternally mopping up the mess with a
towel, a choir of telephone boxes singing to her. She fishes out
the thick clots that disturb the even flow of blood and lays them
aside, carefully, in the red liquid udders, a xylophone of
contraceptive sheaths. Thick, rounded jellies, like bath oils. The
balls of my father, my brother, my lovers. My hypnotist.

# The Other Side of Summer

For three summers Julia had been building the wall. There was some contractual clause stating that Grange Cottage should not be visible from The Dell, which faced it, and the new neighbours were adamant that a barrier be constructed between the two houses. Julia could not be bothered to argue. She began searching for large grey stones, bought two bags of sand and cement, and started work.

Grange Cottage was three miles from 'civilization' and was surrounded by only four other houses. Regular trips were made into town throughout the day – a forgotten comic for Stephanie, meat for the dog, extra bottles of milk – yet the family never seemed disorganized. I would 'call in for coffee' and invariably become involved with the tasks at hand; so if Julia went into town for extras, I went along too. Julia liked to make her visitors part of the family and when she started the wall our trips became regular. At first, Adrian went to collect the enormous bags of sand and cement, until his back gave way. 'It always happens during the holidays,' said Julia, and laughed, proud of her own physical immunity. So we went together and I feigned interest, discussing prices in relation to weights. I agreed with her every time that we had certainly made a bargain purchase.

It was a warm July day when we began. When I say 'we' I mean that I filled buckets with water from the kitchen and made regular cups of tea and coffee, waitressing to both invalid and builder. Sometimes I attempted to smash the larger stones with a hammer, but usually gave up in exasperation when I was able to chip only atoms of dust from their surface, though I was convinced I put heart and soul into the effort. Julia would laugh and mimic my action before bringing the hammer down again, splitting the stone into four or five substantial chunks.

Most of the time, I sat and watched. It was the pattern of three summers. On that first day, Julia was like a child on Christmas morning, having so many toys and not knowing which to play with first. She stood contemplatively and then moved slowly around a huge pile of stones, gathered from the nearby quarry during the week; observed them from different angles, unable to decide upon which to handle first. I have never seen anyone become so involved with physical work as did Julia that summer. It preoccupied her totally. She was possessed. Oblivious to her daughter, her husband, and to me. Only when she successfully picked the 'right' stone from the pile of hundreds, and fitted it perfectly into position, did her eyes resume their usual childish sparkle and smile. Then she stepped back, admiring it balanced in position and asked me what I thought.

'It looks fine.'

'But don't you *see*?' she asked. She didn't require an answer. What I was never able to see was something that should obviously have been perceived. I continued, in my ignorance, filling buckets.

Julia's mortar had to be exactly the right texture and her frustration showed in thin red veins under her eyes if the consistency did not obey the demands of her trowel. She pushed the dry ingredients into a pointed heap in a wide, shallow bucket, and dug out the middle to make an 'island'. She said that that was what Adrian said when he poured milk into the middle of Stephanie's scooped-out dish of dry Ready Brek flakes. Julia frowned. 'But it's not an island,' she said, pouring water into the hollow, 'it's an oasis.'

She pushed the slope of sand and powder gradually into the water, willing the concoction to meet the right texture. The movement of her arm stiffened as the mixture became thick and she added a little more powder, a drop more water until, again, the satisfied glow of success lit up her face and summoned her body back into action.

She carried the bucket to where the stone lay balanced and checked it again for its weight and general appearance in the wall as a whole.

'You don't think I ought to put it at the front, do you?'

'Yes, why not?' I answered.

'But it's a bit big, really. I think I'd better leave it at the back.'

'Yes, I think it'll be better there, too.' My answers were mechanical, in agreement with everything she said: firstly, because she never listened and, secondly, because the stones obeyed only her. The foundation stones were laid in a double row, to give more body, Julia said, and as she intended the 'best' side to face her own house, the positioning of the 'good' and 'bad' was an important issue.

'Definitely one for the back,' she said, picking out a motley-coloured shape. Satisfied with her decision, she scooped cement into the space. She picked up the stone reverently, as if about to carry a sacrifice to the throne of God. She laid it carefully on the cement, as if afraid to wake it, and made adjustments – small firm twists between her dusty hands – until it sank into position, as if it had been designed specifically for that space alone. I never spoke. Words would have been blasphemous. Then Julia took a smaller instrument than the one she used to lay the cement. It was like a small pallet-knife and she filled in the crevices around the stone until it merged like an extension of the previous day's sculpture.

'There, look!' She brought the loose cement from the sides into one upward scraping movement, as if scooping dribbled food from around a baby's mouth.

'Mmm, marvellous, wonderful, great.' I ran out of adjectives. I had no idea what to say to her. It was a stone in a wall. Hardly an object of aesthetic wonder. Julia never suspected my bemusement, she was too wrapped up in the whole thing.

As the wall grew, our relationship changed. In some ways, we moved further apart: the conversations we had enjoyed indoors were gone, the eating and drinking through the long hours of Wimbledon. I missed all of it. Julia, on the other hand, went on living day by day, stone by stone. Sometimes I felt guilty because I couldn't see life through her eyes. Cheerful, satisfied eyes. Now, I don't think it was happiness. I was probably far happier than she. But she was contented. The kind of joy that comes with acceptance: acceptance of suffering, evil, the knowledge that there's very little you can do about it; joy in man's very capacity to hold on. But there was a sadness in it, too: most of all during those summer afternoons and early evenings, when her shadow lengthened along the greyness of the wall. What did she see in those few seconds when the stone first clung to the cement, the cracks were secured, and another part of the wall was completed? They were brief revelations. Moments of transparency.

I was used to silence at the wall. It was as if the words knew by instinct which were the wrong moments to speak. We talked less and less. Sometimes we came close. Understanding nothing but the knowledge that we were each searching. Waiting. Hoping. A sense of silence, more peaceful than the absence of movement and sound. We waited for it. An expectant silence, though nothing occurred. Then our relationship was beyond reach. But close. Closer than during the hours we had spent telling each other about ourselves. Knowing about, and knowing. The point at which you pass beyond knowing an accumulation of facts about someone, to simply knowing.

Julia would tell me to listen to the silence: pinecones splitting their stiff winter scales, a continual crackle of life in the forest. She recognized the different birds' cries and, like a frightened animal, heard footsteps long before they became audible to me. Everything was so green. So still. Stephanie played on the lawn, hunting for four-leaf clovers. She tried to find one for each of her parents and for me. Once she found two and asked if her father would be unlucky because she hadn't been able to find a third.

'He can share mine,' said Julia. 'I'm lucky enough for two.' Stephanie smiled.

The second summer was a particularly bad one and Julia did very little work on the wall. It put her in bad spirits. She stood in the kitchen and gazed out through the window to the dark, wet stones. She moved noisily about the house, as if in the belief that the rain had been sent to taunt only her. I was glad of it. I sat indoors, hoping to resume something of our former relationship, pick up in the middle of an old conversation. It was impossible. Everything we said seemed to have been uttered so many times before. Our words were stale and we wearied of each other's company. We sat in the kitchen waiting for silences that never came. Only the incessant tapping, followed by the sudden gushing of the rain; lightning illuminating the silhouette of black trees, thunder rocking the air, wind shaking the cones from their branches.

'I hate this country,' said Julia. She never amplified the statement. As she stood again at the window, mentally building the next stage of the wall, I knew she could never leave – the country or the house. They would have to carry her away by force. The wall had taken a part of her it would never let go.

Behind the melting rainwater glass they were like separated lovers, unable to communicate because of unforeseen circumstances arising since they made their original plans.

Occasionally the sun broke through, but for the most part the rain kept the surface too wet to allow for further construction.

'I must finish it,' Julia would say, 'the neighbours say it's in the contract. It has to be finished.' She became obsessive about its completion, as if sensing that something would stop her. To compensate for her lack of activity, she talked about it. Incessantly. How she had dug the foundation, measured it, arranged the position of stones so that they curved almost in a full semi-circle, two arms welcoming her as she came from the house. It was her only topic of conversation. My sympathies transferred to her family. How did Adrian communicate with her? Perhaps he had fantasies about burying her in it. I certainly did. Sometimes, holding the sharp pallet-knife, I imagined stabbing her. I built up a mental picture in which, after killing her, I laid her neatly across the top of the wall in a bed of wet cement; watched her sink slowly, inch by inch between the two layers of stones, her body thickly consumed with the rise of concrete on either side. A grey coffin. When I smashed the stones with the hammer I thought of creeping up behind her crouched body when she was working meticulously between the cracks, and slamming it down with as much force as I could on her skull. Watching the white bone fly into millions of pieces, set into the wet cement like broken glass.

I didn't return to the cottage that rainy season. I had nothing more to say on the subject of walls. Also, Julia had bought two goldfish to amuse her when she was unable to work. She sat and watched them with the same concrete euphoria, ignoring me sometimes for half an hour at a time.

The following year was one of the hottest summers on record. During the fourth week of unbroken sun, I cycled over to Julia's one afternoon. She had made considerable progress with the wall and it stood well over four feet for most of the way along. I leant my bicycle against the side of the house and went in at the back door, which was open. Julia was nowhere to be seen in the garden and I hoped, on entering the house, that she would be sitting in her usual seat, occupied by some other task. She was not.

'Hello!' I called. There was no answer. I called again. Stephanie came into the room.

'Mummy's outside,' she said, and disappeared. I returned outside. I heard scraping and knew that Julia must be near the wall.

'Hello!' I called again. Her head appeared briefly over the top from the other side. She had caught the sun on her face and looked healthy and happy.

'Hi,' she said. 'Take a seat.' She indicated a small stool on the opposite side of the wall from which she was working. I sat down.

'How are things?' she asked. 'I haven't seen you for ages.' A feeling of insecurity, speaking to an unseen figure, a voice set in concrete, made me pause.

'I said, how are you?'

'I'm fine,' I answered at last. 'And you?'

'Great. I've been working really hard.'

'I can see.' I felt ridiculous, perched on the tiny milking-stool, addressing the air. I looked around, embarrassed, and hoped no one was watching this first sign of madness. I was not invited around to the other side and felt it would be wrong to ask.

'How's Adrian?' I had the awful suspicion she was just tucking the last of his little finger into a wet crack.

'He's fine. I think. We're all fine.' We were getting nowhere. The small, precise chippings and scrapings alienated me further from my friend. Suddenly, she broke the awkward silence between us. The scraping stopped.

'Do you know, I've been thinking . . .' I prepared myself – the most recent cement on the market, the newest acquisition of stones . . .

'I don't think I'm an atheist in the same way as Adrian. I mean, he doesn't believe in anything.' I remained seated on the other side of our strange confessional, surprised at hearing Julia talk about anything that didn't have its roots in concrete. I was the anonymous priest.

'. . . and there must be *something*.' She paused. We had often talked about religion and it had always ended up the same: Julia criticized the church and the hypocrites attending it, and cruelly ridiculed many of my own beliefs and feelings. I had learnt not to expose myself.

'It would be wonderful to think, to know, that somewhere there was something greater than all this.' I assumed she was making a wide gesture with her arms by the rise in her voice that sent the words more clearly to me. I conjectured how the blind form pictures by voices; yet, the more Julia talked, the less I was able to remember her face, as if with each word she were talking herself away. I felt that if I looked behind the wall her physical presence would have disappeared, yet her voice be continuing soulfully on.

'I've always felt that I didn't need God. He was for people who didn't have much, people who couldn't cope. I've always had everything I've wanted. I can honestly say I've been happy. But I think I'd just like to test Him. Know, once and for all. Give Him a litmus test like we did with acids and alkalis at school. Take this – whoever, whatever you are. Red, I'll believe. Blue, I'll know I've been right all along.' There was a scraping sound of one continuous movement from left to right along the wall; then the spongy slice of the pallet-knife tapping on a cushion of cement. 'I'd just like to know, that's all.'

I was lost. From my confessional seat, I felt I ought to recommend six Hail Marys, tell her to beg forgiveness, go forth and not sin again. But I remained silent. I wondered what she had seen – again in the final shifting of a stone into place. I made coffee and returned to the stool while Julia worked, more quickly, it seemed, than ever before.

'This summer it will be finished,' she said. 'It will,' she repeated, as if doubting my belief in her integrity and assurance. She spoke with the force of will, urging herself into the state of mind she knew its completion required. During that one afternoon the confessional rose between us by another layer of thick, grey stones. When I stood up, it topped my head by two inches. Julia had disappeared. I imagined her dark head close against the wall, intimate and secretive, sharing something to which I was an outsider. Our farewells met in the grey silence of confession. She would go on blindly, building stone on stone, layer upon layer, until she came to the God of her strange acquaintance.

It was my last meeting with Julia. Towards the middle of the summer I received a letter in which she told me that the wall was almost finished. The tone was one of urgency, as if she were writing under pressure. A week later I heard from Adrian. Julia had been rushed to hospital with a suspected tumour. Three days later she was dead.

At first, I remembered our times together before she had started on the wall. I recalled whole conversations, the tiniest detail of insignificant events. And then, as suddenly as these images came, they disappeared. When I thought of the past three summers, it was as if Julia had never been at all. I tried to bring into focus the features of her face; I saw only the stony stare of the wall; the sound of her voice – the rough, rhythmical movement of her tools.

I returned to the cottage, hoping to stir the hard, grey memories back to life. It was an early evening in late August. Adrian and Stephanie were not at home. I stood outside and stretched my back against the cool wall. I listened. The evening was as I remembered it. Warm, green, the early evening sun resting on the red stone of the cottage, pine trees thick against the pink sky. The wall had grown higher, but it was unfinished, its serrated top exposed and uneven. I pressed the curve of my spine into it; the stones on either side wrapped their horseshoe arms around me. I felt the drawing of that grey strength that had dissolved Julia. Now it claimed my memory of her. The garden was totally silent: a silence not of peace, but a silence that is the consciousness of absent sounds: pinecones waking from their sticky winter sleep; the soft scraping of a knife; the slow, perfect sinking of a stone in wet cement.

# DEIRDRE MADDEN

## Hidden Symptoms

When Theresa was small, she thought that the saddest thing she had ever seen was a Bavarian barometer with a little weather man and a little weather woman. It was so sad that always when Hans was out Heidi was in and vice versa: never together, always alone, so near, so far, so lonely. Poor little gaudy wooden painted people! One wet day, in pure compassion, she had tried to winkle the little lady out of her niche by means of a hooked finger, so that she could join the little man in his lonely vigil, but with a loud crack the mechanism broke, and the barometer was later thrown away.

When she was older, she went to the circus. Chimps in frilly knickers or dungarees performed clever tricks and then beat together their pink palms in a manner which seemed to give credence to Darwin, thrilled with their own smartness. It did not make her laugh: that, too, she found pathetically sad. Older still, in supermarkets, her heart ached to see tins of soup for one. Each tiny red tin evoked for her so poignantly the homes of lonely pensioners, and grim bedsitters where all the coathangers were made of wire, and the solitary soup-drinker might at any moment be plunged into darkness by an expiring meter.

In later years, she smiled when she thought back to these notions, but there had been truth, undeniable truth, in them, for when something happened which was truly dreadful it was the little peripheral pains which made the central agony so inescapable and so intense.

At the beginning of the summer which marked the end of her first three years at university and the twenty-second year of her life, she was shocked to discover, while rummaging in the attic, how very ugly Rose was; Rose who had once been her favourite doll.

Had she truly loved and lavished affection upon this grimy thing, this object made of cold, hard plastic with baked-on eyes, a seam running from ear to ear across its moulded head, and 'Empire made' stamped on the nape of its neck in tiny letters? From this I was inseparable? she wondered, perched on the edge of a tin trunk. She sat amazed that she could have loved so hideous a thing, and on returning to her room she picked up with suspicion a large china egg of which she was particularly fond. Why did she like it? Would the day come when she found it ugly? Charmed in the shop by its elegant shape and the cool, smooth translucence of the china, she had bought it as a gift to herself: it was, therefore, not liked because imbued with the wishes of a friend or relative who had given it to her; nor did it have the virtue of being antique, by which it would have proved that it had been beautiful for at least a hundred years, and therefore might well continue to be beautiful for years to come. She liked the egg, thought it beautiful, but could not say with conviction that that was how she would feel about it forever. And yet surely some things were absolutely beautiful: but why, and how did one recognize them?

Life became a series of evaluations and increasingly her confidence in her judgement was wavering, melting away, so that by this time only on things literary would she pass judgement with any degree of assurance. That assurance, at least, was still strong: the following afternoon, when asked for her opinion on an article which she had just finished reading, she did not hesitate to say firmly: 'Trash.'

The question was asked in a Belfast city-centre café, and the questioner, on entering, had noticed at first not Theresa, not that she was drinking tea and eating a doughnut, not even that she was dressed completely in black: he had noticed nothing except that she was reading a certain local 'little magazine' and that there was a seat free at her table. He quickly sat down beside her, ordered a cup of coffee and as she turned the page smiled and said, 'Good article, then?'

'Trash,' she said firmly, taking a packet of cigarettes from her handbag and continuing to read.

'Oh,' he said, deflated. 'Why?'

'Because', she replied, waving a match to extinguish it, 'it supports the view that Belfast, bombed, blitzed, beaten and bankrupt though it may be, is undergoing some sort of literary renaissance, that it is becoming a type of cultural omphalos, which I think is a nonsense. Badly written, too.' She flicked ash into a little tin-foil ashtray, and her questioner seemed disgruntled.

'Lots being written,' she admitted, 'but this writer tries to compare it to the Irish Literary Renaissance. Cretin.' She turned to look at the man beside her. He had, by this stage, noticed her dark clothes, dark hair, pale skin, her general angularity and her plain face, but he was taken aback by the large, brown eyes, which had a pronounced cast, so that even while she looked at him she seemed to be looking elsewhere. She wondered who this person was, with his two gold finger-rings and a very pronounced after-shave, who had looked so put out by her candour.

'Whose little boy are you, anyway?'

He took the magazine from her hand, turned to the head of the offending article, and pointed to the name: 'Robert McConville'. He was pleased to see that she went slightly red, but she shrugged her shoulders and said, 'You've got a lot to learn then, haven't you?'

'And to what do you owe your great literary authority?' he said.

'I know a lot about literature,' she said frankly. 'I've read a great deal, and I can tell the difference between good writing and rubbish.'

'Are you a writer, too?'

'No,' she said, 'I'm a student,' and the expected sneer appeared on his lips. 'Go on, then,' she snapped, 'boast to me of how little you know about literature, tell me how many times you failed your O-Level English – now which play is it that has Portia in it? – and yet it hasn't stopped you being a writer, has it; go on, give me all that, that's today's line, isn't it?'

'I have a degree in English from Queen's,' he said, piqued.

'Then why smirk at me?' She ground out her cigarette, put her magazine in her bag and stood up.

'I'm sorry,' he said, for she looked very angry and upset (although later he wondered why he had apologized, as it was she who had insulted him).

'Oh, forget it,' she said, 'it's foolish to argue over a little thing, I don't know why I did it. Excuse me, please,' and, moving past him, she left the café.

Although it was late June, it was cool and overcast as Theresa returned home, and West Belfast looked bleak from the bus window. Had it been a city abroad, in France, say, or Germany, she would have been frightened, equating its ugliness with constant danger, but she could cope with Belfast, because she had watched it sink since her childhood from 'normality' to its present state. She even found this new Belfast more acceptable than the city of her earliest memories, for the normality had always been forced, a prosperous facade over discrimination and injustice. Just as when she was small she had been very ill and the doctor diagnosed the illness as measles (for some reason the spots had failed to appear), Ulster before 1969 had been sick but with hidden symptoms. Streets and streets of houses with bricked-up windows and broken fanlights, graffiti on gable walls, soldiers everywhere: Belfast was now like a madman who tears his flesh, puts straws in his hair and screams gibberish. Before, it had resembled the infinitely more sinister figure of the articulate man in a dark, neat suit whose conversation charms and entertains; and whose insanity is apparent only when he says calmly, incidentally, that he will club his children to death and eat their entrails with a golden fork because God has told him to do so; and then offers you more tea.

She alighted from the bus two streets ahead of her usual stop, bought two fish suppers in the chip-shop and then hurried home, where her mother had plates and cutlery waiting by the hearth. The local news was beginning on television as they unrolled the greasy white packet and tipped chips onto the plates. The first item reported was the funeral of an RUC reservist who had been ambushed on his way to work earlier that week. Theresa, with a hot chip in her mouth, frowned and turned to BBC2 before the screen could show the flowers, the hearse, the coffin, the widow; she turned the sound down and they ate in silence, until her mother began to grumble about a visit which she was obliged to make that evening.

'Don't lie to me, you can't wait, you love every moment,' said Theresa, and her mother groaned, for the lady whom she was to visit was struggling to bring her children up to be cultured. 'Do your Shakespeare for Mrs Cassidy, dear,' she would say, and her ten-year-old son would obediently go down on one knee to declaim a portion of blank verse in a loud, ranting voice. 'If I have to listen to thon' wee warthog playing "The Merry Peasant" on the piano once more, I'll walk out, so I will. Boring old snob.'

'Nice Mrs Boomer. Clever little kiddies. Wish I was going. Give us a chip.'

While her mother was preparing to leave, Theresa went upstairs to fetch a book. As she returned, she put her hand on the door-handle of her brother's room and paused, but she did not go in, descending instead to the parlour, where she passed the evening alone, reading, smoking and thinking.

Robert also had a duty visit to make that evening, to his sister and her family, the very sight of whose little red-brick terraced house always oppressed him and filled him with a powerful sense of the need to escape; a sense which was, in spite of its strength, vague, abstract, foolish even, when he seriously thought about it. For this had once been his home and he had escaped, he thought; he called only to please his sister, he called from freewill and choice. If he really wanted, he need never go to that grim, narrow street ever again. Gloomily he rang the bell and his sister opened the door, beaming in delight when she saw him.

The whole family was at home: Rosie; her husband, Tom, who was watching television and nodded at his brother-in-law, 'What about ye, Bobby,' (Robert loathed abbreviations); and their little son, Tommy, who was playing with Lego on the floor. Rosie and Tom both hoped that the baby due in the autumn would be a little girl.

'Tea, Robert? He refused but she insisted, heaving herself from the chair and shuffling into the kitchen. Tom said nothing. Robert rubbed his hands over his eyes and wanted to flee the place. He ran an eye around the room. Why were these houses so uniform? he wondered, looking at the brown-and-cream suite with wooden trim and the acrylic carpet with its busy pattern of abnormally large autumn leaves. Was there a working-class parlour in Belfast that lacked these fittings? A right tat palace this is, he thought. Above the fireplace was a huge picture in a broad plastic frame of a little boy with tears pouring down his cheeks, a work which should have appealed to none but sadistic pederasts. On the opposite wall was a large block print of

Constable's *Haywain* with an excessively blue tint to it. In between were a string of horse brasses and two plates which had been there since before his mother died, one bearing a picture of Pope John XXIII and the other a picture of John F. and Jackie Kennedy. There was a sunburst clock of wood and metal and on the window-sill a clown of Murano glass. Tommy, still on the floor, was now sitting up eating liquorice torpedoes out of a crumpled bag. They look like pessaries, Robert thought dully, and shivered with vicarious nausea as the child slid another little torpedo into its plump, wet mouth. Rosie came back with a cup of tea and two Jaffa cakes for Robert just as the local news was beginning on television, and together they watched the funeral of the RUC reservist. 'Good sauce for the bastard,' said Tom and Rosie frowned, looking at Tommy, but said nothing. She was sitting by the window, her head near to the gaudy glass clown, and as Robert drank his tea he watched her, wondering what it must be like to see the world through his sister's eyes, unable to empathize with the strange sensibility which could look around this room and perceive beauty; which could see aesthetic worth in, say, acid-green pampas grass.

'More tea, Robert?'

'Thanks.'

When the main points of the news were over, they made conversation together, Rosie claiming that she felt fine. The doctors said that everything was alright and the only worry was that the summer would be a bit tiring, what with the heat and Tommy under her feet all day during the school holidays. Tommy himself said that Goldie, his pet fish, had died. He had made a wormery in the redundant round bowl, and Robert was obliged to go out to the back scullery to see these new pets, visible at intervals between the soil and the glass. Rosie told him innocent gossip about neighbours whom he had almost forgotten through absolute indifference; he said that his work was going well, Tom talked sport and at seven o'clock Robert had fulfilled his duty and left.

After such visits, Robert always liked to go straight back to his flat, which was near the University. There was, he thought, a smell in his sister's house: not a bad smell, but the smell of people and cheap food: a smell of poverty. He felt it clinging to his clothes and skin, and he removed it immediately on his return with a hot shower and lots of male toiletries which smelt bitter, sexy and expensive. As he dried himself afterwards, Count Basie on the stereo, he took comfort in looking around his flat at his possessions: the pale wicker furniture, his French theatre posters and a cunning little water-colour of two deck-chairs. In his heart of hearts he despised himself for gaining any sort of peace and comfort from such trivia, but their power as symbols of successful escape from the squalor that was home was, to him, undeniable.

I love my squint, thought Theresa, as she tried to gaze at herself in the mirror late that night. The man in the café had seemed distinctly disconcerted by it. It was hers alone, untraceable to any ancestor, unlike her nose and legs which she had inherited from her mother as definitely as one might a grandfather clock and a pair of Meissen candlesticks. She found it slightly weird to look at her mother's First Communion photograph, where the little sepia legs below the frock of white watered silk had just such an artful kink in them as her own legs did. Hamlet, I am thy Father's spirit, an' begob it was an' all, for you could tell the young fella off the Da by the nose on him. People even said that she looked like her grandmother, who had died before Theresa was born, and vestiges of that dead face were then looking back at her from her own reflection. How strange and arbitrary it all seemed to be, people marrying, mating and mixing genes; unavoidable choice and chance producing cocktails of children with inherited traits and yet still new people with their own particularities, like Theresa's squint. She wished suddenly that her father had not died when she was so very young.

I'll probably meet again that man whom I insulted, she thought as she got into bed. Belfast was so small, incestuous almost, in the way paths crossed. And she hated that; she was still bumping into people who sympathized with her, O that's the girl, even once or twice on introduction they remembered or at least conjectured, you could see it in their eyes. Only one of hundreds and the case short, obscure: what of those whose losses were famous and had made the English papers, *Newsweek*, history?

A light summer rain beat softly on the window. So little mattered. The temptation to make one's response as big as the disaster had to be resisted, for in truth what could one do, save collapse down to the horror of little details and keep living? She had read somewhere that there was a museum to the Holocaust in Israel, and that one of the exhibits was a tiny broken shoe upon a pedestal. 'But what can we *do*?' Inexorable time: often it was truly too late to do anything.

A mere two days later she had her comeuppance. While browsing in a bookshop she was brightly accosted by Kathy, who was her only friend from Queen's and beside her stood the insulted journalist.

'Hello, Theresa, are you buying, or just looking? Do you know my boyfriend, Robert? He's a writer.' Theresa smiled at both definitions, made with such pitiful firmness and pride.

Robert grimaced. 'We met a few days ago, in a café. Theresa didn't think much of my last article.'

'Well, it wasn't very good, now, was it, Robert?' said Kathy firmly. 'In all honesty, you have written much better. He's compiling a book now,' she added to Theresa, 'a directory of Northern Irish writers. It'll be very comprehensive.'

'How interesting,' said Theresa politely, fixing her strange eyes upon the writer and smiling. He stared back coldly. Kathy, while grumbling about having to remain in Belfast during the entire summer, removed a pen and a little notebook from her handbag. 'Come and see us next Tuesday,' she said, leaning on a pile of Royal biographies to scrawl down the address. 'Seven o'clock, I'll make dinner.'

'Thank you,' said Theresa, taking the proffered little page. She smiled again at Robert and this time he smiled back, but thinly.

Theresa was glad to see that the address given was evidently that of Robert's flat, and not of Kathy's home in Harberton Park, where she lived with her mother. Theresa's confidence, vacillating when concerned with anything save matters literary, became suddenly and surprisingly firm when faced with the phenomenon of Mrs O'Gorman. In short, she had the lady nailed, and on the strength of one brief meeting would have said that Mrs O'Gorman was a ghastly woman with the same conviction with which she would have affirmed that *Ulysses* was a good book.

The account of Paddy Dignam's funeral in *Ulysses* always brought Kathy to Theresa's mind. When she read of the unidentified figure by the grave whom a reporter later erroneously named as 'McIntosh' (because the unknown gentleman was wearing one), she always thought of her friend who, at college, by simple non-appearance at lectures and tutorials, made a mystery of herself. Kathy who? Her very sex was in question: a notice pleading for an essay appeared on the departmental noticeboard for a Mr O'Gorman, written by a tutor who thought that the K. O'Gorman who was on his class list but who had attended no tutorials was a lazy young man instead of a lazy young woman. Meanwhile, Kathy's presence was adding sparkle to parties, plays, concerts, wine bars and bedsits: she was in evidence everywhere but the Arts library. She made it a point of honour to read as few of the set books as possible, preferring in their stead things obscure, obscene, quaint and curious, so that she had read *Barrack-Room Ballads*, but not *The Prelude*; *Fanny Hill*, but not *Wuthering Heights*; and *The Tibetan Book of The Dead*, but not *King Lear*. She also kept an astute eye on the Belfast cultural scene and in conversation would make claims to the friendship of writers, artists and actors with whom, in reality, she was merely acquainted. Possibly her only sincere friendship was with Theresa, who cared nothing for Kathy's considerable prowess as a social climber but who was immensely fond of the kindhearted and sensible person whom she perceived under the exuberant exterior.

In the summer exams every year, Kathy would scrape a minimal pass, dependent always on the copious notes which Theresa gave her to photocopy and cram. It was through the operation of this favour that Theresa had the misfortune to meet Kathy's mother.

Kathy and Theresa never socialized in each other's homes at Theresa's implicit request, and so when she went to Harberton Park one day to retrieve some lecture notes which she needed urgently, it was the first time that she had ever seen the large, elegant detached house which was the O'Gorman home. As Theresa ascended the steps, the mirthful sounds of half a conversation were audible through the open door, drowned suddenly by a peal of barks, both deep and shrill, as three dogs rushed out of the house and began woofing and snapping at her ankles. One was a Dalmatian, one an Afghan hound, and one an ugly little thing with a mashed face, like a genetically defective cat; and all three barked constantly, the Dalmatian jumping up and putting its large paws on her skirt. She was too shocked to run or scream and only realized how frightened she was when a fourth bark joined in: 'Toby! Prince! Down, boy!' Mrs O'Gorman called off the two larger dogs and scooped up the ugly little one in a jewelled hand. 'Who are you?' she snapped. 'What do you want?'

'Kathy, please,' said Theresa weakly, conscious mainly of the blood booming in her ears, and the startled beats of her heart.

'She's not in.'

'Poetry notes,' Theresa whimpered, and the woman turned her back and went into the house, returning a moment later with the tatty folder of yellow cardboard which contained almost everything Theresa had ever learnt about Augustan poetry.

'Thank you,' she said, but she was talking to air. The woman had gone and the telephone conversation was resumed. Theresa left quickly, for the two large dogs were still on the top step, panting and slavering hungrily.

Kathy later apologized for her absence.

'You did get the notes?'

'Yes,' said Theresa, too embarrassed to elaborate, although she soon discovered that such conduct was not without precedent. Mrs O'Gorman was an ill-mannered snob who treated her daughter with scant regard, much less her daughter's friends, and so Kathy tried to keep friends and mother as far apart as possible. Although the two lived together, it was in a constant state of acrimony. Kathy was an only child: she told Theresa that her father had died when she was a baby and she had an inferiority complex about her lack of family life.

For a long time after the incident with the dogs, Theresa had a perverse fascination with the event. Such conduct in a mother was so strange. Common sense told Theresa that being a mother did not automatically free one of ill-temper and boorishness, and so of course she knew that it was wrong of her to use her own mother as a rule-of-thumb for the world – as wrong as it was irresistible. Everyone could only but be found wanting.

One day, years previously, a hoary old man named Harry, six foot two and with hands like a mole, had come to do odd jobs in the house, and when Theresa returned from school she saw in the kitchen a plateful of enormous scones, each one about four inches across.

'Sufferin' Isaac, Ma, what's wrong with the scones? Did you lose the small cutter?'

But her mother had replied no, that their size was intentional, because she had made them for Harry and she had thought that big scones would be easier for him to manage than dainty little normal ones. Theresa always remembered setting down her school-bag and gazing at the scones with something approaching reverence. Universal love on a thick delft plate with puce roses: she had thought then, 'I shall never be better than this, I shall never be anywhere nearly as good.' Thoughtfulness to the humble level of an old man's dexterity in eating scones. Never neglect the little things in life. The rest of the poor world could only fall short.

(Mrs O'Gorman fell further than most: Theresa imagined her forcing Harry to eat his own sandwiches outside. In a thunderstorm.)

The day before the dinner party, Theresa phoned Kathy.

'You are coming, aren't you?'

'Yes of course, Kathy.' She paused nervously. 'Kathy, you haven't told your friend about Francis yet, have you?'

'Who, Robert? No, not yet,' she replied.

'Well, don't,' said Theresa quickly. 'I mean, I'd rather you didn't. I – it's hard to explain – I hardly know why –'

'Forget it,' said Kathy's voice, disembodied and kindly. 'He'll never hear about it from me, if that's the way you want it: I promise.'

'Thank you. Thank you very much indeed.'

'No problem. See you and your appetite tomorrow at seven. Don't forget now. 'Bye.'

Theresa replaced the receiver, feeling foolish. It was almost as if she were ashamed of what had happened. Anyway, she thought bitterly, who cared now except her mother and herself? Who else had ever truly cared?

The evening evolved strangely. Theresa brought a bottle of Blue Nun and complimented Robert on his flat. 'It says a lot about you.'

'Thank you,' he said, genuinely pleased, not sensing the irony. The room screamed of the persona he had created for himself: short of whitewashing the walls and writing I AM AN INTEL-

LECTUAL in large red letters, it could not have been made to 'say' more. Kathy, in a dress of burgundy velvet with an antique lace collar, served out a vegetable stew which they ate with brown rice as an accompaniment and the Chieftains as background music.

'We'll have to go over to Queen's in a week or two to collect our exam results,' Kathy said. 'It's barbaric, pinning them up like that. It reminds me of those old B-movies about Oxford, jostling to see if you got through: "It's beastly luck, Carruthers, Mater'll be so disappointed at my being sent dhine." God, I wonder if I'll make it again this year?'

Robert said that exams were always a temptation to destruction for him: he had been fascinated by the simplicity with which he could undo a year's study, just as when, on a clifftop or at a high window, he was attracted by how simply his life could be ended. 'One little step forward and I die. If I leave this room and do something utterly mundane for the next three hours – browse in a bookshop or eat sausage rolls in the Union – I can quickly end forever my university career.'

Theresa agreed. Exams inspired her, too, with a feeling of awesome power rather than of knowledge. They talked about the University and about literature until the door was aggressively knocked and a friend of Robert's entered, uninvited and inebriated, his eagerness to contribute to the conversation equalled only by his thirst. He was a struggling playwright with manic eyes and a belligerent manner.

'You,' he said, taking the glass of Blue Nun offered by Kathy and stabbing his finger at Theresa. 'D'you write plays, you?'

'No,' she said, 'but I write lots of prose.' (Something which Robert had not known until then.)

'Prose is nothin'. Prose is useless. Ye ought to write plays. Plays is the only useful art.'

'Useful? In what way?'

'Useful! Bloody useful! D'ye know what useful means, even? Plays are social, they're about people, so they are, you get things done with plays. People see themselves on a stage and then they know,' he added mysteriously.

The discussion became intense thereafter.

The newcomer drank all the wine at an amazing rate and Theresa deliberately baited him, saying flatly, 'Drama is the bastard child of literature,' and, 'Drama is, of all art forms, the most unsatisfactory and the most inferior.' Robert was amused by her total coolness while, visibly tongue-in-cheek, she drove the playwright almost to tears of anger and frustration, and each statement was a goad, calculated, and honed to cruel sharpness before being lunged with heartless success at its target. When Robert tried to join in, the playwright told him to shut his bake, he was only a critic, what did he know; later he asked Robert where he had dug up this 'bourgeoise hoor' (Robert, oddly, thought at first that he meant Kathy), and eventually told them all that they were a pack of fascists before lurching off drunkenly, taking the empty wine bottle with him.

'Oooh, that was funny,' said Kathy, as Robert sat a bowl of fruit before them. 'He's a lot less interesting when he's sober, but he's rarely that.'

'He's decent enough,' said Robert, 'just a terrible bigot.'

'That's not what's wrong with him,' replied Theresa. 'It's the direction his bigotry takes. All great writers were bigoted – Joyce and his like – but bigoted about their art. If writers get too obsessed with other things, like politics or the state of the world, their art becomes less important to them. Your man doesn't take his plays seriously enough. He only thinks of them as tools to serve some end, not as ends in themselves, and the plays suffer; they're bound to.' She took up an orange and began to peel it. 'Fascists, indeed; he's a half-fascist himself for all that talk of "the people". He judges too much, he wants to change things, change people. This is wrong and this is wrong, I say so, I say that it must be changed and this is how. If he had any intelligence and ability, he'd be downright dangerous.'

'Aren't all great social reformers just as you've described him?' asked Robert.

'All great dictators, rather. What is a dictator, anyway, but a misguided social reformer? And an artist is something different again.'

'And what's that?'

'An artist', she said, 'is a person who composes or paints or sculpts or writes.'

'Oh, come on, Theresa,' said Kathy, who was lying on the floor languidly chewing an apple. 'That's a rather élitist view, isn't it?'

'No, I don't think so – just rather traditional. People like your man make it sound very easy to be an artist. I think that it must be difficult – very difficult indeed.'

'What do you write about?' Robert asked. Theresa waited for a few moments before answering and when she did she looked at him in a calculating manner, as if to register the effect which each word had upon him. It made him doubt her sincerity.

'I write about subjectivity – and inarticulation – about life pushing you into a state where everything is melting until you're left with the absolute and you can find neither the words nor the images to express it.'

'It sounds frightening.'

'It is.'

'I don't understand that,' said Kathy.

'It doesn't matter,' said Theresa, suddenly brisk. 'It's late, I must go home.' They had difficulty in persuading her to stay, and eventually she remained only for a quick cup of coffee. She then thanked them and left.

Kathy and Robert remained in the flat, cradling their warm, empty coffee-cups in their hands and listening to the soft music of the stereo. It was a long time before Robert spoke.

'Kathy?'

'Yes?'

He stroked her head as one might stroke a cat.

'Are you going home tonight?'

She raised herself up from the floor and he leaned down from his chair; she kissed him and said, 'No,' pulled herself up into his lap, kissed him again and said that if her mother was not used to unannounced absences by now, then she ought to be; then kissed him long and deeply, sighed and murmured in his ear that she loved him. He did not believe this, but he kissed her back.

They made love and Robert lay awake for a long time after Kathy had fallen asleep beside him. He tried to understand what Theresa had been getting at when she spoke of subjectivity: he could think only of evil and violence. He was not sure that he understood anything about evil, but by God it was easy to assimilate! Every day he could take huge mysterious lumps of evil into his consciousness and the only worrying result was that he did not worry. That very day he had been upstairs in a bus which had been overtaken by a lorry carrying meat from the knacker's yard. For well over two miles he had looked down into the tipper, which was full of skinned limbs: long, bloody jaw-bones; jointed, whip-like tails. It had been a horrendous sight, but he had not averted his eyes from the mobile shambles: he had gazed unflinchingly down into it. This was how things were. He had looked at so many ugly and evil things, unsubtle as a lorry-load of dead meat, and he had said in his heart that this was how things were. He had accepted that lorry. He accepted too much.

He remembered television news reports, where the casual camera showed bits of human flesh hanging from barbed wire after a bombing. Firemen shovelled what was left of people into heavy plastic bags, and you could see all that remained: big burnt black lumps like charred logs. And he could look at such things and be shocked and eat his tea and go out to the theatre and forget about it. He could cope when it did not involve him personally. Now he found himself wondering how he would feel if it was Kathy whose flesh was hanging from barbed wire in thin, irregular strips and shifting in the wind like surreal party streamers. How would he feel if the soft little body beside him was to be translated into an anonymous black lump and shovelled into a plastic bag? He tried to tell himself that it was only a ghoulish thought, but he knew that for so many people this sudden change was a reality in the people whom they slept with, ate with, lived with and loved, and his own lack of empathy saddened him. In the darkness he touched Kathy's sleeping shoulder, and suddenly felt as lonely as Adam.

Gently he awoke her, kissed her and stroked her; whispered lies in her ear. She murmured and giggled, half-awake and half-sleeping. He desperately wanted to bury his fearful loneliness in the blackness of the room and in her thin, warm body, but sex solved nothing: there was only panic and the illusion of union; nothing could protect him. Now he hated himself for having visited his morbid thoughts of violent death upon this innocent person beside him, for he had not really been thinking about her, nor even about how much her death would mean to him. He was afraid that his own innocent body might be destroyed violently and quickly and he had been too cowardly even to imagine such a thing, visiting his fear upon Kathy instead. Suddenly, incredibly, he wanted to cry.

'Robert? Robert?'

But he did not answer her and he did not cry, because he was ashamed and embarrassed and he did not love her.

They kept lumber up in the attic and Theresa found there, on the day after the dinner party, a dead Red Admiral caught in a cobweb. Other cobwebs were spun in arcs across the window-pane, catching the sunlight in their fine rainbow strands. Mentally, she recited a fragment of poetry which she had learnt for her exams:

> Upon the dusty glittering windows cling,
> And seem to cling upon the moonlit skies
> Tortoiseshell butterflies, peacock butterflies,
> A couple of nightmoths are on the wing.
> Is every modern nation like the tower,
> Half dead at the top?

She half-remembered a legend from somewhere which said that butterflies were the souls of the dead. She touched a little wing with the tip of a finger and some of the bright colour dusted off; the brittle corpse shifted in the web. 'The souls of the virtuous are in the hands of the LORD and no torment shall ever touch them.'

She sat on the edge of the tin trunk and wished that she could talk with Francis, for she wished him to help clarify a dream which she had had the preceding night. It concerned the school which they had both attended as children and, with the weird particularity common to dreams, the dominant feature had been the school's radiators, covered with chipped blue paint and always tepid. Above the radiators were tiled window-sills, ranged along with pots of geraniums. The dream had been so vivid that she had even seen and heard the grit of the soil grate between the pots and the saucers placed beneath them to catch the drips. She had also glimpsed, briefly, the overall layout of the school, and on waking she had been puzzled, for she had dreamt of doors and windows in places which she sensed were not quite right, and now she could not remember what the school had really looked like. Was her waking memory accurate, or had the dream been the truth rising to the surface now after the passing of years? Everything was confused: never again would she be able to picture the school to herself with any confidence; now all was a jumble of dream and supposed reality. And never again could she ask Francis for confirmation or clarification, because Francis was dead. She was alone now, and at the mercy of her own memory and imagination.

Perched on the edge of the tin trunk, she began to cry for him as she had not cried for a very long time, reflexively, almost, she could not stop herself and it hardly occurred to her to try. And while the body cried (the eyes wept, the mouth wailed and the fists tried to wipe away the tears), her mind seemed independent of this spontaneous grief. Something within her, calm and apparently rational, was thinking that it was impossible for her to continue living without him, that she needed him as she needed air. She did not believe that she could bear the loneliness of being in this world without him.

Such absolute loneliness had come to her the first night after his death, when she went to bed. Lights out, she put her head down and then, too, she had started to cry automatically. When they were children, she had fingered the pink satin bindings on the edge of the blankets until they were frayed and split; and Francis, before sleeping, had plaited the fringes of the rug. Always for her to be in bed in a dark room was to be in a place timeless as the sea. Now she lay under those same blankets and rugs and a cold stiff sheet, but everything had changed. The fact of his death was something which she would have to take to bed with her for the rest of her life, a new reality which ended innocence as absolutely as lost virginity; ineluctable, irreversible. On waking, his death would still be there. For every moment of every day until she also died, his death would be there, and if she forgot about it for a moment, a week, a year, even if it were possible for her to put it from her mind forever, it would not change the truth. His death would still always be there, waiting silently to be recognized and remembered.

When she had stopped crying, she lit a cigarette and while she smoked it tried to control her thoughts. It was dangerous to think too much about his having been murdered: that was to risk being lost in bitterness and hate. She tried to make herself think only of the pain of loss: that in itself was enough.

When she had finished her cigarette she brushed some ash from her knee, and left the attic.

Three days later, Robert received a brief, polite letter thanking him for a most interesting and enjoyable evening. That afternoon, on emerging from the revolving doors of the Central Library, he discovered the writer of the letter standing on the top step, her irregular eyes narrowed in concentration as she lit a cigarette.

'You'll kill yourself with those things,' he said.

'Good,' she said, after a slight pause, looking at him sideways. He said that his car was parked nearby and he offered her a lift home.

'Are you going towards West Belfast?' she asked.

'Yes, I'm going to see my sister. I can leave you off.'

She thanked him and they walked to the car together. When her cigarette was finished she immediately lit another. She spoke little. He wondered if she was shy, and as he drove up the Falls Road he glanced over at her and decided that she was most definitely not.

'You must meet Rosie,' he said with insincere warmth as he turned into the street where his sister lived, thinking that the encounter might be revealing.

Unlike Robert, however, Theresa did not react with perceptible revulsion to the vulgarity which came out to meet them at a front door bristling with knobs, knockers, brass numbers and bell-pulls. She did not start at the sheer ugliness of the living-room and, although he cringed at Rosie's attitude of good hostess, she did not.

Only Rosie and little Tommy were at home. The latter lay sleeping on the sofa, one arm stretched out Romantically and the other clasping a tatty cuddly toy: the dead Chatterton with a Womble. Rosie shook him awake to meet the visitor and, smitten with shyness, he stuck his face in his mother's armpit.

'Come on, now, none of that. Show Theresa the good boy you are. Do Shakin' Stevens for her.' From her apron pocket she produced a ten-pence piece as a bribe. 'Go on, Tommy, do Shakin' Stevens for her. Go on, do Shakey.' She waved the coin enticingly before his nose and a pudgy, covetous fist shot out to grab the money, but she raised her hand higher. 'No, Tommy, only when you've done Shakey for Theresa.' His eyes flickered sadly. He was torn between timidity and greed, but timidity won and he would not perform.

Rosie went into the kitchen to make tea and took Theresa with her, while Robert eavesdropped shamelessly from the living-room. Their conversation centred around the object which Robert probably hated more than any other in the house: a small plaque which hung over the sink and incorporated a stump of grey plastic to represent the Madonna, a few flowers of coloured tin, and the words 'A la Grotte Benie j'ai prie pour toi'. He could hear Rosie saying that if her Premium Bond came up she would to to Lourdes; she had always wanted to, but unless she won something it would be years and years before she could ever afford it. And to his amazement, the Basilisk was heard to reply that she had always wanted to go to Lisieux because her real name was Marie Therese; she was called for the Little Flower.

Robert at this point congratulated himself on having brought her to the house. This was a new side altogether! Little Flower! He almost snorted aloud in scorn. Then he heard his sister's voice say very softly 'Robert doesn't practise his religion any more. It's very sad, he got sort of – cynical – as he grew up.'

'Oh, that often happens,' he heard Theresa answer airily. 'People read things and they get fancy ideas in their heads; they think they know it all. He'll grow out of it.'

'I doubt it,' said Rosie solemnly. 'He's twenty-eight now.'

And Robert was furious to realize immediately on Theresa's re-entering the room (although she gave him neither grin nor glance to intimate this) that she had known all along he was listening in, and that her last remark was a deliberate gibe to which he could not reply without revealing that he had been ear-wigging.

For a long time after that, every time he saw a flower or heard one mentioned he grimaced to think how inappropriate a symbol it was for his angular and defensive friend. To savour fully its absurdity, he stopped one day before a florist's window in Royal Avenue, where the display of blooms was exact and exotic as a Rousseau jungle; and Robert started in surprise when a florist's face suddenly appeared through the foliage, bright as a naif tiger. She removed a green tin vase of Baby's Breath and retired, but her action had exposed to Robert a much more significant vase. It contained bunches of Tiger Lilies, magnificent in their beauty and perfection, and yet when Robert looked at them closely they unnerved him. From the heart of every flower started long, whip-like stamens, each terminating in a blunt, dark and dusty anther. The thick, creamy-white petals were prickled slightly towards the centre of each flower and the fleshy points were stippled bright red, as if with blood. He imagined a heavy, cloying perfume. If she were any sort of flower, he thought, this was it: not a soft, sweet-smelling innocent little blossom, but this bloody, savage, phallic, heartless flower. He thought of how incessantly she smoked, and wondered why he found her so frightening.

At Robert's mother's wake, seemingly countless women with tired faces who were fresh from kissing her corpse and touching their Rosary beads to her hands had grasped Robert by the forearm and quavered, 'Your mother was a saint, son.' His mother died when he was twenty-two, his father having long predeceased her, dying when Robert was eight. Sometimes it bemused him to think how slight the effect of that first death had been upon him, and how faint were his memories of his father; so faint that, ludicrously, he even wondered at times if he had imagined him. Outside a Christian Fundamentalist Church on the Donegall Pass, he had once misread the words of their Wayside Pulpit and saw on the virulent pink poster not 'Have You Ever Thought Of God As Your Father?' but 'Have You Ever Thought Of Your Father As God?' And in a strange vision the God in whom he did not believe became one with the father whose existence he also doubted. The unreal Supreme Being flashed across his mind as a mild little Belfast man with a loft full of pigeons and a weak heart. People also praised him highly after his death. 'He'd have given ye two ha'pennies for a penny, your Da.'

As Robert grew up, he found it increasingly difficult to live with his mother. He did not understand her. He did not understand the strange, intense religion which dominated her life. He had no patience with her saints, her statues, her novenas, her holy pictures, her holy water, her blind, total, absolute faith. As a child, he had disliked religion because it made him feel guilty and he became increasingly disenchanted as he grew up. By the time he left school he did not believe in God, nor did he want to.

He was a total disappointment to his mother, rejecting both her religion and the petit bourgeois aspirations which she nurtured on his behalf. She wanted him to marry a nice Catholic girl from a decent Catholic family; a teacher or nurse, for choice. She wanted him to 'get on', to get a good steady job, and although she was pleased that he went to university his choice of subject – English Literature – dismayed her. Although uneducated herself, she was astute enough to know that an arts degree was not an instant passport to a highly renumerative or socially acceptable career. He refused to study law, refused teacher training, refused to apply for a clerical post with the Civil Service. And although all this vexed her a great deal, perhaps they could have muddled along together with minimal acrimony had it not been for Robert's total lack of religion.

'What does it profit a man if he gain the whole world but lose his soul?' How often had she said that to him? She believed that everyone had their own particular cross to bear in life and he was obviously hers. Sometimes she looked as though she actually had to carry all six foot two and twelve stone of him around on her frail and narrow back. Her face was tired and sad during their habitual disagreements, but only once had she lost her temper and that was on the unforgettably embarrassing day when, in the course of tidying his room, she found a packet of contraceptives. When he came in that evening she faced him with it, and he saw that she was deeply shocked: her own son was a damned soul, an evil and wicked person. What she had found proved his perdition to her as conclusively as a box of black tallow candles.

Robert's memory operated in a cruel and unfortunate manner, clouding his happy memories and sharpening the unhappy; and so when he thought, reluctantly, of scenes which he would rather forget – scenes of pain and anger and embarrassment and grief – they always returned to him in absurdly vivid detail. He could still feel the terrible cringing shame of that moment when he walked in and saw the offending packet sitting at the extreme edge of the kitchen table, as far away as was possible from half a black-crusted bap swathed in tissue paper and a bone-handled knife, smeared with butter and jam to its hilt. He saw the wedding ring bedded into the red flesh of his mother's hand which trembled with what he perversely imagined to be fear: he was genuinely surprised when she flared out angrily.

'Aren't you the big fella, eh? Aren't you the smart lad? Will ye be so smart if some of yer lady friends has a baby? Then what'll ye do?'

'Oh come on, Ma,' he had mumbled, 'the whole point is that they won't have babies.'

At this she had lost her temper completely and began to hit him, her anger immense but her blows pathetically weak and puny. With one short, effortless movement of his arm he could have shoved her out into the back scullery to cool off in the company of the mangle, a red net sack of Spanish onions and a meat safe, but he could not bring himself to do it. Instead, he stood there gormlessly while she hit him, and wished that her thumps were more powerful and painful and worthy of resistance. At last, worn out, she started to cry and left the kitchen: he could hear her sobbing as she clumped upstairs to her room.

Home life was extremely frosty for a very long time after that and the eventual thaw was never complete: they were never on the same footing again. She still railed at him frequently for being irreligious and immoral, but never again referred to the row or its cause. They were more polite to each other than they had been before. He was quite surprised that she did not insist upon his leaving home; in fact, when he broached the delicate question one day, she said disarmingly, 'Why would ye do that? D'ye think I'd put me own flesh an' blood out on the streets?'

'I'd get a flat,' he said foolishly.

'Ye've no money,' was her pragmatic reply. 'Ye'll be time enough when ye're earning.'

The following year, Rosie married and Tom moved in, Robert left university, started working for a local arts magazine and moved out. But he was under no illusions. He always knew what his mother thought she was up against, and she developed a way of looking at him that made him shiver. She saw him as damned but not past redemption, and his lack of the desire to be redeemed was a real torment to her.

She died almost a year after Rosie's marriage. On the day she was hospitalized, Robert was sitting by her bed when she opened her eyes and gazed vaguely around the ward.

'Ma,' he whispered, 'it's me, Robert. Is there anything I can do for you?' And she had slid her tired, watery eyes sideways, looking at him with ridicule and pity. As if he needed to ask what she wanted of him! He was spoiling her death; he was the unfinished business which she would take to her grave. He hoped she realized that she was not responsible for whatever was wrong in him. Did she know that people who didn't believe in God (and who didn't want to – could she understand that?) – such people could not change to belief at a moment's notice merely to oblige their mothers.

But she had looked away again, closed her eyes and three hours later became comatose, remaining thus for three more days, at the end of which time she died.

Theresa's mother stretched up and ripped off a little page from the wad of months stitched together beneath a reproduction of Murillo's *Flight into Egypt*. 'First of July,' she said, scrunching up June in her fist. 'Feast of The Holy Blood.' Theresa warmed the teapot and tossed two tea-bags into it; her mother threw the crumpled page into the fire and then glanced over the list of feasts for the new month. 'Our Francis was a martyr, wasn't he?' she said.

'I suppose he was,' Theresa replied, 'but he had no choice, had he?'

'What do you mean?'

'I mean martyrs usually have a choice; if they deny their religion they're allowed to live, and if they won't deny it, well, they martyr them. And they just killed Francis because of his religion, he had no choice.'

'How do you know?' said her mother.

She paused. 'Well, yes,' she said, 'you're right, I don't. We don't know anything at all about what happened to him, only that . . . I suppose he was a martyr.'

She made the tea, poured it out and they drank it without speaking. Theresa also had a cigarette to calm herself, angry at having set up that little exchange. Such talk reminded them of how very little they knew of the circumstances in which Francis had died. Once, while reading a terrorist court case in the paper, her mother had said, 'Maybe when they catch the person who killed our Francis, we'll find out more,' but Theresa found the thought of this horrifying. Unlike her mother, who was haunted by the idea of the 'someone' who had killed her son, Theresa could hardly believe that such a person existed. Only on two occasions had she been completely convinced of the reality of Francis's murderer, and she had found it overwhelming.

It first happened shortly after his death, when she awoke from a nightmare in the small hours one morning and realized that just as it would be impossible to find Francis now, no matter where in the city or the world one went, so also it would be impossible not to find somewhere the man who had killed him. That person was somewhere out there as surely as she was in bed in her room, and his invisible existence seemed to contaminate the whole world. She lay awake until morning, afraid to sleep in the darkness which contained him.

A few days after that, she arrived too early for an arranged meeting with Kathy in a city-centre pub. She bought a drink and while she waited she looked around at the other customers, the majority of whom were men, until slowly the thought of the man who had killed her brother crept back into her mind. Those men who were laughing over in the corner; that man with reddish hair and big, rough hands who was drinking alone; even the white-coated barman, cutting wedges of lemon for gin-and-tonics: any one of them might have done it. She gazed at each of them in turn and thought in cold fright: 'Is he the one? Did he do it? Is he the man who murdered Francis?' It was, of course, improbable, but it was possible, and that grain of possibility took away the innocence of every man in the pub, and of every man whom she would ever see in the city. Every stranger's face was a mask, behind which Francis's killer might be hiding. The barman approached her table and said, 'Will I get you another drink?' She could not bear to raise her eyes to look at him, but shook her bowed head in refusal of his services. From that day on, Belfast was poisoned for her. She could not conceive of Francis's killer as an individual, as a person who might be arrested, tried and punished, but only as a great darkness which was hidden in the hearts of everyone she met. It was as if the act of murder was so dreadful that the person who committed it had forfeited his humanity and had been reduced to the level of pure evil. He had dragged the world down with him: everyone was guilty.

It was a hot day. She took another cup of tea and a cigarette out to the back yard, a tiny flagged area where a few drab flowers grew in tubs between the dustbin and the coalhouse. The smoke trailed up from the cigarette between her fingers like a fine filament of grey silk. She slitted her eyes and looked up at the bright sky. All of July to get through. All of August. All of September. All of her life.

At the beginning of July, Theresa and Kathy's examination results were released. They met in the city centre and walked out nervously together to the university, found their names on the boards and then went to Robert's flat.

'Crack the Bollinger,' said Kathy gleefully when he opened the door. 'I made it again, albeit by a whisker. Needless to say, Theresa here breezed through.' They went inside and Robert produced a bottle of cheap sparkling wine. 'Not Bollinger, but the best I can manage,' he said.

'It'll do,' said Kathy. 'Keep the vintage stuff for the finals.'

He opened the wine and while they drank Kathy happened to mention the flags and bunting which they had seen up along Sandy Row in preparation for the Twelfth.

'I think that the way in which society tolerates the Orange Order is ridiculous,' said Theresa. 'I mean, they even encourage them by televising their tasteless marches. Can you imagine the National Front or the neo-Nazis being treated like that? Can't you just hear the television commentary? "And the sun is smiling down today on the men of the Ku-Klux-Klan."'

'Oh, come on, Theresa,' said Robert, 'that's a bit strong. The Twelfth processions are not that bad. They're just a bit of folk culture. They are vulgar, I'll grant you that, but surely it's best to let them march; isn't it harmless that way?'

'Harmless? You seem to forget, Robert,' she said stiffly, 'that the Orange Order is, first and foremost, an anti-Catholic organization. They hate Catholics, Robert, and hate is never harmless. It worries me that intelligent Protestants can't see that, but when it bypasses an intelligent Catholic then I'm no longer worried, I'm afraid.'

'I'm not a Catholic,' he said shortly, and was startled by the vehemence of her reply.

'Oh, come on, Robert,' she snapped, 'spare me that. I know your background and it's about as Catholic as you can get.'

'But I don't believe in Catholicism. I don't even believe in God. Religion's a load of eyewash as far as I'm concerned.'

Theresa laughed cynically. 'Just tell me this: if you were found in the morning with a bullet in your head, what do you think the papers would call you? An agnostic? No, Robert, nobody, not even you, is naive enough to think that. Of course you don't believe: but there's a big difference between faith and tribal loyalty, and if you think that you can escape tribal loyalty in Belfast today you're betraying your people and fooling yourself.'

Kathy was startled to see the turn which the conversation had taken, but already it had gone too far for her to stop it.

'Christ, Theresa, with people like you around it's no wonder the country's in the state it's in,' said Robert.

'And if we were all like you it would be a right little Utopia, wouldn't it? You must have really enjoyed life under the Stormont Government. Do you feel like a second-class citizen, Robert? Do you feel that people hate you because you're a Catholic? Well, you ought to, because they do. Don't believe one half of the liberalism you hear, for do you know what they really think we are? Expendable vermin. They don't care how many of us are killed, because we breed fast, and so the numbers go up again. They'd like to see us all dead. The ones with the tattoos and sashes sweating under the weight of a Lambed drum may be the only ones who'll show their hatred but, believe you me, there's a hell of a lot more of them have it hidden in their hearts.'

'She's a fanatic,' said Robert to Kathy, 'a bloody, raving fanatic.'

'I'm not,' said Theresa, standing up, 'but you're blind and self-deluded. Don't ever say that you weren't warned, or that you didn't know.' She walked out and Robert and Kathy were left there, stunned by the way in which the little celebration had ended. They sat in silence. Robert topped up their glasses but still they neither drank nor spoke. Against his will, Robert found himself thinking of the first night of a friend's play which he had attended with Kathy only the previous week. A sizeable group of friends, Robert and Kathy included, had gone for drinks afterwards and the course of the conversation had turned first to politics and then to a particular politician. They had laughed at him. They had ridiculed the way in which he maintained power by playing on the fear of unintelligent people, telling them only what they wanted to hear. They had imitated to perfection his booming, hectoring voice, and laughed as if he were some great harmless buffoon; but then there had been a lull in the conversation and someone had said, 'Mind you, there's a lot of truth in some of the things he says.' No one had contradicted this. Kathy had looked across at Robert, and Robert had felt afraid.

Kathy now picked up her glass. 'Robert,' she said slowly, 'remember that play we went to see last week?'

'Yes.' His voice was harsh, daring her to say what was in both their minds. 'What about it?'

Cravenly, she sipped her cheap wine.

'It was very good, wasn't it?'

Late that night, Theresa lay in bed, unable to sleep. It was two years to the day since she had left for Italy with Francis. She could hear the noises of the road: traffic, footsteps, voices. As the night wore on, the sounds became more infrequent and increasingly bizarre. When she heard a drunk man singing 'Melancholy Baby', the booming amplification of which suggested that he had borrowed a large plastic traffic-cone from adjacent roadworks to serve as an impromptu megaphone, she sighed, picked up her alarm clock and held its luminous dial close to her eyes. 2.25. The voice of the lonely singer tailed off into the darkness. The clock ticked.

She began to think of all the people in Belfast who were drinking or drugging themselves into bearable insensibility that night. People would be hitting other people in the face with broken bottles. People were avowing and making love to people for whom they truly cared nothing; other people were screaming hatred at those whom they really did love. People were destroying things, daubing walls with paint and breaking up telephone boxes; joy-riding stolen cars into stone walls. In hospitals and homes, people were watching others dying, hoping and praying that the inevitable would not happen, while other people were planning murder. People elsewhere were trying to commit suicide, fumbling with change for the gas meter or emptying brown plastic bottles of their pills and tablets which were bitter and dry in the mouth.

And there are, she thought, there must be, people who think as I do.

Whenever she tried to define for herself her own feelings, she kept coming up again and again with the same images: a wall, a pit, a hole. When Francis died, she felt that she had fallen into a deep, dark pit, with cold smooth sides, out of which it was impossible to climb. She did not deny her desolation, nor believe that she could escape from it either by self-stupefaction or by trying to make others suffer as greatly as she herself had done. She lay in bed, sat, stood or walked and she said nothing and did nothing. She waited, and already this waiting was a progress. She had gone past the stage of the panicked desire to escape to a place where his death was not, for she knew now that in all the world no such place existed. She did nothing, for she did not know what she could do that would be of help; there was nothing possible but to sit and feel this pain of her loss and loneliness wander through her soul. She thought with bitterness of people who said that they wanted to live intensely, 'in extremis'. She did not believe that they understood what they wanted: only a perverse and masochistic mind would think this a desirable state. She did not want to suffer: she wanted to be happy, even though she did not think that this was a laudable desire but truthfully there were moments, and this was one of them, when she would have changed eternal joy – eternal anything – for mere temporal and finite happiness. She wanted to have Francis back with her. She was saddened by her capacity for forgetfulness: the particular inflexions of his voice, the texture of his skin: she had become too used to his absence. She felt a sudden dread of death which was not fear of dying herself, but of being passed over by death, of being left behind, alone. Morbid fantasies concerning her mother flooded her mind. Mammy walking out of the house and having half her head blown away by a stray bullet. Mammy in a shop when a bomb explodes and her body bursting into a scattered jumble of bloody pieces. Mammy being burnt alive in a firebombed restaurant. Mammy –

'No,' she said aloud, 'no, this is foolish and childish, this fear that she will be killed.' But it was the thing which, in all the world she dreaded most. And it was not an illogical fear, for Francis had been killed and Belfast was small: it might well happen again.

At the end, she thought, death must be desirable: Jane Austen heaving her last spiked breaths to say, when asked what she wanted, 'Nothing but death'; the wrinkled Sybil, lying withered and motionless save for a bright and flickering eye, who said to the inquisitive boys, 'I want to die.' She could only think that, after he had been so severely tortured (stabbed and beaten and burnt), Francis, too, had felt relief to be at last released into death. And Francis (terrible irony) was the only person in the world whom she had loved so much that she would have died for him.

For what the undertaker called 'obvious reasons', the lid of the coffin was not removed at any stage of the funeral ceremonies. When they trundled the solid lozenge of pale wood into the hospital's chilly mortuary chapel prior to the removal of the remains, all Theresa's grief was overpowered by anger against the God who could have prevented this but who had permitted it to happen. She would not love such a God and she decided immediately that she would not believe in Him. The undertaker led them in a decade of the Rosary but she did not join in; she stood trembling by the coffin and looked with shock and tenderness at Francis's name engraved upon the little chrome plaque.

Yet to decide not to believe: what did that mean? If God existed, He existed and her refusal to believe could not alter that. The simple withdrawal of her faith (or anyone's, or everyone's) could not destroy God. She had never in her life doubted His existence for a single moment, and she did not doubt it now. This was a problem of love, not faith. God was real: she was quite free to hate Him.

But where did Francis now come into this? If there was no God, death was the end and the people who had killed Francis really had destroyed him absolutely, leaving only a body which was too terrible for his own family to see and which would soon be rotting in the grave. This cruel, hated God was her only link with Francis and if she lost God she lost Francis; if she could stop believing in God, she would have to stop believing in her brother.

Each alternative was dreadful: a God with a divine plan, part of which was that Francis should be tortured and shot; or no God and no plan, so that all this was chaos and there could never be any justification or explanation and might really was right. Some people really did have the power to take away the lives of others and no one could ever vindicate or expiate their acts. And she knew that her ineluctable belief did not leave her free to choose her alternative and although she had resented it deeply only moments before, it offered the only possible shred of comfort.

They concluded the prayers and as she followed the coffin out to the hearse she resigned herself silently to belief in God and knew that she would have to learn to love Him again, although there was resentment and little understanding in her heart.

As one walks across St Peter's Square in Rome, the four rows of Doric pillars which form Bernini's Colonnade merge and shift so that they seem to increase then decrease in number and their colour changes from golden-grey to deepest black. There are, however, two small stones in the vast, cobbled square which are the focal points of the sweeping grey arcs and, when one stands upon these stones, all four rows fall into order, so that one sees only a single row of pillars.

Theresa and Francis had found these stones; Francis had stood on one and said simply, 'This is what it's like when you begin to believe that God loves you.'

She had asked him then how his belief in God affected him, and he had said, 'I feel as if I'm being watched all the time, as if a big eye is looking at me and through me for every second of my existence. I see God in everything, but God also sees everything in me. There are eyes everywhere: the sun, moon, stars, every light and every window, but worst of all are the eyes of people. God looks straight out at me through the eye of every human being, asking me to look straight back at Him. But I know that I can't, because I'm not good enough, and I can feel the eyes catch on me like hooks. Everywhere I look, I see only eyes, God's eyes, God telling me what He did for me and wanting to know what I'm doing for Him; God looking and looking and looking and wanting me to try to look steadily back.'

'That sounds terrible,' said Theresa. 'I can imagine few things worse.'

'Oh, there's something infinitely worse,' he exclaimed.

'Which is?'

'Not being looked at at all.'

The huge square was thronged. People grouped themselves around the fountains for photographs; tourists scurried in groups behind guides, some of whom brandished a little flag, a closed umbrella or a plastic flower. 'Just look at all these people,' he said, 'a fraction of all those who are now in the Vatican, in Rome, in Italy, in Europe, in all the world; think of all the people who ever were, who are and who will be, and then think that you are just one amongst them all, and that no one in particular is looking at you. No matter how good family and friends are, they can't look you absolutely in the eye always and forever: it's never perfect, never total. Other people never understand fully and never love fully. Then they die. Oh, I'd much rather be looked at than not!'

And so he had known even then the best and most dreadful truth.

When they had finished speaking, she put her arm through his and they walked across the square to the basilica. In spite of the heat and the deep blue sky against which the building loomed, the associations which she instinctively made were of coldness, not warmth, as she remembered the souvenir snow-storm which she had owned as a child. The real basilica evoked the flooded plastic edifice and its cold, breakable beauty still was there: she felt that the frail cupola, gilded within, could be shivered easily as an eggshell ('for Thine is the KINGDOM, the POWER and the GLORY') just as she had shattered the dome of the snowstorm. Without water, the model basilica had looked pathetically shoddy and small.

Once inside, she tightened her grip on Francis's arm, for as they walked around looking at the beautiful things, at the paintings and statues and magnificent altars and marble floors, she had felt a terrible passion for this God of whom he had spoken, this God who looked and looked and Who wanted you to return His gaze; but she was conscious of Him through Francis's words and not through the lapis lazuli, the alabaster or the white Carrera marble. They stopped in front of the Pietà, and she thought, idly, were it not for the distance and the plate glass, how much damage I could so quickly do with a hammer or a hatchet. And then Francis had broken into her thoughts, saying softly, 'Were I to break that, I would only be breaking stone. People do not look for God, they look only for bits of metal and stone and glass. They come for art's sake; they don't believe.'

'And without belief,' she said, 'it's just a piece of white stone.' He replied that, even with belief, it was nothing more, that it was merely a thing so very beautiful that it obstructed what it ostensibly stood for, which is infinitely more beautiful and which cannot be destroyed.

And that same evening, they had found by chance the little church which houses Bernini's statue of Saint Teresa of Avila in Ecstasy. The air inside was fusty with the smell of burnt wax and stale incense, the church dim and almost empty. Together they stood before the statue, not speaking, until Francis whispered, 'It's absolutely beautiful. That's what it is to be lost in the eye which never closes or looks away.' She knew what he wanted and she could understand his desire to be in that state, to be like St Teresa, stunned into ecstasy by union with God, but she could not fully share that desire and it frightened her. The little white feet were shockingly still among the panicked, ruffled marble folds of the habit. And Francis was looking unflinchingly at the gilded arrow in the hand of the angel. Suddenly, his sister had felt very lonely: she would never feel so lonely again until he died. She turned away, for she could not bear to look at him, and she waited at the back of the church until he was ready to join her.

They left Rome the following day.

Snuggled down in bed with the duvet tucked up around his chin, Robert, with the fascination of a small child, watched Kathy putting on her make-up. She was sitting at the far side of the room before a pier glass which Robert had bought in Smithfield, although she was using mainly her own little hand mirror which caught sharp flashes of yellow morning light as it streamed through the uncurtained windows to brighten and soften the whole room. She had put Robert's dressing-gown on over her underwear; the rest of her clothes were draped over a large wicker chair nearby. Not for the first time Robert thought about the possibility of her moving in with him, and of how strange and lovely it would be to have her clothes and possessions permanently in his home. The otherness of women fascinated him. 'The opposite sex', therein lay the mystery, so different and yet still human! Her clothes were beautiful, piled there in sensuous disorder – her jacket of plum velvet; her soft grey silk blouse, her pale stockings, translucent as rosepetals.

From where he lay he could not, of course, savour the great richness of their smell, that sweet smell which they had acquired from contact with her body. That smell itself was a mystery; a glorious unnamable blend of perfume, cosmetics and something that was Kathy.

If there really were such a thing as magic, he thought, it had something to do with women's bodies.

He watched while Kathy stretched open her deepset eyes by carefully drawing a mascara brush across each set of eyelashes in turn, an action which he found slightly alarming for the way in which it momentarily lifted the eyelid away from the eyeball. She then smeared a purply-coloured powder on the lids and her eyes remained miraculously wide, their naturally piggy look lost. He watched while she changed the shape of her face by carefully dabbing her cheekbones with an ochre fluid; and while she painted her lips deep red. She kissed a tissue and painted them again, then turned a countenance like a water-colour towards the pier glass to survey the final effect. She saw that he was looking at her looking at herself in his mirror, and without turning round she bounced a smile off the pier glass and across the room to him. The smile revealed a tiny speck of lipstick on her teeth: she carefully wiped it away. She then gathered together all the little bottles and tubes and replaced them in their small corduroy make-up bag, checking in turn that the lid of each was tight.

Robert would have gained a distinctly voyeuristic thrill from watching anyone transform themselves from the sleepy-eyed and tousled person who crept out of bed in the morning into the dressed and groomed creature who normally faced the world: that it was Kathy simply made it more aesthetically pleasing. As a child, it had been a revelation for him to discover that Miss McGuire, the harridan who taught him when he was in Infants, was not born wearing her brown tweed pinafore. She had to undress herself and go to bed every night and she had to dress herself in the morning in layers, just as Robert himself and his family had to do. It took some believing that other people's clothes were like his own and not all of a piece, like the paper clothes which Rosie's cardboard dolls wore, hanging over their printed underwear from little tabs at their shoulders. It was hard to believe that other people had real lives utterly independent of his own and, more amazing still, that in the humblest and most mundane features these other lives were just like his own. (Oh, the sight of Miss McGuire that Saturday morning, buying a quarter of cinnamon lozenges! And his father's mirth afterwards as he told his mother, 'If ye'd seen the eyes of him, near out on two stalks, he thinks she comes up out of the floor to teach him and then goes back down again!'). Of all his childhood fancies, this had been the most powerful and the most comprehensive. It was the only one about which he was loathe to speak, because it still existed in a residual, but strongly perceptible, form. He liked it when his girlfriends stayed the night with him instead of going back to the empty façades of their family homes to wait for their next cue into his life. By staying and sleeping with him and letting him see them putting on their make-up and their clothes in the morning, they seemed to extend their existence; to re-create themselves. He liked that: it helped confirm reality for him.

Kathy was now brushing out her hair. She fastened it up with two combs of tortoiseshell plastic, then moved across the room to a chair by the window and sat in profile to him, looking out into the street.

What was in her mind? Most likely her own sins, he thought. He had never yet met a woman with the guts for atheism; they were all cringeing with at least vestigial Christianity at heart. A few nights before that they had inadvertently begun to talk about religion and when he asked her outright if she believed in God she had said, 'No,' but with a 'No' so reluctant and so diffident that he did not believe it. He had teased and nagged her, 'You do, you do, go on, admit it,' until at last she lost her temper. 'Alright, so what if I do? You can be a right pig, Robert McConville, a right bully.'

So what? It put the power of real sin in her hand. Amorality was a bland business, but Kathy was immoral, and spectacularly so. She believed in free choice for right and wrong, and she wilfully, gleefully, chose wrong. It was exciting to dabble with perdition. With a mixture of alarm and sadness, he had listened to the discourse which she poured in his ear one night in bed a short time after he had first known her, a long seamless speech concerning her mother. 'So-then-she-said-and-then-I-said . . .' She told him about the scene there had been when her mother found out that she had been sleeping with her boyfriend, information which she had volunteered not because she had to, but because she wanted to annoy. 'I hope she's happy now she knows that I'm as bad as she always said I was.' It was mainly because of this that he did not believe that she loved him, in spite of her frequent claims to the contrary. He didn't care about being loved but he despised her for lying about it. She had practically admitted to her mother that she did what she did only for the sake of sex and sin, not love. Why, then, would she not admit it to him? As well him as another. Damn, he would make her admit to it, just as he had made her admit to her sneaking religion.

'Kathy,' he said, softly, perfidiously, 'penny for your thoughts.' Would she say something cosmetic and coy; – 'I was thinking about us'? She shook her head and said nothing.

'Kathy? Come on, tell me.' She was silent for another moment before speaking.

'I was thinking about Theresa,' she said.

'Oh *her*,' he snorted, disappointed at the inaccuracy of his guess. Now there was one person whom he would not want to see prove their reality in the morning. He would have preferred conclusive evidence that she was merely a figment of his imagination, a bad-tempered, chain-smoking hallucination.

'Yes, Theresa,' said Kathy crossly, 'and you needn't take that tone when you're talking about her.'

'Oh, but Kathy, she's so belligerent, so aggressive. You saw the way she got at me the other day, making a personal attack out of a political discussion.'

'You deserved that, Robert, and don't try to tell me you didn't. She said no more than the truth. If you thought about it at all you'd see that she's right.'

'I do think,' he said indignantly.

'No, you don't. Oh, come on, Robert, admit it: you pride yourself on being apolitical, away above all that. It doesn't even interest you.'

'Well, there's no need for her to be so bloody ardent.'

'There's nothing wrong with being ardent, Robert. It's better than being apathetic.'

He did not like the direction this exchange was taking; now he would either have to lose face or let it develop into a full-scale row. 'She smokes too much,' he eventually said lamely. 'That really gets on my wick, so it does. Is she on commission from Rothman's, or what?'

'It's nerves,' said Kathy.

'Nerves? What has she got to be nervous about?'

'She hardly smoked at all when I first knew her,' said Kathy, which was not an answer to the question which he had asked; and saying that she had been thinking of Theresa had not been strict truth, either, for although she had been thinking of her while putting on her make-up, by the time she moved to the window she was thinking of Francis.

Theresa and Francis were twins. They started at Queen's the same year as Kathy and all three were in the same class. They soon developed the custom of meeting each day in the Union for coffee and Mars Bars, while Francis, the most inveterate and most inept doer of crosswords she had ever met, attempted the Simplex puzzle in the *Irish Times*.

'Twelve down. Bubbles on the skin. Eight letters. No idea.'

'Blisters. Easy-peasy,' she crowed. 'Gimmie another.' After his death, Theresa had given her as a keepsake a *Daily Telegraph* book of crosswords in which every single puzzle had been attempted, but not one of which was complete.

From the first she had preferred Francis to Theresa, because she was reserved while he was genuinely shy: he made a much greater effort to be friendly than his sister ever did. They were always together. Sometimes Kathy wondered if Theresa resented slightly her friendship with Francis. She was hurt and surprised when he left college after the Easter vacation in first year, for he had not given even a hint that he was thinking of such a move. When she asked Theresa about it, Theresa said crossly, 'Oh, Francis! Don't even start me on that. He said he was leaving Queen's because he couldn't get to grips with it, as lightly as you like, as if it was an evening class in O-level crochet or something. We can't get wit out of him, you might as well talk to the fireplace.'

'What will he do now?'

'I shudder to think.'

He took a job filling shelves in a city-centre supermarket. Kathy saw him often between his leaving university in the spring and his death that autumn. She used to call into the supermarket and saw him in his brown overall, stacking up jars of instant coffee or putting price labels on tins of condensed soup. She asked him why he did not try to find a more interesting job.

'I like boring work,' he said. 'It leaves my mind free for higher things. Anyway,' he added, 'I don't expect to be here for very long,' a remark which, with hindsight, she understood even less than she had done at the time. Her friendships with Theresa and Francis became consolidated for their being conducted separately. She was immensely fond of Francis, who had the most tender and lovely smile she had ever seen. When Francis smiled at her she felt important and loved; although in sustained conversation he failed utterly to maintain eye contact, his glance flitting from his shoes to displays of cornflakes to huge yellow posters saying 'Low Low Prices'. Before they parted, he always dared to look her in the face once more.

He took her out to lunch a few times, to a seedy little café where the sandwiches indecorously turned up their crusts to reveal their fillings; and a solitary, stale pork pie lurked under a perspex dome like the control of a scientific experiment which had gone horribly wrong. 'Have a fly's graveyard,' he would say, 'or a wee cement biscuit, they're nice.' Kathy was often lonely and then she would envy Theresa her gentle, eccentric brother. She had never known two people so close. She wished that she was half of such a loving couple. Maybe if she had had a brother or sister, it might have been like that. It wasn't fair that she was an only child with a mother who didn't care for her and a dead father whom she couldn't even remember, and a fluctuating fund of men, none of whom had ever really cared for her any more than she cared for them. But then Francis died, and she felt guilty for envying Theresa. She knew that the greater the love, the harder it must be now.

She would never forget the first time she saw Theresa back in college after the murder, sitting at a table in the Union, and looking abnormally solitary. She looked incomplete and shockingly different; even her hair and clothes seemed bereaved. Kathy had been unable to approach her then and had gone away and cried and cried. Looking at Theresa alone, she had felt intense pity and fear.

'Think kindly of her, Robert, please. You don't understand her.'

'And you do?'

'Not completely, but still better than you do.' She came over and sat beside him on the bed. 'It's wrong for you to judge her, you mustn't do it.' She leaned against him and put her arms around his neck, thinking how very lucky she was to have Robert. At least somebody loved her.

Robert gently removed the plastic combs and ruffled her hair. Bloody women. He would never understand them. He thought Theresa a most unlikely friend for Kathy and wondered what the attraction could be. Probably that of an unplumbed opposite, he guessed. Theresa's strange eyes had their effect seemingly without any willed effort on her part; her gaze was like that of an indolent cobra. She was a right oddity, he thought. In a way she wasn't really like a girl. Never before had he met anyone so angular and androgynous; indeed, never before had he known anyone for so long and so little considered their sex. It had only really come to his attention some two days before their recent argument, when he had been again obliged to give her a lift home from the library. On reaching her street, the door-lock on her side was stuck, so he had leant across to open it and as he did so, through the thick fug of cigarette smoke which permanently hung around her, he had smelt the faintest whiff of a light, flowery perfume. He felt not the tiniest frisson of sexuality, but a major tremor of shock: for the first time ever, he was conscious of her body. It begged more questions than it answered. He wondered if she was a virgin, but balked at the notion, for he shuddered to imagine what it would be like to kiss her, much less sleep with her. Kissing Theresa, he thought, would be dangerous and painful; it would sting the lips as it did to kiss a poisoned Bible or a religious statue daubed with Belladonna in a Jacobean tragedy. To embrace her would be like driving an iron spike into his chest.

One day when he was small, a wasp had stung him at school. Miss McGuire applied her sovereign remedy for stings, which was malt vinegar painted on with a long-handled sable brush, but he had continued to weep pathetically (the smell of the vinegar was almost as bad as the sting). Miss McGuire then kissed him on the cheek, and he immediately forgot both smell and sting in the shock of discovering that her face was as warm and soft as his own. He still felt that it would be eerie and unnerving to discover by experience that Theresa's body was as warm, soft, mortal and sexual as that of anyone else.

'She never talks about her family,' he said.

'No,' replied Kathy, 'and neither do you.' She leant over and kissed him on the lips, which made it physically impossible for him to either answer this retort or to ask any further awkward questions. For the first time that morning, he guessed correctly what was in her mind but although he knew she wanted to keep him quiet he could not know the reason why. The ruse worked, however: it provided sufficient distraction to turn his thoughts away from Theresa. He considered her now, together with the other women whom he knew. Theresa, Kathy, Rosie, his mother – what did any of them truly think and feel? And why? None of them were deliberately mysterious and yet they were all a mystery. He wished for understanding for the sake of pure curiosity rather than for the love which he might have had for any of them. There was always an obstruction. He had never felt real unity with any woman, worse, he had never once even reached a consensus by which they agreed to differ. He had drifted away from all the girls he had ever known with no more ultimate intimacy than there had been when they first met. He looked down at the crown of Kathy's head. Did he really want to understand her? No. Did he love her? No, and if he had been mistaken about what was in her mind when she was sitting at the window he was convinced that it was an error of time only. She did delight in what she was doing; he was her sin, he furnished the glamour of her being 'bad'. So be it. He put his hand under her chin to raise her head and saw, to his puzzlement and utter exasperation, that her eyes were filled with tears.

A black-and-white photograph of her parents' wedding hung over the china cabinet in the parlour, and Theresa's attention was drawn to it again and again and again. She wondered how her parents – how anyone – went through with a white wedding, for she could never countenance even the possibility of it for herself. She thought that weddings were unspeakably vulgar and almost primitive in their hidebound custom and attention to detail: the white dress, the communal meal of cooked meats and a tall cake, the speeches, dancing and confetti, the crude remarks lipsticked across the windscreen of a car festooned with toilet paper and old boots. The unhappy happy couple were at least spared the Eastern ignominy of having their entire extended family beating at their bedroom door, demanding proof of recently lost virginity. As The Preacher said, there is nothing in the world that is new and white weddings, Theresa thought, like the popular press and much television, are greatly dependent upon unoriginality and repetition for their ultimate success.

It was partly because of this that she found it hard to believe that her mother remembered her wedding day as a real day and not merely in terms of black-and-white photographs, a few dried flowers, some cards and telegrams and a yellowed tulle veil. These objects, like holy relics or objects in a museum, alienated Theresa from that to which they pertained, rather than bringing them closer, their frail, folded, dated state stressing for her how very old they were and how far in the past the event had been. It took an effort to remember that her parents' wedding-day had been a real day, a day with weather and milk deliveries. She could never fully catch and hold that idea, so that the day remained a series of images. She could make no satisfactory substitute for experience. Her isolation from her parents' marriage made her sad, because it was a part of her isolation from her father and it made her very sad to think of his having died before she was old enough to remember him.

Somewhere in the house there was a large manilla envelope containing an eclectic array of photographs of her father. There were some fuzzy little snaps stapled into covers of ginger cardboard to form tiny books; and a studio portrait of him when he was twenty, in which he was grinning at the camera with well-fed confidence. There was an oval sepia print of a scruffy little boy with a skew-whiff Eton collar; and a tattered class photograph taken when he was nine, and upon which he had later indicated his own tiny image with a heavily inked 'X', completely obliterating the face of the child directly behind him. Theresa's favourite photograph of him was one taken by a street photographer years before her father's marriage. He looked so young and happy, as unaware of death as he was of the eye of the camera. What had happened before and after that instant when, as he passed innocently down the street, a clicking shutter had made of him an eternal image for his unborn daughter? Around him, the city spawned and died. There was a cigarette between his fingers; moments later he would have extinguished it; an hour later smoked another and that evening bought a new packet, moving away from the moment of the photograph and towards his own death. History of some sort had been made that day, for there was never a day so dull that the newspapers had no headlines, but what was for her its only significant event was unrecorded. No paper carried the leader: 'Patsy Cassidy Snapped by Street Photographer'. She would have given a year of her life to know the day and hour at which that photograph had been taken. She felt that such knowledge would have given her the power to pluck and save her father from the flux of time.

It was even worse for poor Kathy, she thought. Her mother absolutely refused to talk about her husband, of whom there was not a single extant photograph. Mrs O'Gorman evidently bore her bereavement through such silence and negation, but it was a source of deep resentment for her daughter. 'He might as well never have lived,' she said bitterly.

As children, Theresa's father and mother had travelled frequently on the same local train; he and his father going from Belfast to visit a rural grandmother; she and her mother coming up to the city for a day's shopping. On every journey, the train stopped at Lisburn Station and the children saw a large metal advertisement which read 'DON'T BE MISLED: CAMP COFFEE IS THE BEST'. Independently, they both thought that misled was pronounced 'mizzled' and wondered what on earth it could possibly mean. Only after their marriage did they discover their shared misunderstanding.

So they met and married, then honeymooned in Clifden, a town which Theresa had never visited and never wanted to visit. She accepted her mother's evocation of Clifden as she accepted Dostoevsky's Petersburg. Each place was conceived in the memory, language and discourse of others, and then took life in her own imagination: the illusory streets and squares and people rose before her. It would be futile to look for these towns, not because they had changed but because in the form in which she saw them they had never truly existed.

This honeymoon Clifden, then, was a dream, and the real

nature of her parents' short marriage, the first days of which had been spent there, was also impossible to pin down. Once, only once, had her mother let slip: 'It wasn't all roses,' and while this did not give the lie to the stories which she told of a kind and happy husband, it showed that the truth was only partial. She wished that her mother would say, 'He was sometimes selfish and thoughtless and mean – but only sometimes; I loved him, so it doesn't really matter.' While she did not know the whole story, her father remained an affable but unreal stranger. She could not love him.

She could understand her mother's tendency to romanticize the memory of someone simply because they were dead: she did it herself with Francis. As if it had all been so perfect! Never a cross word? At times there had been nothing else. She could make herself forget almost completely the bitter rows they had had when he left university, but that did not mean that they had never happened. When she thought back now, she was still angry, she still thought that she had been right and Francis had been a fool, a stubborn fool.

'A supermarket, Francis? A bloody supermarket?'

'Yes, Theresa, a supermarket. I have to do it. It's what God wants for me now.'

'Before He formed you in the womb He knew you, and decreed that you be a filler of shelves, is that what you're trying to tell me? Are you to be a voice crying in the wilderness, "10p off Heinz Beans, this week's special offer"?'

He did not reply to that, but left the room, slamming the door behind him. She never missed a chance to mock and goad him. 'I hope you're ambitious, Francis, I hope you aspire to high and noble things, like the bacon counter.'

He had once said, 'You'll see,' but she never did. She still felt that she had failed in not managing to browbeat him back into college and she resented that he had proved his will stronger than hers by not yielding. She still could not see, and believed that she never would see, the virtue of his taking that brainless, pointless, futureless job. She might suspect his motivation, but she could not understand it.

He had had an exaggerated sense of the importance of his own life. He felt so strongly that life was a huge, blank, malleable and significant thing which one had a moral obligation to use fully and properly, that he had eventually frightened himself into doing nothing at all. He had dabbled in various things – painting, playing the piano, geology – but never with any great conviction, and his halfhearted plans and projects always came to nothing. Eventually he gave up, and waited for that one big thing, that one act or event which would qualify his whole life. It was as if by taking the job in the supermarket he was trying to hoard all his energy – trying to hoard life itself – for that one instant of action, union and justification. It was similar to the way in which all the trivialities of an artist's life become subsumed by the grandeur of his greatest work; but Francis, she thought, had been no artist. He had, however, been happier at the supermarket than at Queen's, there was no denying that. It all seemed so unimportant and foolish now that the fearfully conserved life was ended. The overwhelmingly significant thing now was her love for him. Even if she thought that he had been foolish or that he had shirked life, her love would have to accommodate these things because they were a part of him.

Where was Francis now? What was Heaven? A place of total and unqualified love; a place where there was never, ever the need to say 'and yet', 'in spite of' or 'nevertheless'.

Towards the end of July, a television documentary was broadcast concerning former terrorists who were now living in exile in America, unextradited and unrepentant. Theresa's mother insisted that they watch it, although Theresa herself had strong misgivings. One man, wearing beach clothes and sitting on a white iron chair by a sunny terrace, deprecated with a wave of his hand the luxury in which he now lived. He spoke of the dangers of his position, and said that he was wanted by both the British Army and various paramilitary organizations. In a voice which had acquired a strong American twang, he spoke of internal organization and communication; cell structures and factions; divisions, battalions and volunteers. Then the interviewer asked him about the actions which had led him to his present exile.

'Did you kill members of the security forces?'

'No comment.'

'Did you kill civilians?'

His eyes flitted left and right, looked slyly at the camera, and then looked away again.

'No comment.'

'Did you ever take part in any purely sectarian killings?'

He gave a little smile of exasperation.

'No comment.'

As Theresa had feared and expected, her mother broke down and cried. 'I knew this would happen,' she said, and switched off the television, her mother's sobs sounding even more wretched and distressing against the sudden silence which this afforded. Her mother, her sweet, kind, thoughtful mother, who had made big scones, now lay wailing on her chintzy sofa. 'I hope they rot in Hell for what they did to Francis, God curse them and their kind.'

'They're not all in California ate'n steaks and melons,' said Theresa roughly. 'The one that did Francis is probably lyin' drunk in a gutter in Sandy Row.'

'Does that make it any better? He's alive an' doin' what he wants. Francis is lyin' in Milltown.'

Theresa also began to cry then. She would never see him again in this world, never never never never never. She thought that Francis had been beaten; he was an absolute victim. She resented even the longevity of little old ladies with velveteen hats and bile-green knitting, who clung to the railings for support as they toddled up the road to mass and who, merely by staying alive, had in some way bested Francis. Francis was a failure; he had failed even to continue existing. Now they would have to live out the rest of their lives without him.

'Uncle Bobby?'

'Yes?'

'What do you call a dwarf covered in cement?'

'Give up.'

'A wee hard man.' Tommy crowed with laughter and leapt across the sofa.

'Uncle Bobby?'

'What, Tommy?'

'What's big an' warm an' furry an' would look good on a Protestan'?'

'A fur coat?'

'No, an Alsatian dog.'

'Tommy, you stop that,' scolded Rosie. 'That's not a nice joke, who told you that?'

'Daddy.'

'Well, it's not nice. C'm on, feet off the sofa and out with ye; away out to the back scullery an' play with yer worms.' Tommy stumped reluctantly out of the room and Rosie wearily drew her hand across her forehead. 'God, yer up agin a brick wall tryin' to bring them up right in this day an' age, aren't ye?'

'Yes, indeed,' said Robert with sincerity, although he thought that she could have simplified her task considerably by marrying someone other than Tom, Provo or Provo sympathizer or whatever the hell he was, the miserable get. Robert had once seen the butt of a gun sticking out from under a bed in the house, and every time there was an army raid Rosie smashed a few plates or cups and got edgy. Wouldn't it be like the thing for them to lift Tom just when the baby was due? Wouldn't that be a nice picnic? As he thought this, he heard the sinister whine of an army Saracen passing and against this convenient noise he deliberately asked Rosie, 'Do you ever – ah – worry about Tom?' She, with equal deliberation, chose to be evasive, by not associating the sound and the question.

'Worry? Aye, he wants to be there when the baby comes and that worries me alright. He goes to these classes in the Royal and sees films about it and things, but he has no more notion than the cat, Robert.' The very thought of seeing a baby being born made Robert feel queasy. How could Tom countenance such a thing? God, but he hated him! He hated him for being so consistently cheerful and irresponsible and happy. He hated him for the way he was always trying to inveigle him, Robert, into talking politics, with his 'British war machine', and his 'revolutionary struggle' and his 'imperialist oppression' and all his other clichés, and his unfailing way of concluding, 'Amn't I right, Bobby?' His arguing unnerved Robert as much as it annoyed him, for Tom was persuasive and articulate: in spite of his jargon, he knew what he was talking about. It did not matter whether Tom was right or wrong: what mattered was his blithe and total conviction that he *was* right, which Robert could counter only with ill-informed and badly thought-out arguments, made mainly for the sake of argument. The whole Northern Irish political issue wearied and bored him.

He had met Tom by chance in the city the previous week and had been obliged, with great reluctance, to go for a drink with him, over which Tom had told him a story about an old woman named Eileen who lived in the same street as Rosie and himself.

'Last week,' he said, 'Eileen, she slipped an' fell at her own front door. There was a foot patrol of Brits goin' past and they stopped to give her a han' an' Eileen of course was effin' an' blindin' an' tryin' to beat them off, the more they were tryin' to help her, seein' as how they were Brits. Well, the leg was brave an' badly hurt, so she got it all strapped up an' three days later she's sittin' on a chair by her door with the leg propped up before her on a stool. What comes along, but an army lan' rover. It slows down, see, an' one of the Brits sticks his head out of the back an' he calls to her, "Hello, Eileen, how's your leg?" An' Eileen, Eileen, she calls back, "Still hingin' from me arse."'

Tom almost choked with laughter as he came to the punchline of his joke, which Robert did not find particularly amusing. A stream of words drifted into his mind to describe the noises Tom was making: 'a coughball of laughter leaped from his throat, dragging after it a rattling chain of phlegm.' They were splendid words but they were not Robert's own, and as he watched Tom laughing and coughing he wondered which was worse: the claustrophobia of Belfast or the verbal deficiency which prevented him from adequately describing it.

Rosie sighed and shrugged away the thought of Tom as spectator at her confinement. 'I saw your girlfriend the other day,' she said, 'in Clonard.'

'Kathy?' he exclaimed in amazement. 'In Clonard?' He did not know, nor care to know, all Kathy's movements when she was from him, but he could not believe that the chapel of a Redemptorist monastery was one of her haunts.

'No,' said Rosie, 'not Kathy. I don't know any Kathy. I mean Theresa, the girl you brought here.'

'Oh, Theresa,' he said. 'Were you speaking to her?'

'Yes. She's nice. I feel sorry for her.'

'Why?'

'I don't know: there's just something about her.'

So the Basilisk went to Clonard, did she? One day when she was outside the library having a fag he would leave a note on her absented desk saying, 'Nymph in thy orisons be remembered all my sins.' Rosie broke into his thoughts.

'Who's Kathy, then?'

'My girlfriend,' he said shortly. 'It's through her that I know Theresa.'

'Oh.' She looked hurt and resentful, but he would still tell her nothing. She was bound to have already a fair idea of his lifestyle, but the details would shock her. To suspect was one thing, but to know was quite another, and he was afraid that he would alienate her in exactly the same way in which he had alienated his mother. It would have been little comfort to her to say: 'Rosie, I couldn't tell you the things even if I really wanted to.' There were things of which he was too ashamed. He could never tell her about what he had done on the night of their mother's death.

On the evening when her remains were brought from the house to the chapel he had, immediately on returning from the short service, gone up to where she had been laid out. He was taken aback by the ravished air of the little room. A small oleograph of the Sacred Heart had been tilted askew on the wall by the press of mourners. A few velvety petals had dropped from the little vase of roses on the dressing-table, the mirror of which was sheeted. On top of the chest of drawers were long pennons of paper which were printed with crucifixes and all stuck with beaded rods of creamy wax. The pennons were crumpled and torn as a result of having been removed from the candlesticks in great haste by the undertakers. Then he saw the bed with its quilt depressed and slightly dragged to one side, as if his mother had been merely sleeping there for half an hour in the afternoon, rather than lying in her coffin. But you could rumple beds with something other than sleeping or death, and that very night he brought a girl back to his flat and frightened her with passion.

She in turn startled him afterwards by saying suddenly, 'I spy with my little eye something beginning with B.T.'

'What?'

'Black tie. Who's dead?' she said playfully.

'My mother.'

He felt her body stiffen and her voice changed.

'When?'

'Last year. I bought the tie for her funeral; it must have fallen out of the wardrobe.'

'Oh,' she said. There was a pause, then he felt her body relax again. 'God,' she chuckled, 'you had me worried there for a minute.'

He regretted his cowardly lie, even though the girl would probably have fled the place had he told her the truth. She never knew that she was turfed out early the following morning so that he could prepare for the funeral. Rosie would think he was an utter monster if she knew, and perhaps he was. If he had slept with a girl and was then told that her father had died the previous day he would have been shocked, so he felt that the shock of others was justifiable. He tried to remember the girl's name, and felt with a pang of regret that his grief had taught him nothing. He realized that Rosie was watching him beadily, and he fidgeted uncomfortably in his chair.

'The less you know about me the better, Rosie,' he said.

'Better for you or for me?'

'For both of us. I'd best be off.' He stood up.

'Robert, sometimes I wonder why you come here at all,' she said, her voice hardening with uncharacteristic anger. 'D'ye like to remind yerself how far ye've come? Cos I'll tell you something – it might not be just as far as ye think.'

Little Tommy held to his eyes an oblong of red plastic, thrice dimpled, in which had nestled some of Mr Kipling's Exceedingly Good Jam Tarts. He saw the world in the round; rosy-pink when the light was strong and changing deeper to red as the light dimmed; and he saw it roughly because of the way in which the plastic was stippled. The view he obtained of his home city was thus narrow, inaccurate and highly coloured: defensible in a five-year-old peering through a piece of cake-box packaging, but not in the older citizens who shared his vision. The violence and political struggles had effected less change than was generally acknowledged: it had not altered Belfast's perception of itself. It remained an introverted city, narcissistic, nostalgic and profoundly un-European (this latter in spite of one's now being able to purchase there croissants in tins).

Robert worked hard that summer, primarily in the fine arts department of the Central Library. He frequently raised his eyes to the little artist's pallets which formed part of the stucco ornamentation around the ogee'd skylight, and inwardly he groaned. He felt that he deserved something better than the boredom of summer in Belfast, and the dull, uncreative work on which he was engaged. He had vaguely expected a more exciting, a more fulfilling life, and only in instances did he realize that it had not materialized and that it probably never would. In lucid flashes, he feared that this tedious summer was a microcosm of his whole future life: lonely, frustrating, dull, dragged out in a lunatic, self-destructive city. He could not have defined the life he wanted; could not have named another person whose art or scope he desired. Perhaps every life was unsatisfactory; perhaps the feeling which predominantly united humanity was not loneliness or love, but a deep sense of failure. He knew no one whose life seemed a fair compensation for the horror of having to die.

The only new person whom he had met that summer was the unlikable Theresa whose newness and surliness gave her at least a certain novelty value. She also frequented the fine arts department, and was there almost as often as Robert, her desk piled with books and papers, journals, magazines and literary reviews. Her labours seemed even more aimless and unsatisfactory than Robert's, lost in a welter of paper, reading erratically or scribbling in a large red notebook. At worst she was killing time in the library, putting in a summer which had to be got through in some way; at best she was trying to make sense of things through what she read and wrote, but it gave her little comfort. Her own definitions were unsatisfactory; but what she read frequently confirmed her fear that loneliness was inescapable.

'Death is like a fisher who catches fish in his net and leaves them in the water for a little while; the fish is still swimming but the net is around him and the fisher will draw him up – when he thinks fit.' She wondered if people in general shared her iceberg mentality: was it common to feel that only a tiny facet of one's self was exposed and communicable to others, with the rest locked in ice, vast, submerged and impossible? She caught Robert's glance as it passed between his desk and the stucco, and she surprised him with a tiny, timid smile.

Possibly other people were like this unconsciously, and did not realize how little they were known and understood by those around them, nor how little they knew or understood of themselves. Her daily life was very mundane that summer. She idled in the library and in bookshops, frequently had lunch with Kathy and went to occasional films, plays and art exhibitions. She went to mass often and lived quietly, peaceably, with her mother, who did not realize just how few friends her daughter had. Except for Rosie, who thought that there was something sad about her, no one realized that practically her every thought was an unhappy one, and that she was being quietly ground down by constant, nagging, absolute distress. She complained frequently of being tired, exhausted even: no one could understand why. She wondered if sometime she would scream aloud what often screamed in her mind: 'No! Leave me to have my own life!' If only he had been a husband or a lover, anything but a brother. His death had pitched her into love as much as grief; rather, it let her see how deeply and hopelessly she had been steeped in love, in utter passion for him since the day of their birth. But he was her brother and now he was dead, so that this love was exclusively of the family; worse, of the grave. She swung from feelings of betrayal and revulsion at the idea of similarly loving anyone else to desperate loneliness from the knowledge that she could not do so. She thought that love should not make her feel so trapped, but it did, and she felt it beyond her power to change this.

Her mother told her that she was wasting her summer.

'You ought to take a holiday before you go back to college.'

Theresa shrugged indifferently.

'Go abroad,' her mother said.

'No.'

While in Italy with Francis, she had had a bar of sandalwood soap, and in the course of the journey the atmosphere of that summer had seeped into the soap, so that forever afterwards the smell of sandalwood made her immensely sad, evoking the hot, crowded trains, with their little pulldown seats in the corridors; fusty churches; great art; bitter coffee; and the shabby hotels and inns where they had put up. In Trieste, they found lodgings from a tourist office, where the girl was so anxious that they did not confuse the two inns of the particular street to which she was sending them ('The other one is not at *all* nice') that they became convinced it was a brothel; a conviction strengthened when they saw how very seedy was the establishment to which they had been carefully directed. While the owner was copying their names from their passports for registration, Francis whispered to Theresa: 'You wouldn't see that in Ireland,' and nodded towards two framed pictures hanging on the wall only inches apart; one a gaudy print of the Madonna and Child, the other a highly erotic etching of a female nude.

Trieste was a forlorn port whose glory had crumbled away when an empire fell and left it sitting bleak, uneasy on a frontier. Theresa and Francis soon wondered why they had gone there, for there was little to do or see, and that little obscured by a sea mist which hung persistently over the bay for the few days they were there. They stood down by the harbour, where dry grass sprouted between broken cobble-stones and diseased, scabby pigeons picked around their feet. Francis claimed that he could see things in spite of the fog. He pointed out the Miramare, the Faro and distant ships, but Theresa could see nothing.

'It's your poor wee turney eye,' he teased her, 'that's what's wrong. Mustn't Mammy have been fierce disappointed when you were born and she saw the eye rollin' in your head? I can see her sittin' up in bed in the maternity ward with the baby in her arms, shakin' it and tiltin' it to try to get the eye to roll into position, like one of those games you used to get in the lid of a tube of Malteasers at Christmas, where you had to roll three ball-bearings into three wee dimples.'

'Meanie,' said Theresa. 'I'll have you know that some people find my eye very attractive.'

From Trieste they went to Venice, and only a few hours after their arrival she fell ill with cramp. She told Francis to go out and leave her to suffer alone in peace, and promised that she would meet him by the door of St Mark's Basilica three hours later. When the time came, she felt weak but sufficiently well to walk the short distance from the pensione to St Mark's Square, which she had not yet seen.

A drawing-room indeed; elegant, timeless, beautiful. Here was where the Doges had thrown rings of flowers into the water to marry the city to the sea. Real ladies in heavy trailing silk dresses had moved beneath the loggia, and all seemed fused to a timeless perfection, the past and the present, the fictional and the religious. It was evening, and the sun fell slantingly against the walls of the Palace; the sky was turbid and promised thunder. Some light rain had already fallen, and the stones of the square were bright and wet. There were many people there, mostly tourists, all strangers; and then suddenly she had seen Francis's face materialize out of the crowd, as familiar to her as her own foot or finger. This was what she had been seeking, and the faces of all those other people were masks, dross, distortions, faces which were wrong: suddenly the only right and real face in Venice had appeared.

As she watched him move across the damp marble towards her, she felt a sweep of love which was the sole complement to the loneliness she would feel before the statue in Rome, and this loneliness and love would be fused together in the black moment of grief when she learnt that he was dead.

In Venice, a man with an umbrella hat had tried to sell them handfuls of birdseed, which they refused, and they refused more vehemently the photographer who attempted to hand to them a toy gondola on which was perched a miserable-looking little monkey in a blue-and-white-striped knitted suit, with a small hole in the seat of the trousers out of which hung a long, long tail. Francis had impressed her with his knowledge of the history, art and architecture of the city, and with the sensitivity of his response to the beauty around him.

'You're wasting your life, Francis,' she said. 'Please, why don't you think again? Change jobs, or go back to college.'

He frowned. 'It's too late.'

'Nonsense, it's never too late, how could you . . .'

'I mean for college. It's too late for me to apply for re-entry for this autumn.'

'Next year, then.'

'I don't think so. I don't know, Theresa. I'm sure of nothing. Look, leave it and I'll see in the winter, when I'm home and settled, alright?'

'Alright, then.'

But before the autumn ended, he was dead.

The coda to that summer was a day spent in Lugano when they were on their way home, and by the side of the lake they saw a small boy with golden-tanned skin and a navy sailor-suit who was tossing little pebbles to break and break again the lake's still surface. He was quite unaware that he was being watched, and Theresa and Francis looked at him for a long time before Theresa spoke.

'If we had been here a hundred years ago, we might well have seen such a child.'

Francis continued to look at him and did not answer her for quite some time, then said, 'Yes. When you think of that and continue to look at him he ceases to be a particular small boy and becomes the eternal small boy. We're all like that. Everything we suffer has been suffered before, everything that gives us joy has been enjoyed before. Nothing is new: but that doesn't make it any easier to suffer.'

'And joy?'

He smiled. 'It doesn't diminish joy.'

And the summer's final image was a little Lugano fountain, the basin of which had been painted sky blue. People had dropped coins into the water for wishes and good luck, and the blue paint was marked with brown or green rings where the coins had lain and corroded. A stream of bright, fresh water spurted to the sky through a thin bronze pipe, and as it tumbled down to the painted bowl it caught and warped the sunlight. They dipped their hands in the cold water and accidentally their fingers touched. Now, when she tried to visualize the distant Heaven where Francis was, her imagination balked and she could think only: perhaps a well of light: perhaps a stream of bright water ascending to the sun, spurting upwards and away from a small, blue, painted, tainted bowl.

Night had fallen. Robert sat by his desk and stared obliquely at the window, behind which a perfect image of his room was suspended in the dark air. He arose and walked to another chair, so that he, too, was now reflected and was thus substantially within and insubstantially without. Glumly, he stared at his dark *doppelgänger*, which stared back as it floated above the street in its intangible apartment. Could this room and this person, who looked so solid and so real, actually be a mere reflection, nothing more than a trick of glass, air and light? Yes, it was just that, and he found the realization liberating. The reflection looked like him but it was not him: this is me, he thought, refined to perfection. A shadow upon glass could not feel worried or lonely. It could not have a sister or a girlfriend or a dull book to compile. Its body could not feel pain. I should write to the papers, he thought, and say political initiative be damned! The solution to the Irish crisis is for everyone to live by night, to put strong lights in their rooms and draw back the curtains and so make a whole new population identical to the one here now in all things but reality. Let these dark illusions live our lives for us: they will do it much better than we can. For how can a reflection hate? Or be bigoted? Or kill? How could it ever know the futility of suffering? He gave a little laugh which his dark double mirrored. He wished that he could stop being himself and become that double so that he could be dissolved into nothingness when the morning came.

He turned from the window and looked back into his own room. It made him feel ill. He wondered why he accumulated so assiduously this arty clutter of books and prints and rugs and trinkets; such having and hoarding struck him as rather pathetic. Often he felt genuinely queasy just to think of the vast glut of personal possessions in the world. On his way to the library in the mornings, he tried not to imagine all the things which people around him in the streets had recently used; tried to keep at bay a nightmare vision of countless tea-bags and crusts and tooth-brushes and combs and bus tickets and socks. Too much reality was hard to bear. He liked to see the private lives of girls in the morning, but one at a time, please! What fascinated him singly revolted him en masse, and the most haunting image he retained from reading about the Holocaust was that of the liberating Allied troops finding the vast mounds of clothing which had been taken from the prisoners on their arrival, including the swallow-tail coats and expensive evening dresses of some wealthy Viennese Jews arrested at a gala evening.

He had gone back to Rosie that afternoon to end a week of festering ill-feeling, although he had gone not knowing whether it was to demand an apology or to make one. In the event, neither happened. Rosie received him kindly and behaved as if nothing had happened, until he brought the subject into the open.

'Oh, let's forget it,' she said. 'It's not important, we all lose the rag now and then, what does it matter?'

She made tea for him and their subsequent conversation was overlaid by bangs and thumps from the upper storey, which he presumed, correctly, to be caused by Tom. After a time the banging stopped, they heard heavy feet on the stairs, and then the feckless beast stuck his head around the living-room door, giving a surprised grin when he saw Robert.

'What about ye, Bobby, I never knew ye were in. Nobody tells me nathin' around here.'

He had been assembling a cot for the new baby and had come down to tell Rosie that the job was complete. With characteristic bonhomie, he insisted that Robert come up to see his hand-iwork, and so they all trudged up the narrow stairs to a tiny back room, where little Tommy was waiting with the new cot.

'There,' said Tom, picking up a small, thin mattress printed all over with pandas. 'Bung in this yoke an' Bob's yer uncle.'

'Bob is my uncle,' chirruped Tommy and they all laughed, except Rosie, who only smiled and tenderly stroked the veneered chipboard. Watching their innocent delight, Robert realized that he saw before him a thing rare in modern times: familia intacta. They had problems and would have many more; in so many ways he found them pathetic, contemptible, even, but there they were, undeniably real, united and happy. He thought of the other families he knew, broken or decimated, and remembered reading somewhere that the family was the only social unit which could survive beyond the grave. Hamlet, I am thy father's spirit. Two bright Cumberland eyes had peeped from a bonnet, their owner insisting, 'Nay, Master, we are seven.' Tom and Rosie beamed shyly at each other and Robert's throat tightened. He hated himself for being moved by scenes of such maudlin sentimentality; it was worse than crying at *The Sound Of Music*. He could never see himself in the role of family man, but here, in this tiny bedroom, he now felt the lonely pangs of a monk who, on Saturday afternoons, watches at play the children of men and women who have come to the monastery for blessings, honey and fortified wines, and knows that he will never have a family of his own.

What did it matter that all Rosie's taste was in her mouth? He looked up from his chair to the print of a van Gogh self-portrait which he had acquired a short time before one of Rosie's rare visits to his flat.

'Who's that?'

'Van Gogh. It's a copy of a painting he did of himself. Do you like it?'

'He could have smiled.'

He had tried then and he tried now to imagine Vincent beaming down from his frame, jolly and avuncular, but at both attempts he failed. Now he, Robert, had at least the grace to smile.

Rising from his chair, he crossed to the window. For a moment he again looked out into the phantom room and stared deep into the eyes of his dark fetch until he could bear it no longer. Abruptly, he let the blind drop.

Theresa looked at her hand where it lay on the pillow by her face, and with the heightened perception of extreme pain noted the details of her fingers: the tiny vertical ridges along the nails, the arrangement of the lines in the skin across her knuckles; the conspicuous absence of half-moons. She was relieved that she had not risked going to the library that morning to startle the other readers by falling over her desk with a low and horrible moan. She had realized what was happening at breakfast-time and now, two hours later, the pain had arrived, intense as a knife wound. For two days she had felt like a piece of rotting fruit, and now she cried and moaned and bit the pillow and swore and cursed everything with the comprehensive rage of someone in extreme, inescapable pain. The most spectacularly obvious feature of pain was its unfairness, descending like a dark bird of prey at that arbitrary moment to her frail and mortal body, rather than to the equally frail and mortal body of someone else. Why me? Why not? She cursed the nurse who, years before, had answered her wail, 'Is there anything can cure this?', by giving her two aspirins, patting her head and saying, 'It'll be better when you're married, dear.' Every so often, she screamed aloud from utter despair that she could not escape from this weak, hateful body, from anger that this piece of agonizing rubbish was the only thing which kept her from death. She deeply resented the extent to which she *was* this body. She kept turning to look at the clock – the passage of time was her only hope. Twenty minutes, half an hour, three- quarters, and the agony had ebbed away, leaving her weak and whimpering, like a half-drowned person washed up upon a beach; by the time an hour had passed, she had already forgotten how awful it was.

It was always the same. When she was in the depths of pain, across the fragments of resentment and self-pity would flash the amazed thought: some people live like this. Some people's lives centred around intense and constant pain every single day, so that they could do nothing but suffer and be, their whole existence telescoped into the eye, womb, bowel or leg in which the pain lived, like a savage and belligerent animal. But only when in pain herself could she empathize with this, for immediately afterwards, although her mind of course remembered, her body instantly forgot. By that afternoon, she would be ashamed of the fuss which she had made over a little cramp, and although while in pain she would have done anything, literally anything, to escape, when it was over she knew that she would do nothing to prevent its inevitable recurrence. This was how some people lived, and this was how Francis had died. She felt that she needed to endure occasionally the communion of extreme agony which was beyond the power of memory, much less imagination. She held pain in a certain awe.

It was hard, however, to accept the power of the body over the mind: one cannot simultaneously read Yeats and cry into a pillow and so in defiance that afternoon, although still feeling weak and tired, she bundled herself up and went down to the library. Her presence was her only triumph for, try as she might, she could not concentrate. She sighed, fingered the pages of a review, popped a Polo mint into her mouth and stared idly at the book shelves. Looking at the spines of erudition intimated to her all the knowledge that lay before her. She knew a little about literature: how insignificant her knowledge of music and art; how non-existent her knowledge of anything scientific! $E-mc^2$ and everything was relative, but what did it *mean*? Perhaps most demoralizing of all was her ignorance of her own pitiful body, which had made her suffer so much that morning. Where, she wondered, are my kidneys? How big is an ovary? What shape is a pancreas? She tried to imagine her lungs and saw them as a bigger version of the sheep's lungs which she had once seen being fed to a dog and which had been like two red-and-white mottled sponges, but her own lungs would be lightly lacquered over with a fine ginger tar. Then she saw mortality coming, saw a surgeon peel back her skin, lift away the frail cage of her ribs to reveal her lungs, still warm and moist and mottled. They rose and fell, rose and fell, while the surgeon gently stroked the surface with a long, white sterile forefinger.

Even they don't know it all, she thought defiantly. The body still kept its secrets and always would. They had not yet fully unravelled the mysteries of the long, dark ribbons of chromosomes coiled and replicating at the heart of every cell. They had put men on the moon, but Theresa's body remained an undiscovered country.

Robert came into the library at that moment, and saw Theresa before she saw him. He thought that she looked even worse than usual. Glancing up, she saw him and thought, 'Please, don't come over.' He walked straight across to her desk.

'Hello,' he said. 'I have a message for you from Kathy. She wants you to go over to her house this evening, she wants to talk to you about something.'

'You don't know what it is?'

'No. She said go any time after five and she'll give you tea.'

Theresa was silent. She was very tired, and had foreseen an evening of coffee, toast, cigarettes, vacuous television and then sleep, sleep and more sleep. She didn't want to trudge over to Harberton Park and risk being insulted by that horrible woman again.

'She said that if you can't go you're to phone her and she'll arrange to see you tomorrow.'

'Sounds important.'

'Quite.'

Theresa sighed deeply. 'Very well then. I'll go. You've no idea . . . ?'

'No, none.'

'Oh. Well, thanks for the message, anyway.'

Theresa knocked timidly at the door, afraid that she would be again surrounded by a trio of yapping, snapping dogs, but there was silence until she heard Kathy's heels clatter across the parquet floor of the hall.

'Come in.'

Her eyes were red, and when Theresa stepped into the house the two girls saw themselves reflected, side by side, in a vast oval mirror. They both looked pale and ill.

'You're safe this time,' said Kathy, in a very stilted voice. 'I have the three dogs locked in the garage, and the bitch is out, and I know that's a terrible thing to say about your own mother, but wait till you hear what I have to tell you. Food first.'

She led the way to the kitchen, where she put the finishing touches to two plates of chicken salad, put coffee in the filter for later and cut two large slices of gâteau. They carried the food through to the dining-room on a tray, and ate sitting on fat, red velvet chairs with cabriole legs. Neither of them ate much, pushing pieces of chicken and lettuce aimlessly around their plates with large silver forks. Theresa noted that, although Kathy was obviously deeply distressed, in her own home she still fell into the role of good hostess, and had not neglected napkin rings or a posy of flowers in the centre of the table, the colours of which matched the designs on the china and the table linen. It seemed such a ridiculous façade when she was obviously so upset and eventually Theresa said, 'Look, give me that. Make the coffee, forget about the cake and tell me everything.'

'It's about my father,' said Kathy. 'You know I told you that he's dead.'

'Yes,' said Theresa.

'Well, he's not.' She was struggling to keep her voice steady. 'He's alive. He lives in London.' From her pocket she drew a crumpled envelope. 'This letter arrived this morning. He wrote to say that he didn't know how much I knew about him, but that he was sorry for all the time lost. He wants to see me. He sent me a cheque so that I can go over to London to see him. Can you imagine it, Theresa? Can you imagine it? I thought that he was dead!'

'Some people might be very happy to receive such a letter.'

'Happy? My father deserts my mother and myself when I'm a baby; she divorces him and tells me lies, tells me he's dead, and then he waits over twenty years before he cares enough to ask if I'm living or dead. That's supposed to make me happy?' said Kathy angrily.

Theresa sat quiet, trying to imagine how she would feel if the dead father of the street photograph, with his smile and cigarette, were to suddenly write to her and suggest that they meet. That the neverness of death could be so suddenly reversed . . . It was little wonder that Kathy was distressed.

'He's married again now,' said Kathy slowly. 'And he has two little girls. Their names are Cissie and Lizzie. Isn't that nice? Cissie is ten and Lizzie is twelve. I'm sure they're sweet, Theresa, just

225

think, two little girls, I have two little sisters . . . I . . . Theresa . . . I . . . I can't . . .'

She broke down and cried and cried and cried. Theresa fetched a box of paper handkerchiefs and let her cry her fill. When she was calmer and wiping her eyes with her fists, Theresa said cautiously, 'May I ask you something, Kathy?'

'What?'

'Does Robert know about this?'

Kathy gave a huge sigh. 'No.'

'Why not?'

She took a deep breath and replied very slowly.

'I wanted to tell him. That was one of my first reactions. Tell someone. Tell Robert. So I phoned him and said that I wanted to meet him for lunch and he agreed. So we met. Theresa, I could not tell him. I wanted to, I tried to, but it would not come. I sat there waiting and waiting and said to myself, now, now, tell him now, but I couldn't do it. I opened my mouth and either I said something else or closed my mouth again without having said anything. Eventually he said that he was going back to the library, so I asked him to give you a message if he saw you: to ask you to come here this evening.'

'I see.'

'My mother's away for a couple of days: that'll be a nice showdown when she comes back. I'll never forgive her for this. I'll never forgive either of them.' She paused for a moment, then said, 'But Robert . . . It worries me so much that I couldn't tell Robert, for I felt at first that it put a big gap between us, and then I saw that this gap had always been there, and that this just made me admit to it. Lately I haven't known what to make of things. Sometimes I feel in my heart – this sounds terrible, but it's the truth – sometimes I felt that he really despised me because I loved him so much. I felt that he was using me. And sometimes I even wondered if I loved him because he was there – because there was no one else, so perhaps I was using him too . . . God, Theresa, it's such a muddle, I hardly know who I am anymore, nor where to go nor what to do.'

'Sleep on it,' said Theresa. 'Wait for a few days before you decide anything. Things like this need time to settle.'

'Yes. Yes, I suppose so. Thank you for listening to all this, Theresa. You have no idea what this means. You're the only one, you know,' said Kathy, and for the first time that evening her voice was firm and steady. 'You're the only real friend I have: you're the only person that I really and truly love.'

Robert and Kathy sat in the Bonne Bouche Café, taking Earl Grey tea and little buns. Kathy looked prettier than Robert had ever before seen her, with her long, dark, silky hair piled artlessly on top of her head, little coils and tresses escaping from their fetters at the back of the neck. He could not help but wonder what went on in the mind beneath all that hair. For over a week now she had been acting oddly. She wouldn't sleep with him and when he was in any way affectionate towards her, it seemed to make her either sad or annoyed. There was something rather cold in her recent conduct and when he had asked one night what was wrong she had replied, 'Nothing', so vehemently that he had been afraid to ask again. And now here she was, saying that she was leaving Belfast within two days.

'To go where?' he asked.

'London.'

'Oh.' He paused for a moment, then she saw panic and horror in his face as he jumped to the wrong conclusion. She went very red and looked away.

'Don't be so horrible and suspicious, Robert, it's only for a holiday,' she muttered crossly.

'Really?'

'Yes, really,' she snapped.

'Oh. This is all very sudden, isn't it?'

'I suppose so, but what does that matter? I'm bored with Belfast and college'll be starting up again soon enough. I just felt I needed a break before that.'

'Are you going alone?'

'Yes. Yes, of course. With whom did you imagine I might be going?'

'How would I know who you might go off with?' he said harshly. He realized that he was glaring angrily across the room and intimidating a rather elderly waitress, so he lowered his eyes and tried to speak calmly.

'What will you do over there?'

She poured out more tea. 'Go to the theatre, go to the art galleries, go out to Kew to see the pagoda, watch the changing of the guard: the usual things one does when in London, I suppose. It's only for a week, you know.'

'I hope you enjoy it,' he said, with all the sarcasm he could muster.

'Yes, so do I,' she said lightly, then she abruptly put down her teacup. 'Do you want to talk to me about something, Robert?' she asked angrily. 'Do you want to have one of those heavy what's-gone-wrong-with-our-relationship discussions?'

'Do you?'

'No.' He glanced at her little hand, which was resting on the table-cloth: she noticed this and immediately withdrew it.

'You will wait for me, won't you, Robert?' she taunted him. 'You will be good while I'm away?'

Robert stood up, hurt and confused. 'That', he said, 'I cannot promise. Enjoy yourself without me.'

'I will,' she replied, and she had to call it across the café, for he was already at the door.


Robert had found Belfast dull and tedious even with the palliative of Kathy's company. Without it, he found his loneliness and boredom verging on the unbearable. He had many other friends and he now made an effort to see and entertain them, but he missed Kathy inordinately. He wondered and worried about her going off like that so suddenly, and he regretted deeply the row in the café. With anyone else, the bed would not have been cold before he was at least attempting to charm a replacement into it, and he was surprised to find that he now could not bring himself to do this. He missed her in every possible way, and every so often he hated himself for missing her, and told himself that she wasn't worth it.

In his flat he found a silk scarf which bore her smell, and a copy of Thomas Mann's *The Magic Mountain*, which bore her book plate. He tied the former around the bar at the foot of the bed and attempted to read the latter, remembering Kathy's enthusiasm for it, but found it impenetrable. He forced himself to plough through the novel, but retained little, save perhaps the image of the girl with the handkerchief and orange perfume, and the passage concerning X-rays as a means of seeing into the diseased, mortal, dying body of a woman, which he found both disturbing and oddly titillating. On the fourth evening after

Kathy's departure, he had just wearily cast the book aside, wondering if Kathy had been lying when she said that she enjoyed it, and uncorked a bottle of cheap wine to blur his misery when the doorbell rang. His astonishment when he opened the door and found Theresa standing there was total.

'Good evening.'

'Hello.' He stared at her blankly.

'May I come in, please? It's rather cold out on the step.'

'Of course.' He opened the door wider and she passed through into his room, a strong smell of cigarettes trailing in her wake.

'I see you're reading *The Magic Mountain*.'

'Yes.'

'Wonderful, isn't it?'

Robert made a non-committal noise as reply. 'Why have you come?' he asked bluntly.

'Social call,' she said with a sweet smile, as she removed her jacket. 'Alright?'

'Yes. Fine.' He went into the kitchen and brought out another wine glass.

'May I put on some music?'

'Yes.'

Soft clicks from the stereo were succeeded by strains of Wagner. Her strange behaviour in his own home made Robert feel uneasy. He offered her a glass of wine which she accepted but left sitting untasted in front of her for a long time, and she did not speak. Slowly the truth dawned on him: she was carefully, lucidly and extremely drunk, and just as he realized this she downed the glass of wine in a single gulp and began to speak.

'Come the revolution, Robert, what do you think will happen? Will the weak merely overthrow the powerful? The poor overthrow the rich? Or is it possible that at last the ugly will overthrow the beautiful? The uncultured overthrow the cultured? More wine. Do you ever think about that, Robert?'

'No,' he said, reluctantly refilling her glass.

'Well, you ought to, because we need to know whose side we'll be on when it happens, oppressors or oppressed. Whose side are we on now? We need to know that first.'

'I see,' he said, seeing nothing.

She was quiet for a few moments, then said, 'Wonderful music.' They listened to it for a few moments, then she added, 'He was Hitler's favourite composer, you know. The Israeli Philharmonic still refuses to perform his works.' Wagner soared on. 'Today, Robert, all art aspires to the condition of muzak. It is the noise against which real life happens.' She spoke very slowly and carefully. 'This is the century which has seen art become more debased than at any other time. Because there was a war, Robert, with concentration camps where a string quartet played Mozart while a man who liked good music had a line of people pass before him and he decided which of those people should live and which should die. Things happened in those camps, Robert, and in that war, which were so terrible that art could not cope with them, and just as all the paintings and music and books in the world were unable to prevent those things happening, afterwards the artists found that they could not produce books or paintings or music which could express that horror. But no one admitted this. The artists would not openly admit defeat. They were like priests who stop believing in God but who keep on going through the motions of religion rather than trying to face or find an alternative. And so more books and paintings and music have been produced since that time than ever before. Because people need something pretty to hang on the walls of their living-rooms. They need agreeable noises to flood their ears. They need stories to distract them from the passage of time. They need art, Robert, to clutter their minds, because if they did not have art they would be forced to look into the silence and emptiness of their own hearts. And the artists conspire with them in this. This is the art we need now, Robert.'

She got up, lifted the needle from the record and the room was at once filled with silence.

Robert put his head in his hands, unable to believe what he was hearing. He cursed his luck at being invaded by a drunken female philosopher.

'Doesn't this bother you, Robert? You're supposed to be a writer.'

The 'supposed' found its target. 'No, it doesn't bother me,' he replied grumpily. 'You're trying to say that art is, or should be, dependent upon politics, and I don't believe that. You're trying to give art a moral function.'

'That's what it had long ago.'

'Well, not any more.'

'That's what I'm trying to tell you!' she cried. She drank her wine and filled her glass again. ''Truth is beauty, beauty truth.'' You still believe that, Robert?' He did not reply. 'What does art do?'

He would not reply.

'What does art do?' she yelled.

He shrugged, not wanting to get embroiled in this pointless row. 'It makes you more alive,' he said eventually.

'You try telling that, Robert,' she said, 'to all the people in this world who are suffering and dying.'

As she spoke, he remembered the moment of his mother's burial, when he had suddenly felt that he was the person in the coffin who was being lowered out of life. He was conscious of familiar faces growing smaller around a rectangle of light: then silence and darkness. An overwhelming sense of the absolute futility of his life and labours swept over him and he heard Rosie say in a small, sad voice, 'It makes ye wonder what it's all about.'

'Christ Almighty, Theresa!' he exploded. 'Leave me be!' He gazed at her with revulsion as she cowered in a huge, white, wicker chair: sullen, skinny, pale, cross-eyed, drunk, grotesque. It was a very long time before she spoke again.

'Why don't you write about the troubles here, Robert?'

'I don't want to.'

'Why not?'

'They don't interest me. I don't understand them.'

'God curse your indifference. What does understanding matter? Nobody understands. Some people say that they can see both sides, but they can't. You can only ever see one side, the side you happen to be on. But you haven't the guts for that, Robert: you haven't the guts to be partial, ye spineless liberal.'

'Don't you think it's time you were going?' he said coldly, picking up her jacket.

'No.'

'It's very late.'

'I haven't said all I came to say.'

He tossed her jacket onto a chair. 'Say it, then, and go.'

'Kathy has gone to London to see her father and sisters.' She saw his face change. 'I thought that might interest you.'

231

'Her father's dead.'

'So you think. And so she thought. But he's not. He's alive and well and living in London. And he's married, with two little daughters. Sisters for Kathy. So you see, Robert, you've lost her.'

'What do you mean? She's coming back.'

'But not the same as she was when she went away. She's found her family, Robert. You know she won't be the same again.'

And Robert understood perfectly.

Theresa began to cry. Had this happened only moments before, he would have sworn at her and possibly put her out into the street. Now he was so preoccupied that he scarcely noticed it, and they sat there for some time, she weeping pathetically, he silently thinking while all the anger and resentment and misery drained away, leaving him peaceful and calm.

Eventually, he glanced at the clock. It was well after midnight. Theresa was still whingeing at the far side of the room, and looked even more grotesque than she had done earlier. He did not know precisely where she lived, and doubted if she knew, either, by this stage. In any case, he decided, he couldn't send her home in such a state, he would have to keep her here. He went over to her side and said, 'Come on, Theresa, enough's enough. Time for bed.'

He tried to overcome his revulsion: it was like steeling one's nerves to pick up a toad. He moved to touch her sleeve, but she shrank back into the chair. 'Come on,' he said firmly, and grasped her by the hand. It was clammy and cold. Against her will, he pulled her up out of the chair and dragged her towards the bedroom door, but she began to wriggle and scream until at last he had to manhandle her into the room. As soon as he released his hold she fell to the floor. He pulled the door closed, dashed back to the living-room and gulped down the little that was left of the wine. He hoped she would stay where she was, because he knew that he would not be able to bring himself to touch her again. He marvelled that he had been able to do it at all.

Robert spent the night coiled up uncomfortably on the sofa. For a long time, he could hear Theresa crying in the bedroom with all the venom of an angry baby. Just as he was on the point of dropping off to sleep he thought how desperately confused and distressed she must be: when he put his arm around her waist to heave her into the bedroom, she hadn't even known who he was. Three times she had called him, 'Francis'.

The following morning, he discreetly pretended to be sleeping when he heard the click of the bedroom door. He felt her sweep quickly through the room and he heard the sound of the front door closing. He arose, tidied the flat and spent the rest of the day wondering if it could all have been a strange dream. That night, however, he had sensuous confirmation of its reality, for when he went to bed he found that the pillow and sheets reeked of cigarettes.

'I can't understand how you could do this to me, Theresa, I simply can't understand.'
    'I'm sorry.'
    'Sorry's not good enough. After what happened to Francis, if you had thought at all you'd have known that I'd be distracted.'
    'Look, I said I'm sorry,' Theresa snapped. 'I can do no more. What do you want, blood?' She had never known it was possible to feel so ill.
    'You still haven't said where you were, Theresa,' her mother persisted, and Theresa exploded in anger.
    'Leave me alone! I'm a grown woman. I'll do as I please and answer to nobody.' A wave of nausea succeeded her rage. She ran from the room and spent the rest of the day in bed, feeling angry, guilty, confused, worried and very, very sick.

The following Friday evening, at around 7.00 p.m., Robert's telephone rang.
    'Bobby?' said an exited voice.
    'Yes, Tom?'
    'It's Rosie. She's away in to have it.' He was phoning from the Royal Victoria Hospital and said that they had left Tommy with a neighbour. This was part of a pre-arranged plan by which Robert was to collect and mind Tommy until such time as Tom returned and so, resigning himself to a long night, he gathered together a book, half a bottle of whiskey, a few chocolates with which to bribe his little nephew, and left.

Tommy was tired but excited and Robert had some difficulty in washing, undressing and coaxing him into bed. He had never babysat before, and was indeed so little used to the company of children that he found it distinctly unnerving. It was a great relief when Tommy was at last tucked between the sheets. Even with the child out of sight, however, Robert still felt ill at ease in the tasteless house which had once been his home, and out of the corner of his eye he looked at the things around him: a few scattered, shabby toys; Tom's ashtray, full to overflowing; a crumpled copy of the previous day's *Irish News*, with the form marked in red ink; and an expanding wooden clothes-horse, draped with tiny, damp vests. In the kitchen, his sister's apron hung from a nail, pink, limp and sinister. He always hated being in people's homes and rooms in their absence: it seemed an intrusion. He could never defeat the feeling that the people concerned were really dead and that their dross of belongings was all that remained to make vague, painful, pathetic final statements about them. Sometimes deserted rooms could seem even more artificial, like theatre sets at the end of a play's long run, waiting empty and idle for the stagehands to come and dismantle them.

Every small object in the house seemed a talisman capable of evoking lost souls, and he thought back to the time just after his mother's death when Rosie was attempting to sort through her belongings. Robert had come across his sister sitting on a sheepskin rug in their mother's bedroom, sobbing into an old, torn sweater, which he gently removed from her hands. He sent her down to the kitchen and himself started to sort through the contents of the dressing-table, but it made him unspeakably sad. He felt it was a great affront to her memory as he bundled together the shabby clothes, worn shoes and dingy underwear. He remembered the day she had found the contraceptives in his room and felt very conscious both of being 'her son', and of falling far short of what she had thought her son ought to be. He wished that among her effects he might come across something surprising, but he found only things which he might well have expected: broken Rosary beads, a few photographs and old birthday cards, a box of cheap, ginger-coloured face-powder, and a Relic of St Martin de Porres, which was attached to a large safety-pin. He remembered thinking when he had finished –

There: her little soul laid bare before me and I still do not know, I still do not understand.

He watched the late film until the television whined into closedown, and when he unplugged the set he could hear the sound of heavy rain pattering on the pavement. Tommy called for a glass of water, which Robert brought to him. The snout of a grubby Womble protruded over the top of the eiderdown.

'Mammy'll be alright, won't she, Uncle Bobby?'

'Of course,' said Robert, thinking of everything that could possibly go wrong, and imagining his sister screaming in pain as she bled to death. 'Your mammy'll be grand, and then you'll have a new baby sister or brother.'

Tommy handed the empty glass back to Robert with a look so full of disbelief and cynicism that his uncle had to restrain himself from saying, 'What the hell can you know about childbirth, anyway? You're only five, for God's sake!' Once Robert had told Tommy that there was a fox with big yellow eyes under the bookcase in his flat and Tommy had believed him; and yet when he was told in Bangor to look at the white horses out in the sea he had cried in disappointment because he could see only waves. Robert did not understand children. He went down to the living-room and poured himself a very large whiskey.

He read his book and dozed until 3.30 a.m., when he heard a key being turned in the lock of the front door. Tom had returned.

'It's a wee girl, Bobby,' he said, 'an' the both of them's grand. Two of everything down the side an' one of everything down the middle. That's the way it ought to be, isnit? Whiskey! Good man yerself, Bobby!' They filled two tumblers and sat down by the embers of the dying fire. As Tom drank, his buoyancy gradually subsided. He spoke little, and Robert thought that he appeared rather shaken.

'I seen it all, Bobby,' he said eventually. 'I mean, I knew what it was goin' to be like, an the doctors said there was no problem, but I mean . . . it was rough, Bobby. I mean, it makes ye think.' He paused and sipped at his drink. 'Yer own wife, Bobby . . . an' then . . . then ye think . . . yer own Ma . . .' He paused again and then gave a nervous and violent sob which startled Bobby, and cried, 'I mean, Christ, Bobby, it was fuckin' desprit!' After that there was silence for a long time.

It brought Robert back again to the time of his mother's death, when Rosie's grief had manifested itself primarily as anger. She complained bitterly about every little detail; about the times of the removal of the remains and of the funeral mass; about the body being laid out in the bedroom instead of in the front parlour; about the undertaker's failure to provide a black crepe bow for the front door. Her anger had lingered on afterwards, until the day they attempted to find accurate wording and a suitable verse for the In Memoriam cards. In this matter Tom and Rosie looked to Robert for guidance, but their tastes conflicted. Robert liked things literary which his sister found incomprehensible or pagan, or both; so he tried instead for something biblical which would be both religious and nicely phrased, but 'The Lord has given and the Lord has taken away; Blessed be the name of the Lord' was coldly met by Rosie, who said, 'Really, Robert, we're not Presbyterians.' For well over an hour they struggled hopelessly to find the words they needed until Rosie at last turned violently on Robert and shouted, 'And you're fucking well supposed to be a writer!' All three of them were stunned by this outburst, particularly Rosie. They drifted away from the table without looking at each other. The following day she had handed Robert a torn piece of newspaper and mumbled, 'What about this?' Robert read it.

> Your gentle face and patient smile
> With sadness we recall,
> You had a kindly word for each,
> And died beloved by all.
> We miss you now, our hearts are sore,
> As time goes by we miss you more.
> Your loving smile, your gentle face,
> No one can fill your vacant place.

He handed the paper back to her and said with a little smile, 'That'll do fine.' She also smiled, understanding that she was forgiven and grateful for that forgiveness: but she did not, and never would, apologize to him, mainly because she had a pathological aversion to apologies, but also because she did not fully realize what she had done. She would never know that her words had cut him to the heart.

Tom gradually became more cheerful and soon Robert had difficulty in restraining him from going up to wake Tommy and tell him that he had a new baby sister. Before going to bed, he thanked Robert for babysitting. 'It's true enough, Bobby, family's what counts at the end of the day.'

'Yes,' said Robert drily. He tried to really feel this dryness, but he felt instead genuinely sad. Often he wished that he could cut the stick completely with his family, because they had nothing in common, and yet he knew that he would never do it: he valued them too much. The family was like a living souvenir of an age lost and gone. They reminded him of an antique newspaper which shows how much has changed by simple virtue of its price, print, paper, smell, quaintness and the innocence of its news. For he felt that Rosie and Tom were innocents in the way that people were innocents by chronology, with every generation more world-weary than the one before because of the fresh horrors which they have seen. There was something atavistic in Rosie's and Tom's significance to him, and with great reluctance he had to admit that he needed them in his life.

He settled down to another uncomfortable night upon a sofa, and eventually fell asleep thinking about Kathy.

When he arose the following morning, he found father and son already in the kitchen, dishevelled and delighted, taking tea, bap and Weetabix, chattering excitedly about the new baby, spilling things and laughing. Robert filled a mug with tea and wearily watched them. Within a week, Rosie would be home again, bringing with her a new person: not merely new to them, but utterly new. Robert found this a sobering thought. Every day people died and babies were born, but these events only appeared to have cosmic significance when one knew the people involved. Eventually he slipped out to the hall telephone and dialled a Belfast number. He waited for a few moments, then to his joy heard the desired and familiar voice.

'Kathy?'

'Yes?'

'It's me, Robert.'

'Oh, hello.'

'When did you get back?'

'Yesterday.'

'Oh. How did you get on in London?'

'Fine. I had a nice time.'

'That's good. Listen, Kathy, when can I see you?'

'Well I'm not really sure now,' she demurred.

'Tonight, Kathy. Please.' He glanced towards the kitchen door, pressed the receiver closer to his ear and pleaded quietly.

'Please, Kathy. I have to see you. Come to my flat this evening.'

'I don't know, Robert . . . I'm not sure . . . Look, leave it with me and I'll see what I can do.'

'Great,' he said. 'Listen, Kathy, I . . .' But she had hung up.

He paused for a moment, then consulted the telephone directory and dialled another Belfast number. Another familiar voice answered.

'Good morning, Theresa,' he said smoothly. 'Robert here.' There was a long silence. 'Theresa?'

'Yes?'

'I just thought you might like to know that my sister had her baby last night. A girl.'

'Oh, that's good. I take it they're both well?'

'Yes. She's in the Royal, if you want to see her.'

'I might just do that. Thanks.' There was another silence, which he waited vainly for her to fill, and at last he said insinuatingly, 'Kathy's back from London.'

'Yes, I know.'

This piqued him and he again waited in silence, but she evidently shared Rosie's aversion to apologies. He wondered if she remembered coming to his flat, then decided that she was bound to. He considered saying to her bluntly, 'Did you get home alright the other morning?' but glanced again at the kitchen door and thought better of it. 'Well, that's the score, anyway,' he said lamely.

'Right. Well, thanks for phoning. Goodbye.' She hung up.

Under his breath Robert comprehensively cursed all women, replaced the receiver and returned to the kitchen.

In Boots' baby department, Theresa dithered over bears, rugs, pandas, shawls and tiny hats. The longer she looked, the less able she was to decide, and if an elderly woman had not eventually pointed to the Baby-Gros and said, 'Great yokes, thon', wish we'd had them when mine were wee,' she might never have clinched it, might have wandered off in despair and bought chocolates.

It was four days after Robert's telephone call that Theresa at last mustered the courage and energy to go visit Rosie in hospital. It was to the Royal that Francis's body had been brought for identification and she had not been back to it since that time. She feared hospitals with a primitive and childish fear. This was where strange people 'did' things to you. This was where people's bodies, vulnerable at the best of times, were at their weakest and most pitiful. Everything possible was done in hospitals to maintain life, and still people died.

On reaching the ward, she peeped timidly around the door, afraid that Robert would be there. It was a relief to see Rosie's familiar face amidst the anonymous iron bedsteads, the flowers, cards, Lucozade and grapes; and she was pleased to note that there was no one with her. Rosie was delighted to see Theresa, and proudly handed the baby to her. It fitted snugly in her embrace, and suddenly Theresa felt that she had been waiting unconsciously all that summer, all her life, for that moment when she would take the baby in her arms and feel the perfection of its weight, shape and warmth; as if the baby had been created uniquely for that moment and for her arms.

'Robert thinks it's a dote,' said Rosie, 'but he's not the sort as would say.' Theresa did not answer. The baby wrinkled its face, pressed its tongue between its gum and lower lip and yawned lazily. Its eyes were deep, dark and unseeing, and Theresa thought: the worst fate this child might have would not be to end up like Francis, but to end up like me. Rosie and her baby made love look simple and normal. Theresa wished that it were so and then thought: Perhaps it is. Perhaps it is for everyone except me. What if my body were at this moment drained of all blood and pigment, until I became transparent as glass? Then they would see through to my cold, black, hidden heart, and I would be banished at once from this warm and tender room. Feeling unworthy, she sadly handed the baby back to its mother.

Rosie prattled on happily about Tom and Tommy and the baby while Theresa struggled to keep smiling. She had not thought that the visit would be so deeply traumatic, and she left as soon as she decently could. On crossing the hallway, she saw Robert enter the building and was obliged to dart behind a pillar to avoid him. She could not believe that she had had such a narrow escape. Rosie and a baby had been difficult. Rosie and Robert and a baby would have been impossible.

As he walked across the hallway, unconscious that he was being watched, Robert thought how glad he would be when Rosie at last went home, for then he would no longer have to visit the hospital. His mother had died there, and returning to this place had brought that time back to him in a way which he would never have believed possible. The freshness of his memories shocked him. He had forgotten so much, both of the events and the emotions: now he was forced to live through them all again.

Their mother had remained conscious for less than a day after her admission, then slipped into a deep coma which had lasted for three more days. Days? They had exploded time; he and Rosie had neither ate nor slept while day seeped into night seeped into day; unending, nightmarish; until all terms to express time became meaningless. He thought that he could remember a life which had been lived out somewhere else, in houses, libraries, pubs and bookshops, and began to wonder if it was a dream or a hallucination, for he felt that he had been and would be in that cramped and overheated room for all eternity. He could not believe that there was a world other than this: Rosie, red-eyed, holding her mother's hand to ensure that the small crucifix which she had tucked into the dying woman's slack fist remained there; and a respirator wheezing and clicking in the corner, as if it were the one dying, rather than the still, frail woman upon the sterile bed. She had been connected up to a heart monitor and they had blankly watched the brilliant green line of light wiggle across the black screen, while little numbers clicked in the corner, high and steady, until a few hours before the end. He had felt at one stage a wave of unexpected anger well up in him, and thought, 'If she can't live, why doesn't she die and have done with it?' He wanted to, and was afraid that he would, move quickly forward and pull all the wires and tubes from her body, rip all the machines from their sockets and so get all three of them out of this horror, push the entire family over the brink into grief and release. It was the first time he had experienced coming to the absolute limits of his endurance, only to find that he had to drag himself on past those limits. He had never known that it was possible to suffer so much and still be alive.

The numbers on the screen had dropped swiftly towards the end. When they clicked to double-zero and the green line became straight, Robert and Rosie turned quickly to each other, and each saw in the other's eyes disbelief and shock.

He walked through the door of the maternity ward. Rosie looked up from the baby and smiled at him.

'Guess who you've just missed?' she said.

Kathy did not keep her appointment with Robert, broke another engagement three days later, and it was almost a week after her return when she at last deigned to go to his flat. The meeting was a disaster from the moment he opened the door and said, 'Welcome back. How was the family reunion?'

'Who told you about that?' she said angrily.

'Theresa,' he replied. 'I didn't know that it was supposed to be a secret. I can't see why it should be.'

'And when were you talking to Theresa?'

Robert began to relate the whole story of her visit and the more he talked the more he wished that he had kept silent. Kathy glowered angrily throughout, although he tried to tell his tale lightly, making it a thing insignificant and amusing. Kathy did not laugh. When he had finished she said, 'This is all news to me. I've seen Theresa three times since I got back and she didn't say anything about it.'

'Do you wonder?' he exclaimed with a giggle of desperate mirth. 'It doesn't show her in a very good light.'

'It's not much to your credit, either.'

'I don't know what you can mean,' he said stiffly. 'She came of her own accord and half-plastered. I didn't want her; I thought she was a right pest. She was lucky I didn't throw her out on her ear five minutes after she arrived.'

'Such kindness and charity,' Kathy sneered defensively.

London had confused her. At first she had felt a union with her father and his family, and had delighted in their casual lives. The elder of the two girls strongly resembled Kathy and had many of her mannerisms; her father's second wife, Sophie, was young and friendly. But, as the days went on, a feeling of alienation crept over her. All the little things which distanced her from the family gradually became more obvious. She became increasingly conscious of the children's English accents, so different to her own; and of the fact that they were only half-sisters. One day, as a joke, Kathy referred to Sophie as her stepmother, and both of them immediately realized that it was the truth. From that moment on, they were never completely comfortable in each other's company. Gradually, she admitted to herself that she was not one of the family: it was her father's family, but it was not hers.

The night before she was due to come home, she lay awake in bed thinking of all the little failures and inadequacies of the trip; of all the moments when a word or a look had proved to her (although without malice) that she was only a visitor, and she had been seized with a sudden craving for a family life, a life of her own. She knew all the difficulties and drawbacks, but still she wanted it. Now she was glad that she had not told cynical old Robert why she was going to London. He would have laughed, she thought, if she told him this. He set little store by his own family; he would never understand. As soon as she arrived in Belfast, she missed her father and the family so much that she could hardly bear it. She could not talk about her loneliness, and so translated it into anger. Robert and Theresa had unwittingly given her a convenient target for this anger.

Robert watched her, and knew that Theresa had been right. Kathy had changed; and he worried about the consequences.

September arrived, damp and cold, and Theresa thought with dread of the coming winter. It would bring Francis's second anniversary, the horrors of Christmas, with all its maudlin sentimentality and aggressive bonhomie, followed by the New Year, which she always found unspeakably sad. She did not understand how people could celebrate the passage of time. January: the dead of winter. She would have to drag herself somehow through the dark, dreary months of the young year, until spring came, with Easter, green shoots and the first shred of hope. She seriously wondered if this time she would have the stamina to make it through to March, for it seemed a lifetime away.

Feeling wilful and trapped, Theresa knelt in church before the crucifix, remembering how, when it was veiled in Lent, it had looked like a kite of purple silk. Once, during the unveiling on Good Friday, the priest had dropped one of the elastic bands which held the silk in place, and she had seen it lying on the carpet as she knelt at the altar rails, a long, fine, gum-coloured lemiscate. The stuff of religious symbols was so paltry and mundane: paper and stone and metal and wood and wax; but perhaps this purple veil upon a cross was the best symbol possible. Silk stretched over wood; a symbol concealing a symbol. Things of importance and truth were always layered and hidden. When Francis died, they had placed him in a coffin with a small chrome crucifix fixed to the lid; and she remembered looking at it and knowing that she would never again be afraid to die. In Russia, his coffin would have been carried open to the graveside, but they had not been permitted to see his poor dead face and cold forehead. She remembered tenderly stroking the wood of the coffin and trying to visualize his dear, broken body within. She imagined his features sharpened in death, sharper, sharper to corruption, and then she knew why medieval knights and lords had had statues carved or wrought to represent their own bodies, and placed upon their tombs. These people of marble and brass were first an image of the body which lay beneath, but soon became a dishonest distraction, attempting to belie the hidden bones and dust. Whited sepulchres. Futility. His coffin had been carried for a short distance and then placed in the hearse. Theresa and her mother had found themselves looking at their own reflections, ghostly and bloodless as photographic negatives, cast upon the glass behind which lay the solid coffin and a few bright wreaths of flowers.

She wondered why she worried the memory of his death again and again, like a dog with a bone, for she felt that the death itself was not at the heart of her distress. When she watched his burial, it was as if the gravediggers were tucking him up for the rest of time with a thick brown blanket, living and warm and moist. She knew that in springtime his grave would be greened over with grasses and weeds, and she believed that her brother was now perfected. Too late she wished that she had jumped in with him, so that the gravediggers could cover up the living and dead together: she longed for the soft, damp soil to muffle her ears and gag her mouth, to seal her eyes up in union and death.

Months later, she had scribbled on a scrap of paper, 'I loved him too much,' then tossed it into the fire and watched it burn.

'Do you reject Satan?'
  'I do.'
'And all his works?'
  'I do.'
'And all his empty promises?'
  'I do.'
'Do you believe in God, the Father almighty, creator of heaven and earth?'
  'I do.'

Robert listened as the sacramental words dropped into the still, cold air of the church. It gave him a curious sensation, as if he were attending not a baptism in west Belfast, but a primitive and mysterious religious ceremony in a gloomy, subterranean temple, far distant in both time and space from the reality he knew. That reality was a late Sunday afternoon in September, and already the darkness was pressing lightly against the windows, draining away all colour and so making it difficult to distinguish the saints and symbols depicted in the stained glass. At the top of the church there was a rectangular candelabra, where numerous little discs of white wax were ranged in tiers, their flames waving, guttering and making the air all around them glow, while down at the back, where the font stood, there was little light save from a single candle which Tom's brother was holding in his capacity as godfather. Its flame cast ghastly and sinister shadows upon the faces of those gathered around, and as the bright baptismal water sparkled across the baby's forehead it caught the light of the candle. The child did not cry, but Robert could see its little feet working frantically beneath the shawl.

Theresa was kneeling almost directly opposite Robert, her eyes closed and her head bowed in prayer. With a jolt, he thought: 'She really believes in this. They all do.' They believed that mere water and words and all this theatrical mumbo-jumbo had the power to free the baby from the grip of evil. They believed that this ceremony was absolutely vital for the well-being of the child. They spoke of the devil as if he were lurking behind a nearby pillar. Robert tried to imagine the Devil, and saw him as tall, thin and blood-red, with thick, black hair and cold, dark eyes. He saw the Devil toy thoughtfully with the barb at the end of his long, slimy tail and take particular care to stand very still, lest his cloven hooves be heard to rattle upon the stone floor of the church. Robert felt a nervous giggle rise in his throat, and he bowed his head.

But what if it all were true? God and the Devil. Sin and death. Heaven and Hell. What if this water and light really meant something? What if there were four last things to be remembered instead of just one? He raised his eyes and looked at the little group before him. Try as he might, he found it impossible to understand, or imagine, or empathize with, their belief, and because of this inability he thought that belief must make a huge difference to the way one saw life – saw everything. It was little wonder that he had had such difficulty with his mother, or that he could not understand Rosie or Theresa. Even Kathy would admit, under pressure, that she believed in God. Robert's closest approach to faith in the last ten years had been when he looked at his mother's dead body and found that he could not believe that what he saw was in any significant way the person he had known. More importantly, he could not believe that she was nowhere, that she was simply gone, annihilated. He felt that she must be somewhere, but he could not begin to imagine where; could never have dared to define or name the state or place where his mother now was. Suddenly he understood the drift of his thoughts, and his mind balked in horror. It implied too much for him, and filled him with dread. She is dead, he told himself, dead, dead, dead.

Now, in church, he remembered that moment, and felt pity for believers. The priest talked about evil, and Robert felt afraid. He wished that he had not come. The wax of the candle steadily dripped.

They all went back to Rosie's and Tom's house after the christening, as Rosie had prepared a small buffet, the centrepiece of which was a large fruit cake coated in royal icing and garnished with a pink plastic stork. Robert ensured that Theresa was well supplied with tea, ham sandwiches and sausage rolls, then edged her into a corner and was surprised to find himself bluntly asking, 'Theresa, do you really believe in all that mumbo-jumbo?'

'The christening? Why, yes, of course I do. I wouldn't have been there otherwise.'

'But don't you find it . . . medieval? I mean, it's so . . . so creepy.'

'In what way?' she asked, nibbling on a sandwich.

'Well, for example, what has a little baby got to do with sin and evil and the Devil?'

'Rather a lot, I should think, seeing that said baby has been doomed by birth to life in Belfast,' she said drily. 'Don't try to tell me that there's no evil in this city just because you can't see a Devil with cloven hooves wandering around.'

'Is that what the Devil looks like, then?'

'How should I know? He probably looks like lots of things. He might look a bit like you, who can say?' She smirked and wiped some crumbs from the corner of her mouth. He ignored the insult and persisted with his interrogation.

'But why are you a Christian, Theresa?'

She shrugged and said, 'Because it's a good religion for me.'

'But why?'

She gave a deep sigh and replied in a soft voice, 'Because it's the religion for victims and failures. It's for people who are diseased and depraved. It's for people who are subversive; who can detect and denounce evil even when it looks comfortable and respectable, and particularly when it's in their own hearts and minds. People who can see below the surface of things, and who have difficulty in accepting their own existence. But I'm not answering your question, am I?'

'Aren't you?'

'No. There's only one valid reason for believing in Christianity.'

'And what's that?'

'Because it's the truth. I mean, you can't be a Christian just because you find it an attractive notion, or because it seems comfortable – you soon find out that it's not that, anyway. Nor can you do it for the sake of beauty, because it has too much to do with the ugly, broken side of life. You do it because you have to. If you know that Christianity is the truth, then you have no choice but to be a Christian.'

Robert listened and was lost. He felt as if there were a thick wall of glass between himself and Theresa, for in no way could he relate to what she was saying. It was like hearing someone defending the flat-earth theory, or soberly claiming that they had once caught a unicorn.

'What's the point of it all, then?' he asked. 'Does it make you happy?'

'No. Maybe it's not supposed to. Maybe I'm not a very good Christian. In any case, you do it for God, not for what's in it for yourself. But it does do one thing: it allows you to live with your own conscience. It means that you're at least trying to live with integrity; you know that you're struggling in the right direction . . .' She fell silent and looked away, for she could not find words to express the tensions which lay between faith and the 'however' side of life. Robert could not know what it was like to glimpse perfection and know that that was the state to which one had to aspire, only to see it suddenly offset by the immense imperfection of one's self. She could not explain how weary it made her to know that she would never be good enough.

'I want to go home.'

She said goodbye to Rosie and Tom and thanked them for their hospitality. Robert insisted on walking at least part of the way home with her, and together they set off up the Falls Road. It was twilight. His mother had fallen ill on just such an evening. They had followed the ambulance down to the hospital by car, and on the way he had seen three young girls in pale summer dresses run lightly along the pavement. They had seemed like wraiths in the dusk, and he remembered thinking, 'They are not real and so none of this can be reality. This is a dream from which I will soon awaken.'

Theresa remained silent as they walked. Both were conscious that some reference ought to be made to Kathy, but neither of them could bring themselves to do it. Robert glanced at Theresa and thought it weird that someone could be so near to him and yet so distant in mind and heart. Eventually she said, 'This is where I live. Goodnight.' He watched while she crossed the road to a high, red-brick terrace, and watched until the home at the end of the row had swallowed her up in blackness.

Robert sat at his desk in the library, browsing through a large leather-bound volume of newspapers. Although they were less than two years old, they smelt musty and sour. He turned the yellowed pages with great care to avoid tearing them.

Kathy had arrived at his flat the preceding evening, bringing with her all the books which she borrowed from him in the course of the summer, and had never before troubled to return. He found this ominous. He made coffee while she sat down in the wicker chair where Theresa had sat during her unexpected visit, and when Robert came in from the kitchen with the tray he was annoyed to see her choice of seat, for it was ostentatiously distant from the corner where he habitually sat. He poured out the coffee and put a record on the stereo. She asked politely about his book and he said that it was almost completed. Kathy took a small notebook from her handbag and scribbled something down, then tore out the page and handed it to Robert. 'That's a play to which you ought to refer. It was first produced in Belfast. You should check it out. Get the reviews from the local papers; they'll have them in the library. I think you'll find it interesting.' Robert looked at the page. He had never heard of either the play or the author before. Kathy had also conveniently added the date of production. 'Thank you,' he said.

Their subsequent conversation was sparse, for they had nothing left to say to each other. Robert wondered why it always had to end like this, with a steady drifting to indifference and silence. As night fell, he could see the ghostly room begin to crystallize behind the dark glass, and the clearer it became the more it unsettled him. At last he went over to the window and lowered the blinds. As he passed behind Kathy's chair on the way back, he stopped and tentatively stroked the back of her neck. She swore and jerked her head aside as if she had been stung. 'I beg your pardon,' he said very coldly. Hurt and angry, he crossed to the stereo.

'I think we ought to have a change of music, don't you? What about this one, it's perfect, it's called, "I Used To Love Her But It's All Over Now".'

Kathy stood up. 'Very amusing, Robert,' she said. 'But not quite accurate. You never loved me. But you're right about its being over.' She picked up her coat and left the room. Robert did not follow and from where he stood he could hear the front door close behind her.

As he thumbed through the faded newspapers the following day, he felt sad. He doubted that the reviews would be significant, or even relevant, but he felt that he had to find them as a final and token gesture to Kathy. At last he came to the issue for the given date, and began to scan the columns carefully. The first two pages revealed nothing, and when he turned over the third frail page he saw a large grainy photograph of Theresa. Startled, he read the caption. 'Miss Theresa Cassidy at the funeral yesterday of her twin brother, Francis.' He quickly read the accompanying report, which dealt mainly with the funeral, but revealed to Robert that Francis had been murdered. He then rapidly turned back to the issues for the days immediately preceeding. The report of three days before said that the badly mutilated body of a young man had been found on a patch of waste ground near the city centre. By the following day he had been identified and his name released: Francis Cassidy, 21, a Roman Catholic who had no connections with the security forces or with any paramilitary organization. He had been abducted on his way to work in a supermarket near the city centre. The murder was described as 'particularly brutal' and the motive appeared to be purely sectarian. There was a small photograph of the dead man, who looked so like Theresa that Robert shivered.

The discovery stunned and confused him, and he did not know what to think. Foolishly, he tried to remember what he had been doing around that date two years ago, as if that knowledge could help him to understand or control in some way this dreadful new reality. He could not recall the murder from papers or news reports which he might have heard or read at that time. It had been a particularly brutal and cruel killing, but it was still only one out of so many hundreds of brutal and cruel killings. He looked up at the people around him in the library, reading and writing and browsing and whispering. It shocked him to think of the evils and sorrows which might be in their minds and hearts: no one could see or guess the things which they might have done or endured. He looked down again at the photograph of Francis, and was suddenly conscious of someone standing close behind him. He quickly raised his head, and saw to his horror that it was Theresa, who at that very moment glanced down casually over his shoulder at the book laid open before him. She saw Francis's photograph and her face changed immediately, becoming pale and impassive as a mask. Without saying a word, she turned and walked away. Robert watched her go, and could have wept with embarrassment. He did not know what to do. He could not bring himself to go after her, and in any case he was not sure if that was what the situation required.

Attempting to avert his eyes from the photograph, he closed the heavy volume and returned it to the issue desk, but waited for a long time before leaving the library.

Three times that afternoon, Robert tried to phone Theresa, but each time there was no reply. By late evening he had decided that meeting her again would be so awkward and embarrassing that he wanted to do it as soon as possible and get it over. He therefore drove over to west Belfast and parked outside the house which he had seen her enter on the day of the christening. A light glowed in the bay window. Timidly, he knocked upon the door, and as soon as Theresa opened it felt that he had compounded his error by coming to her home. He wished that he could garble out upon the doorstep all he had to say and then run, but had the wit to know that to attempt this would be the final and greatest insult.

'Oh,' said Theresa when she saw him. She had a few pound notes in her left hand. 'I thought you were the paper boy.'

'May I come in?'

'Of course,' she said, but seemed annoyed, and he did not know if this was because she did not really want him to enter; or because she had intended to usher him in anyway, and the request to be admitted was thus an insult to her hospitality. Feeling wretched, he followed her into a dim hallway, and on through into a small parlour.

'I hope I'm not intruding,' he mumbled.

'Not at all,' said Theresa, indicating a chair by the fireside. 'You owe me a visit.' He sat down and felt slightly more at ease than he had done on the doorstep. Theresa remained standing. On the wall behind her was a round mirror surrounded by a garland of leaves wrought from black metal. Robert gazed thankfully past Theresa's head into the glass, where he could see the whole room reflected, circular and small, distorted at the circumference because of the mirror's convexity. It reminded him of a painting – what was it called? – *The Arnolfini Marriage*, was that it? Robert could see himself in the mirror as if he were the artist who had created all before him, both the room and the room reflected. He remembered from the painting trivial domestic details – a little dog; some oranges; a pair of slippers carelessly tossed aside – and as he thought this he noticed that Theresa was wearing the most absurd bedroom slippers he had ever seen: a pair of mules which engulfed her feet in two clouds of candy-pink imitation fur. Had he not seen them for himself, he would never have believed her guilty of possessing such things.

'When you've finished gazing into the middle distance,' she suddenly drawled, 'you might speak to me.'

'I'm sorry,' he blurted out, and wished that he could escape into the circular reflected room, or that he really were a figure in a painting, with the crabbed inscription 'Johannes de Eyck fuit hic' upon the flock wallpaper, to prove the artifice. 'I'm sorry about what happened this morning.'

'Next time you're checking someone out like that, Robert, remember to sit facing the door.'

'But I wasn't checking you out. Honestly, Theresa, I came upon that report when I was looking for something else. It was pure coincidence . . .'

She raised an eyebrow cynically, knelt down by the fire and lit a cigarette from a small ember which she plucked from the grate with the tongs. 'Funny coincidence,' she said, sitting back on her heels.

'I tell you, it's the truth. I was looking for a play review, look, I can even tell you the name of it.' He took from his pocket the crumpled page which Kathy had given to him, and passed it to Theresa. She glanced at it indifferently, then looked again more closely.

'But this is Kathy's handwriting.'

'Yes,' he said, 'Kathy gave me the reference to check. She said that it was important.'

Theresa looked back at the page, then suddenly to Robert's amazement her eyes filled up with tears and she said bitterly, 'She may have found her father, but she's still her mother's daughter.'

'Theresa,' said Robert wearily, 'I give up. I know that I probably ought to understand all this, but it's beyond me.'

'For someone who's supposed to be educated, Robert, you can

be very dense. But tell me this: did someone as *au fait* with the theatre in Belfast as yourself not find it strange that a significant play was produced here less than two years ago and yet you had never heard of either author or play? And when you couldn't find the reviews, did you not think it odder still?'

'How do you know that I didn't find them?'

'You tell me, Robert. Yes, Robert, yes,' she said, seeing sudden understanding in his face. 'That's the way it is. Sweet girl, Kathy, isn't she?'

'But why did she do it?'

'To hurt me. To get her revenge because I went to see you when she was in London, and because I told you about her father. She doesn't need or want us now that she has her precious Daddy and sisters.'

'Does it matter so much that I know about your brother?'

'Yes,' she said shortly. There had been a time when she had wanted everyone to know, when she had craved pity: Look at me, look at how much I have to suffer. She wanted her suffering to frighten others as much as it frightened herself. That time had passed, leaving inexplicable feelings of shame, as if she were somehow tainted by his murder. She felt guilty for continuing to live while he was dead, and the pity of others now sickened her, for under it she saw contempt. 'It matters a lot. It matters to me.'

Robert tried to visualize the dead boy at home in this cosy room: curled up in a fat armchair; kneeling at the tiled hearth or looking at his reflection in the circular mirror, but his imagination failed him. Francis remained one of those grey people (and his own father was another) whose existence, Robert knew, could be proven, but whose reality he could never quite grasp. 'You have to get over these things,' he said with a hint of impatience. 'Surely your religion must give you some comfort?' She turned on him, more angry than he had ever before seen her.

'Comfort? Why do you miserable atheists always say that about religion? You don't know what it's like to suffer and believe. Where's the comfort in knowing that God Himself had to die because of my sins? Where's the comfort in knowing that I'll never be good enough? Where's the comfort in trying to escape suffering when I know that I ought to cherish it? You're the one who has it easy, because you don't believe in sin or in judgement. You think that when you die there'll be blackness and silence and nothing. You don't believe that you'll ever need forgiveness for all the evil things you've done, and that makes you dangerous. It was people who thought that they were above forgiveness that killed my brother.'

'But you believe that your brother's in Heaven now, don't you? You believe that he's at peace?'

'Yes, but what about me?' she cried. 'What about me? I loved Francis as dearly as I loved my own life, but he was taken from me and tortured and killed. I have to go on living without him, and I have to go on believing in God, a good God, a God who loves and cares for me. Do you think that's easy? I have to believe that my brother's death was a victory. I have to forgive the people who killed my brother; I have to try to love them as I loved him. I have to try to think of *them* as brothers while in my heart I want to hate them: and then you dare to speak to me of comfort? You tell me what's easy about belief. You tell me where the comfort is.'

She was crying long before she ceased to speak, and continued to cry in the following silence. Robert listened to her, remembering how he had once heard her weeping far into the night on the other side of his closed bedroom door. He was awed not by the depth of her faith, but by the intransigence of her will, seeing in her a refusal to be comforted as staunch as his own refusal to believe. He remembered his mother making much of God's mercy and grace, but he did not dare mention it. He wished that he could take her in his arms and weep, too, but his usual revulsion for her body was now compounded with fear, for he felt that if he were to touch her, all that immense anger and grief would thrill through him like electricity and he would be brought down to suffer there with her. Her professedly comfortless faith did do something: it made her grief finite; but he felt that if he were to fall he would fall forever and forever.

'Leave me,' she sobbed. 'Please go away and leave me.'

Robert wanted to speak but could find nothing to say. Feeling wretched, he quietly left the room and her home. As soon as he had gone, Theresa slid to the rug and lay there crying with a total lack of restraint until she was spent and could cry no more. She wondered how long she had been lying there in tears: perhaps for half an hour, perhaps for even longer. Sniffing pathetically, she curled up on the rug until she could touch her feet, then removed a slipper, smelt it, and stroked its soft, synthetic fur against her damp face while gazing at the dusty grey cinders of the fire. She thought of nothing.

After a long time, she heard a single knock upon the front door. She waited, listened and heard a second knock. Raising herself to her knees, she listened again and when the third knock came she arose and went into the hall. As soon as she saw Theresa's face in the ghastly yellow light of the street lamp, Kathy knew that she had come too late.

'Robert's been here, hasn't he?' she said. 'Oh, Theresa . . .' She stepped into the house, but would go no further than the tiny porch formed between the main house door and a light inner door inset with a square pane of glass into which was frosted the image of a bowl of roses. Only a very little light filtered through from the hall and the street by way of the frosted glass and the fanlight: the porch remained dim. 'I told him in such a roundabout way that afterwards I thought: he won't find out or if he does he won't mention it; it doesn't matter. But all day today I couldn't get Francis out of my mind and I thought, of course it matters, of course it's important. I could hardly believe that I had done such a thing, and I couldn't forgive myself. Can you forgive me?'

'Yes,' said Theresa's voice in the darkness. 'Of course I forgive you.'

'I feel so bad about this,' said Kathy. 'It's dreadful to do something wrong, and then know that absolutely nothing can undo it.'

'Kathy, I've forgiven you,' said Theresa wearily. 'I can do nothing more.'

'I'm sorry, Theresa. I'm really, really sorry. Look, I'll leave you now because you're tired, but I promise I'll phone tomorrow. Goodnight. And thanks.'

'Goodnight.'

Kathy left and Theresa returned to the parlour. She reached for the cigarette packet but found it empty; swore and folded her arms in frustration. Then she caught sight of her reflection in the round mirror, and was startled. Who was that person? Could that pale, hunched, ugly little person be herself? She could scarcely believe how intimately she must know the sad hinterland of the red-eyed girl's life, and she approached the mirror timidly, watching with fascination the way in which the image grew. Stopping before it, she was filled with a desire to touch the glass. She remembered when she was a child at school a priest had once come to show slides of the Missions, and halfway through the showing she and Francis had risen, with a shared, single impulse and run across the dark room together to stroke the wall, believing that the bright pictures being cast upon it would magically change its texture. (Francis said afterwards to the angry teacher, 'I wanted to feel what Africa was like.') Of course they were disappointed when their touch encountered only the ordinary wall; but they did distort the image: they did have the satisfaction of seeing the African veldt at dusk ripple across their tiny hands, even if they could not feel it.

Stretching up, she touched the mirror with the tips of her fingers. It was, of course, cold and smooth. What else, even now, did she expect? She withdrew her hand and gazed again at her reflection. Me. The metal leaves framed her as she stood, still and dead as a painting. Could there be anything more wearisome, she wondered, than to stand alone, alone, alone before a mirror? How long would it be, she wondered, until she could go beyond reflections? For how long would she have to continue claiming the face in the mirror as her own? When would there be an end to shadows cast upon glass?

Theresa turned her back upon the mirror, with its cold, circular, distorted room, and looked around the real parlour in which she was standing. She realized that she was very cold. Shivering, she crossed to the hearth, knelt down and tried to rekindle the dying fire.